THE
EVERYTHING.
SALAD BOOK

Dear Reader,

I've always had a passion for food, especially fresh fruits and vegetables, so it's my greatest joy to write this cookbook. As a child, I was constantly in trouble for sneaking blueberries from my mother's garden and sugar snap peas from the neighbor's yard. Thanks to my mother's avid gardening and adventurous cooking, I grew up with a true appreciation for fresh ingredients and multicultural cuisine. To this day, my idea of heaven is attending an outdoor party loaded with a diverse buffet of fresh salads and fruity desserts straight from the host's garden.

I'm delighted to now share my favorite recipes and demonstrate the creative potential of a simple salad. My aim is to display how much variety is possible, with recipes for every meal, budget, schedule, and occasion. Overall, I hope this cookbook acts as an introduction to the amazing world of salads while both inspiring and tantalizing readers with an array of culinary delights from around the globe.

Aysha Schurman

Welcome to the EVERYTHING® Series!

These handy, accessible books give you all you need to tackle a difficult project, gain a new hobby, comprehend a fascinating topic, prepare for an exam, or even brush up on something you learned back in school but have since forgotten.

You can choose to read an *Everything®* book from cover to cover or just pick out the information you want from our four useful boxes: e-questions, e-facts, e-alerts, and e-ssentials.

We give you everything you need to know on the subject, but throw in a lot of fun stuff along the way, too.

We now have more than 400 *Everything®* books in print, spanning such wide-ranging categories as weddings, pregnancy, cooking, music instruction, foreign language, crafts, pets, New Age, and so much more. When you're done reading them all, you can finally say you know *Everything®*!

QUESTION

Answers to
common questions

FACT

Important snippets
of information

ALERT

Urgent
warnings

ESSENTIAL

Quick
handy tips

PUBLISHER Karen Cooper

DIRECTOR OF ACQUISITIONS AND INNOVATION Paula Munier

MANAGING EDITOR, EVERYTHING® SERIES Lisa Laing

COPY CHIEF Casey Ebert

ASSISTANT PRODUCTION EDITOR Jacob Erickson

ACQUISITIONS EDITOR Lisa Laing

SENIOR DEVELOPMENT EDITOR Brett Palana-Shanahan

EDITORIAL ASSISTANT Ross Weisman

EVERYTHING® SERIES COVER DESIGNER Erin Alexander

LAYOUT DESIGNERS Colleen Cunningham, Elisabeth Lariviere, Ashley Vierra, Denise Wallace

Visit the entire Everything® series at *www.everything.com*

THE EVERYTHING® SALAD BOOK

Includes:

Raspberry-Cranberry Spinach Salad

Sweet Spring Baby Salad

Dijon Apricot Chicken Salad

Mediterranean Tomato Salad

Sesame Orange Coleslaw

Aysha Schurman

Avon, Massachusetts

*To everyone whose inner child loves to eat
sugar snap peas straight from the garden.*

An Everything® Series Book.
Everything® and everything.com® are registered trademarks of F+W Media, Inc.

Published by Adams Media, a division of F+W Media, Inc.
57 Littlefield Street, Avon, MA 02322 U.S.A.
www.adamsmedia.com

ISBN 10: 1-4405-2207-3
ISBN 13: 978-1-4405-2207-9
eISBN 10: 1-4405-2555-2
eISBN 13: 978-1-4405-2555-1

Printed in the United States of America.

10 9 8 7 6 5 4 3 2 1

Library of Congress Cataloging-in-Publication Data
is available from the publisher.

This publication is designed to provide accurate and authoritative information with regard to the subject matter covered. It is sold with the understanding that the publisher is not engaged in rendering legal, accounting, or other professional advice. If legal advice or other expert assistance is required, the services of a competent professional person should be sought.

—From a *Declaration of Principles* jointly adopted by a Committee of the
American Bar Association and a Committee of Publishers and Associations

Many of the designations used by manufacturers and sellers to distinguish their products are claimed as trademarks. Where those designations appear in this book and Adams Media was aware of a trademark claim, the designations have been printed with initial capital letters.

*This book is available at quantity discounts for bulk purchases.
For information, please call 1-800-289-0963.*

Contents

Introduction ix

1 Salads for Everyone 1

Salads: The First Meals 2

Salad Versatility 4

The Benefits of Eating Salad 5

Salad Dressings 6

Salad Preparation Tips 8

Salad-Making Tips 9

Salad Storage Tips 12

2 Light Salad Dressings 13

3 Rich Salad Dressings 31

4 Green Salads 49

5 Fruit Salads 69

6 Potato Salads 87

7 Pasta Salads 109

8 Bean Salads 127

9 Poultry/Beef/Pork Salads 149

10 Fish/Seafood Salads 171

11 Quick Salads 193

12 Gourmet Salads 205

13 Creamy Salads/Slaws 225

14 Spicy Salads 245

15 Dessert Salads 265

Appendix A: Classic Salad Combinations 285
Appendix B: Produce Buying Guide 286

Standard U.S./Metric Measurement Conversions 288

Index. 289

Acknowledgments

My deepest thanks to Adams Media and managing editor Lisa Laing for the opportunity, education, and guidance they've given me. My eternal gratitude to my mother Jill, father Don, and sister Leah for their decades of inexhaustible support and endless editorial labor. Many thanks to my amazing friends—especially Tahane, Barbara, Valeria, Dan, and Nina—for all their help, patience, and inspiration.

My love to Ed, who not only kept the family fed when I was too busy writing about food to cook, but also put up with my culinary critiques of each meal without once dumping anything over my head. Finally, my love to Alaina, who never tired of coming up with reasons why the book should only contain dessert and taco salad recipes.

Introduction

CRISPY GREENS, JUICY FRUITS, tangy beans, or creamy pastas; there's something special about every type of salad. Unlike fully cooked dishes, salads have a wonderful way of retaining the distinct flavor of each ingredient. You can taste every green in a cool garden salad and each addition in a warm potato salad. Whether you're an experienced chef or just learning how to cook, salads have a way of waking up your taste buds and your creativity.

The term *salad* evolved from the Latin word *sal*, which means salt, an important ingredient in salad dressing. Bringing out the natural flavor of fresh ingredients is the secret to creating salads, and salt is a historically vital aspect in flavor enhancement. Ancient Greeks, Romans, and Egyptians not only adored salads and salted salad dressings; they consumed the most coveted of all salad ingredients, lettuce. While you may think of raw salads and fancy dressings as modern ideas, ancient cultures reveal that humans have long appreciated the value and versatility of fresh produce.

It's true that modern salads include much more than just fruits and vegetables, but even potato, pasta, bean, and gelatin salads usually combine some sort of raw produce in the dish. Regardless of whether you grow your own succulent plants or choose the perfect produce from a farmer's market, turning raw ingredients into a culinary triumph provides a certain sense of satisfaction.

Fresh salads also offer something rare in modern life: They contain ingredients you can recognize and pronounce. As long as you stick with produce and all-natural toppings, you can create anything from an appetizer to an entrée without including a single mysterious additive in the meal.

Considering the easy preparation and numerous health benefits, it's surprising that more people don't eat a salad at least once a day. Part of the problem is due to a feeling that salads lack variety or imagination, which couldn't be farther from the truth. A pre-packaged tossed salad from the store may be a dull meal to eat every day, but with a little guidance and a few minutes of work, anyone can learn how to take a salad from simple to spectacular.

Think of salads as the ultimate culinary exploration and let the ingredients inspire you. Any ingredient you can consume in raw form can be put into a salad, as well as many foods that require cooking. All four food groups work in a salad, which means you can go wild at the grocery store. It's the perfect opportunity to grab a cheese you've always wanted to try, discover a new dressing to bring out the flavor of carrots, and find a use for the weird fruits you've seen in the produce aisle.

The Everything® Salad Book provides you with an array of recipes to suit every occasion, from fancy gourmet salads you can serve at dinner parties to quick and easy salads that even the fussiest kids will enjoy. You can explore light salads and dressings for low-calorie meals, as well as rich salads and dressings for indulgent meals. Along the way, you'll learn the secrets to making your own salads and dressings, as well as how to select, prepare, and store produce. In the end, it's all about playing with the flavors and textures until you discover your own special way of making the recipe just right.

CHAPTER 1

Salads for Everyone

Salads are found in cultures around the world and throughout history. The loose definition of a salad, a dish composed of mixed raw ingredients, is easily applicable to a variety of creations. The definition of a salad is "loose" because the versatile dish can contain almost any mix of raw, cooked, cold, and hot ingredients. From warm German potato salad to raw American fruit salad, there are recipes for any meal, season, or ingredient preference.

Salads: The First Meals

Salads were one of the first primitive meals created by ancient humans, albeit a culinary accident. Before man discovered pottery or even fire, he knew how to forage for food. A handful of wild leaves, roots, nuts, and berries was not only precious nourishment; it was a crude form of salad. Modern man may have refined the techniques and dressings since those early meals, but the basic principle of mixing fresh ingredients into a healthy and tasty creation still stands at the core of every great salad.

The most popular and recognizable salads contain young and/or leafy plants. Many civilizations recognized the value of fresh spring greens after a long winter subsisting on dried plants and smoked meats. At a primitive level, people understood that vitamins sapped away by the poor winter fare were replenished with the consumption of young and/or leafy spring plants. Thus, salad was not only one of the first meals; it was one of the first popular forms of "health" food.

Many cultural dishes call for some sort of salad and dressing combination, but it was ancient Rome's love of salads and dressing that formed the cornerstone for modern versions of the dish. Like many things, the Romans borrowed their knowledge of salads and healthy food from the Greeks. However, they added the distinct Roman element of indulgence and embellished the simple meals with flavorful sauces and garnishes. In fact, dressing salads with vinegar, oil, and salt was an extremely popular practice during the Roman era.

The Decline of Salads

While salads still existed after the fall of Rome, they did decline in popularity. The medicinal community went back and forth on whether raw fruits and vegetables were healthy or poison. At times people were encouraged to eat fresh produce, and at others, they were warned against it at the risk of their very lives. While modern people may think it silly to avoid eating fresh produce, there was a very serious logic behind the recommendation.

Up until and even into the twenty-first century many civilizations used "nightsoil" to fertilize fields. Nightsoil is simply a polite way of saying human excrement. The ease of disease transmission from excrement to plant to person meant that eating raw produce did carry a significant danger, especially during a time when few people had access to clean water for washing themselves or their food. Thus, it is not surprising that the fall of Rome, and its extensive aqueduct and waste systems, resulted in western cultures turning to safe cooked food instead of potentially dangerous raw food.

The Salad Rises Again

Starting during late medieval times and gaining speed during the Renaissance, Mediterranean cultures helped bring salads back into the mainstream. By the late 1800s, salads were back in vogue among Western civilizations. This is due to both the boom in exchanged ideas due to immigration and to a somewhat more sophisticated knowledge of hygiene. It's also worthy to note that salads gaining popularity and the Victorian era seem to coincide. This may be partially due to the Victorian fascination with personal health and any activities, elixirs, or food items reputed to have health benefits.

FACT

Fannie Farmer is a legend in the world of cooking for being the first person to write a concise cookbook that used measurements. Her cookbook, *The Boston Cooking School Cookbook*, was first published in 1896 and is still available to this day. It included precise measurements, such as 1 cup and ⅛ teaspoon, instead of general amounts, such as a handful and a pinch.

By 1883, the first American cookbook dedicated solely to salads was published. Along with the wave of new salad enthusiasts came new kinds of salads, especially the new idea of molded gelatin salads. After the turn of the century, fancy salad dressings and salad recipe cookbooks were common items in stores across Europe and America. The early twentieth century saw the creation of such timeless classics as the Waldorf salad at the Waldorf Astoria restaurant, the Cobb salad at the Brown Derby restaurant, and Green Goddess salad dressing at the Palace hotel.

Salad in Eastern Civilizations

Many Middle and Far Eastern civilizations also enjoy dishes that can be classified as salads. The most noticeable exception to this rule is China. Due to China's ancient history of large populations and big cities, it has long faced problems with disease and distribution, and thus there are very few raw salad-like dishes. The most popular "salad-like" meals usually consist of pickled ingredients as opposed to raw.

Anthropologists note that a need for fertilized land and human waste removal made nightsoil a natural choice for Chinese farmers, so eating raw food was often a bad idea. In addition, the need to prepare harvests for transporting to faraway cities required smoking, drying, pickling, salting, and other preservation methods. The danger of raw food and reliance on preserved items developed into the logical cultural practice of eating only prepared goods.

Salad Versatility

The wonderfully versatile nature of a salad means it works as any meal, from breakfast to dessert, and with any ingredient combination, from hot or cold to pickled or raw. You can make a salad with vegetables, fruits, meats, cheeses, and beans all in one bowl to guarantee a perfectly balanced main meal or just throw juicy fruits together to make a light summer snack. Winter holiday potlucks, summer picnics, gourmet dinner parties, or school lunches, there's a salad to suit every need.

FACT

Tomatoes are popular in salads now, but they're native to South America and were not available to the rest of the world until the 1500s. The British colonists in America suspected tomatoes, which are related to poisonous nightshade, were themselves poisonous. It took Italy's love of tomatoes to make the fruit popular in Europe, and eventually popular in the United States.

Salad ingredients are also versatile. While it's true that every ingredient provides a special taste, there are ways to substitute a similar item if you need to change a recipe. As long as the ingredients have the same texture and relative flavor, there's a chance you can substitute one for the other. For example, if a recipe calls for Pink Lady apples, you can try different kinds of sweet apples or pears instead.

Leafy Greens

The easiest salad ingredients to switch around and play with are leafy greens. Lettuce greens break into four categories; Romaine, butterhead, crisphead, and looseleaf. Romaine lettuce, also known as Cos, is crisp with a strong and slightly sweet flavor. Butterhead lettuces, including Bibb and Boston, are soft with a mild flavor. Crisphead lettuces, including iceberg, are extremely crisp with a light and refreshing flavor. Looseleaf lettuces, including red leaf and green leaf, are delicate and crisp with a mild to medium flavor.

Other leafy greens break into three general categories; bitter, sweet, or peppery. Bitter greens include chicory, endives, mustard greens, Swiss chard, dandelion greens, and kale. Sweet greens include green cabbage, red cabbage, lamb's lettuce, baby spinach, baby greens, and baby lettuces. Peppery greens include arugula, watercress, red mustard, and radicchio. Generally, baby greens are slightly sweeter than the adult version. Micro greens are tender, sweet, newly sprouted greens only a few inches big.

Ingredient Warning

While many salad items are highly versatile, some ingredients are far from versatile and cannot be replicated fully. If a recipe calls for baby carrots, for example, you can only replicate the texture and not the taste. However, some ingredients you never want to switch or substitute. Red, yellow, and orange bell peppers have a similar sweet flavor and are easily switchable. When it comes to green bell peppers, though, their flavor is much sharper than the others and it will significantly change the taste of the recipe. Red, green, and white onions have relatively similar sweet undertones, but yellow onion is much stronger and may overpower the recipe if used.

The Benefits of Eating Salad

With obesity and poor eating habits turning to epidemic levels, eating a salad every day may seem like a weak solution. However, people who eat one salad a day are much more likely to meet the recommended daily intake of nutrients, regardless of what else they eat that day. Raw vegetables provide an array of vital nutrients, including vitamin C, vitamin E, folic acid, beta-carotene, and iron. Raw produce also has a hidden benefit—

hydration. Due to the high water content in raw produce, it can contribute to your daily water intake and help keep you well hydrated.

Another huge benefit to eating salad is the presence of fiber, also known as roughage. Fiber does not break down in your digestive system the way fats or sugars do. Instead, it stays relatively whole to help scrub out your insides and remove general toxins from your system. It also helps keep you regular, reduces intestinal blockage, regulates weight, lowers bad cholesterol, lowers glucose levels, and staves off hunger. High-fiber produce includes peas, beans, carrots, spinach, apples, bananas, oranges, pears, and strawberries.

Of course, salad health benefits can be limited to dishes with fresh ingredients, such as vegetables and fruits. When you start getting into salads with prepared pastas, meats, cheeses, dressings, and other ingredients, the health benefits may remain high or plummet to junk food levels. The difference usually comes down to whether you're using whole grain pastas, fresh meats, and real cheeses. If the ingredient is highly processed and heavy in artificial additives, you lose most of the healthy aspects. Nevertheless, even a sugar-filled salad with fresh fruit is a healthier dessert than a sugar-filled pie with artificially flavored fruit syrup.

Environmental Benefits

If you choose to grow your own produce or buy locally grown items, eating salads can also have a positive environmental impact. Growing or buying organic produce eliminates the need for pesticides and chemical fertilizers, which in turn reduces contamination, waste, and energy consumption due to production. Even if you don't grow your own or go organic, you can buy locally grown items. Purchasing local produce reduces an item's carbon footprint by cutting out the majority of transportation and preservation required to get the food to your table.

Salad Dressings

The key to using salad dressing is to add just enough to highlight the salad flavors without overwhelming them. In addition to killing the flavor, excess salad dressing weighs down delicate ingredients and makes everything soggy. For the best results, always use less dressing than called for in a recipe. See what the salad tastes like with the minimum amount of dressing, and then add more as needed to balance the flavors to your liking. Remember, salad dressings are easy to pour onto a salad, but hard to remove if you use too much.

Types of Dressing

Vinaigrette and creamy are the two main types of salad dressing. Vinaigrette dressings, such as Catalina and Italian, are an emulsion of oil and vinegar. Creamy dressings, such as ranch and Thousand Island, contain dairy products and/or mayonnaise, which is an emulsion of eggs and oil. The third type of dressing is a general category that covers fermentation items, such as soy sauce, and infused items, such as garlic-soaked olive oil.

ALERT

Regardless of the type, and whether it's homemade or store-bought: All salad dressings need to be stored in the fridge and shaken well before each use, unless the recipe or packaging specifically states otherwise.

Vinaigrette Dressings

The standard ratio for any vinaigrette dressing is three-parts oil to one-part vinegar or lemon juice. The rest of the recipe, such as herbs, is a matter of taste. The most important part of creating a vinegar and oil dressing is to add the oil last. Oil encapsulates ingredients, whereas vinegar or lemon juice helps dissolve and disperse ingredients. The easiest way to make vinaigrette dressing is to mix the vinegar and other ingredients first. Pour the mixture into a jar, add the oil, screw on the lid, and shake like crazy until the dressing is fully mixed. If the recipe calls for hand mixing, a small whisk works best.

Creamy Dressings

Creamy dressings are much more forgiving than vinaigrettes when it comes to the order of ingredients. You can mix most creamy dressings with a blender, food processor, electric mixer, or by hand. The biggest catch to creating creamy dressings is to remember that dairy products tend to amplify flavors, especially citrus juice. Dairy products can also curdle when aged, boiled, or mixed with an acid, such as citrus juice.

Thus, it's important to pay careful attention to recipe instructions and measurements when creating a creamy dressing.

Food Processors Versus Blenders

The two most common electric appliances used to create homemade salad dressing are food processors and blenders. Generally, food processors have higher power and are better at breaking up whole ingredients than blenders. Most processors also come with interchangeable blades so they can chop, mince, or puree as needed. Blenders work best with liquid ingredients and are able to create extremely smooth textures.

If you need to use a blender instead of a food processor, there are a few tips you should know. If the blender stalls or has problems breaking up the ingredients, turn the blender off and use a spatula to scrape the bulkier food out from under the blade. If you need to add something while the blender is on, turn the lid so that the opening and spout line up and then add the ingredient. Depending on the style of blender, you can also remove the plastic plug from the middle of the lid and add ingredients through the hole.

Salad Preparation Tips

It's important to check the produce in your refrigerator for overall quality before preparing them for a salad. You want to remove any slimy or discolored leaves from your greens, cut away the bruises in your apples or onions and discard any spongy carrots or cucumbers. Your salad will end up suffering if you don't check beforehand that every ingredient smells and feels right.

Washing Ingredients

All fresh salad ingredients need rinsing before going into the salad. Leafy greens and delicate vegetables require thorough rinsing in cool water. The crinklier the greens, the more you need to brush your clean fingers over the leaf as it rinses to help knock off any insects or dirt clusters. Packaged produce may be pre-washed so you can skip the cleansing process, but it never hurts to rinse off packaged produce too.

Use a soft cleaning brush and cool water to clean heartier vegetables and fruits. Never use the soft brush for other activities or it may become contaminated. Gently scrubbing ingredients with the brush can help remove dried dirt on a potato or the wax coating on an apple. Avoid using hot water to wash any ingredients, as the water can cause produce to wilt, bruise, and change color. Avoid using soaps or detergents on produce, as the substances may leave more harmful residue on the food than they remove.

ALERT

Be careful not to fall for urban myths regarding salad creation, such as tossing the lettuce into a clothes dryer or washer to spin away the excess water. Not only is this practice ineffective and dangerous, it would make the salad taste terrible. You also never want to soak produce in vinegar to ensure insect-free ingredients, as the vinegar will seep into the items and dramatically alter their taste.

Drying Ingredients

Investing in a salad spinner is the quickest way to dry salad ingredients. Salad spinners literally spin salad greens to remove excess water after rinsing. The spinners are only a luxury, though. Carefully shaking greens in a colander after rinsing and patting them gently with a paper towel can also remove excess liquid. For the best results, shake the rinsed greens, let sit in the colander for a few minutes, shake again, and pat dry with a paper towel. Other ingredients only need a gentle wipe with a paper towel to remove extra water.

Salad-Making Tips

Creating the perfect salad is a delicate art where every aspect, from the ingredient ratios to the type of bowl used, has an impact on your result. Despite the intricacies, learning to make amazing salads is easy. The most important part of creating an amazing salad or salad dressing is to trust your own taste buds. A recipe may call for one teaspoon of garlic powder, but if you're using an old powder, you may need to add more; or, if you hate garlic, you may need to use less. Recipes are just guides; your taste buds are what truly let you know if the salad or dressing is just right.

Salad Texture

While the taste of a salad is always a vital point, the texture of the salad is also important. You can create a salad that tastes amazing, but if every ingredient is one-inch big with a mushy texture, the salad will be boring to eat and the flavors will run together. When you add different texture to the salad, such as thick slices of crunchy celery and thin shreds of creamy Cheddar, you make the experience of eating the salad interesting. You also add interest to the flavor. As the juices from the crunchy celery squirt out with each bite and the sliver of Cheddar melts with other ingredients in your mouth, you taste different levels of flavor from each part of the salad.

Salad Bowls

The type of bowl you use to create your salad can influence the taste and texture of the meal. Salad bowls are large and deep, with steep sides and a small bottom, as opposed to mixing bowls, which are somewhat shallow with wide bottoms.

ALERT

Plastic salad bowls are useful for presentation purposes, but tend to be annoying if used for mixing/tossing purposes. The lightweight containers are often unbalanced due to the small bottom area used for salad bowls. Even if the bowl doesn't fall over on its own, the light material is easy to accidently knock over while you're tossing the salad.

The shape of a salad bowl allows liquids to drain down the sides and pool at the bottom, which helps keep delicate salad from getting soggy or saturated. The oversized nature of the bowl not only aids in draining, it provides a big enough area to toss your salad properly. Tossing room is important, which is why salad bowls are only supposed to be filled ½ to ⅔ full. The remaining space lets you mix the salad without making a mess.

In addition to the shape and size, the material used to create the salad bowl can also have a small effect on your salad. Wooden salad bowls are popular for home use due to their attractive appearance and seasoning qualities. You can rub flavored oils into the wood to season the bowl and thus add subtle seasoning to the salad without using dressing. However, seasoned wood cannot go into the dishwasher and its porous nature can cause health/sanitation issues for restaurants. Metal and ceramic salad bowls tend to be popular in restaurants due to their stability and cleaning ease. The slick bowls also prevent the taste of past ingredients invading the salad, which keeps the flavor free of contamination in a busy restaurant kitchen.

QUESTION

How do I clean a wooden salad bowl?
Although wooden salad bowls should not be put in a dishwasher, they do need to be cleaned. Use warm water mixed with just a drop of soap to wash out the bowl, removing the top layer of dirt without stripping the seasoning or oil from the wood. Rinse the bowl out and wipe dry immediately to prevent damage to the wood.

Tossing Technique

Delicate and/or leafy salads require gentle tossing to mix the ingredients together and coat the salad with dressing. Tossing the ingredients a few inches into the air mixes the fragile items, particularly lettuce, without bruising or ripping them as a spoon would. The most frequent error people make when preparing salads is a lack of tossing. Tossing the salad a few times does little good, especially if you're trying to coat the ingredients with dressing. You need to toss the salad a dozen or more times to fully mix and coat the ingredients.

Tossing a leafy salad also has hidden flavor benefits. As you toss the ingredients, you expose them to large quantities of air. The air causes oxidation to take place in each ingredient, which helps enhance the aroma. Taste and smell are closely linked, as the tongue only truly tastes sweet, salty, sour, and bitter. Flavor details actually come from scent, not taste. Therefore, by enhancing the aroma of the ingredients, you enhance the flavor.

When it comes to mixing fruit, pasta, potato, and bean salads, it's important to use a large spoon to turn the ingredients rather than stir them. Stirring the ingredients can mash the salad, particularly if you have delicate items, such as cooked pasta, cooked potatoes, soft beans, or soft fruit. Think of scooping the salad up and folding it over the top of the other ingredients as a controlled tossing technique.

The three most popular utensils for tossing leafy salad are clean hands, tongs, or salad utensils. If you don't mind getting messy, you can use your clean hands to dig into the salad and toss it together. Tongs keep your hands clean, but you need to be gentle when using them to prevent bruising the ingredients. Salad utensils usually consist of a shallow, serving-size spoon and fork in either separate or tong form. You grasp the separate utensils in each hand and use them to lift and toss the salad.

Salad Presentation

Part of a great salad's appeal is its appearance and the way it's presented. While a salad's appearance may not directly alter the taste of the dish, a visually appealing salad does heighten the sense of enticement and stimulate your taste buds, which helps make the salad all the more enjoyable to eat. You can dress up a salad several different ways for an artistic presentation. Instead of just sprinkling seeds or croutons as a topping, try sprinkling them in a spiral pattern over the salad. Instead of throwing egg slices over the salad, use the slices to create a pattern around the edge of the bowl.

Salad Storage Tips

Most salads, be they fruit, pasta, or vegetable, require refrigeration for storage. Some recipes, such as green salad, may not store well and some, such as pasta salad, may need to chill for a whole day before being served. Most heavy pasta, potato, grain, and meat salads only require a storage container and lid. However, delicate vegetable and fruit salads should never be stored in a closed container. Delicate salads, especially leafy ones, need to breathe or the ingredients will wilt and/or turn mushy.

The best way to store fruit and green salads is to place the salad in a bowl and cover it with a damp paper towel. The damp towel provides moisture to keep the produce hydrated and lets the salad breathe to keep it from over-hydrating. Unless the recipe specifically states otherwise, it's always best to store a salad without any dressing. Placing a dressing-covered lettuce salad in the fridge for a few days will result in little more than a soggy mess.

CHAPTER 2

Light Salad Dressings

Italian Dill Vinaigrette Dressing
14

Sherry Vinaigrette
14

Cucumber Vinaigrette
Salad Dressing
15

Light and Creamy
Chive Dressing
16

Light and Creamy
Horseradish Dressing
16

Agave-Lemon Ginger
Salad Dressing
17

Cilantro and Red Onion
Dressing
18

Creamy Wasabi-Tofu Dressing
19

Cilantro-Lime Tofu Dressing
20

Cobb Salad Vinaigrette Dressing
21

Asian Ranch Dressing
21

Lemon-Ginger Poppy Seed
Dressing
22

Blue Cheese Dressing
23

Dairy-Free Ranch Dressing
24

Low-Cal Spinach Pesto
Vinaigrette
25

Creamy Miso Sesame Dressing
26

Tangy Lemon-Garlic
Tomato Dressing
27

You Are a Goddess Dressing
28

Tangy Honey Mustard
Salad Dressing
29

Chickpea Herb Salad Dressing
30

½ cup low-sodium chicken broth

3 tablespoons white wine vinegar

1 tablespoon lemon juice

½ teaspoon fresh chives, minced

½ teaspoon fresh dill, minced

½ teaspoon sodium-free Italian seasoning

⅛ teaspoon black pepper, finely ground

INGREDIENTS | SERVES 12

⅓ cup virgin olive oil

⅓ cup walnut oil

1 teaspoon shallot, chopped

¼ teaspoon kosher salt

¼ teaspoon black pepper, ground

½ cup sherry wine vinegar

Italian Dill Vinaigrette Dressing

Replacing fatty oils with healthy and tasty chicken broth helps ensure this salad dressing offers full flavor without the extra calories.

1. Whisk together the broth, vinegar, and lemon juice in a small bowl. Mix well.

2. Whisk chives, dill, Italian seasonings, and black pepper into the dressing. Mix well. Pour dressing into a lidded container and chill in fridge. Shake well before each use.

PER SERVING

Calories: 3	Sodium: . . . . 46 mg
Fat: . . . . 0 g	Fiber: . . . . 0 g
Protein: . . . . 0 g	Carbohydrate: . . . 1 g

Sherry Vinaigrette

Walnut oil must be fresh and properly stored. Taste the oil before adding to ensure that it has not gone bad. Refrigerate after opening.

Mix together the olive oil and walnut oil. Whisk together the shallot, vinegar, and salt and pepper in a separate bowl. While whisking, add the combined oil slowly at a drizzle. Adjust the seasoning to taste. Will keep for 1–2 weeks refrigerated. Whisk before using if separated.

PER SERVING

Calories: 208	Sodium: . . . . 49 mg
Fat: . . . . 23 g	Fiber: . . . . 0 g
Protein: . . . . 0 g	Carbohydrate: . . . 1 g

1¼ cups chopped cucumber, peeled and seeded

2 tablespoons white wine vinegar

1 tablespoon flat-leaf parsley, chopped

2 teaspoons cilantro, chopped

½ teaspoon garlic powder

¼ teaspoon salt

¼ teaspoon ground black pepper

¼ teaspoon ground red pepper

¼ teaspoon dried dill

¼ cup extra-virgin olive oil

Cucumber Vinaigrette Salad Dressing

Cucumber not only gives this light dressing a delicate flavor, it provides body, reducing the amount of oil needed in the recipe.

1. Add the cucumber, vinegar, parsley, cilantro, garlic powder, salt, black pepper, red pepper, and dill to a food processor or small blender. Process mixture until silky smooth.

2. Pour the olive oil into the processor. Process for 15 seconds, or until oil is thoroughly mixed in.

3. Pour the dressing into a bottle and cover tightly with a lid. Shake well before each use and store in fridge.

PER SERVING

Calories: 63	Sodium: . . . . 1 mg
Fat: . . . . 6.5 g	Fiber: . . . . 0 g
Protein: . . . . 0 g	Carbohydrate: . . . 1 g

Removing Cucumber Seeds

The easiest way to remove the seeds from a cucumber is to slice it in half lengthwise. Using a melon scoop or small spoon, you just scoop out the seeds from the middle of each half. Once the seeds are gone, you're free to slice and dice the cucumber as needed.

Light and Creamy Chive Dressing

You can mix mayonnaise with a fair amount of water without losing the creamy texture. The water makes the dressing go farther and reduces the overall calories.

1. Whisk the mayonnaise and water together in a medium mixing bowl. Mix thoroughly.

2. Stir the chives and garlic powder into the dressing. Mix well and pour into a lidded container. Store in fridge and shake well before each use.

PER SERVING

Calories:......51	Sodium:.......24 mg		
Fat:...........4 g	Fiber:..........0 g		
Protein:........0 g	Carbohydrate:...4 g		

Light and Creamy Horseradish Dressing

This recipe is all about bite, so don't get stingy with the horseradish.

1. Whisk the mayonnaise, water, and horseradish together in a medium mixing bowl. Mix well.

2. Stir honey, parsley, garlic powder, and onion powder into the bowl. Mix well and pour dressing into a lidded container. Store in fridge and shake well before each use.

PER SERVING

Calories:......80	Sodium:......175 mg		
Fat:...........7.5 g	Fiber:..........0 g		
Protein:........0 g	Carbohydrate:...2.5 g		

2 tablespoons boiling water

2 teaspoons agave nectar

1 teaspoon lemon zest

1 teaspoon ginger root, finely minced

¼ teaspoon kosher salt

¼ teaspoon onion powder

¼ teaspoon ground ginger

¼ teaspoon black pepper, finely ground

¼ teaspoon sweet Hungarian paprika

¼ cup lemon juice

⅓ cup sunflower oil

Agave-Lemon Ginger Salad Dressing

The sunflower oil in this recipe is low in trans-fats, saturated fats, and cholesterol, just like olive oil.

1. Combine the water, agave nectar, lemon zest, ginger root, salt, onion powder, ground ginger, black pepper, and paprika in a glass bottle. Twist the lid on the bottle and shake to mix well.

2. Add lemon juice and oil to the bottle. Secure the lid and shake until thoroughly mixed. Store in fridge and shake well before each use.

PER SERVING

Calories: 57	Sodium: . . . . 0 mg
Fat: . . . . 6 g	Fiber: . . . . 0 g
Protein: . . . . 0 g	Carbohydrate: . . . 1 g

Agave Nectar

Agave nectar is usually located right next to the honey on grocery shelves. The powerful nectar is extremely sweet, so you can use less of it than you would honey or maple syrup. It also has a low glycemic index, which means it doesn't overwhelm your system and cause a jump in blood sugar.

2 tablespoons finely chopped red onion

½ teaspoon ground ginger

3 tablespoons slivered almonds

1 tablespoon sesame seeds

1 teaspoon anise seeds

3 tablespoons chopped fresh cilantro

¼ teaspoon paprika

2 tablespoons white wine vinegar

3 tablespoons fresh lemon juice

½ cup extra-virgin olive oil

¼ teaspoon seasoned salt

Cilantro and Red Onion Dressing

A great dressing for a summer salad that can include any fruits such as strawberries or mandarin oranges.

Combine all the ingredients in a medium-sized nonreactive bowl and whisk to combine. Taste and adjust seasoning as desired. Remix just before serving. Refrigerate any unused portion and bring to room temperature before serving. Shake well before each use.

PER SERVING

Calories: 188   Sodium: . . . . 52 mg
Fat: . . . . 20 g   Fiber: . . . . 1 g
Protein: . . . . 1 g   Carbohydrate: . . . 2 g

Cilantro Crazy

Cilantro, also known as coriander leaf, is the leaves of the coriander plant. The pungent leaves of the fast-growing plant look somewhat like parsley, as the two plants are related. Cilantro is common in both Asian and South American dishes. A boom of cilantro use in high-end restaurants during the 1990s led some people to rejoice and others to start "anti-cilantro" clubs.

12 ounces soft silken tofu

2 tablespoons soy sauce

1 teaspoon wasabi paste

½ teaspoon garlic paste

¼ teaspoon mustard seed, ground

¼ cup rice wine vinegar

¼ cup canola oil

Creamy Wasabi-Tofu Dressing

This light and spicy salad dressing is not only healthy, the tofu gives it an extra punch of protein. However, tofu can spoil, so the dressing only keeps for one week.

1. Place the tofu, soy sauce, wasabi paste, garlic paste, and mustard seed in a blender. Add half of the vinegar and half the oil to the blender. Blend on low until mixture is smooth.

2. Slowly feed the remaining vinegar and oil into the blender. Blend on low until thoroughly mixed. Pour dressing into a lidded bottle and refrigerate until needed. Shake dressing well before each use.

PER SERVING

Calories: 23	Sodium: . . . . 49 mg
Fat: . . . . 2 g	Fiber: . . . . 0 g
Protein: . . . . 1 g	Carbohydrate: . . . 0 g

Homemade Garlic Paste

Garlic paste is a combination of mashed garlic and liquid. It's a popular culinary shortcut because it makes it easy to blend the garlic with other ingredients. To make your own, crush and mince 4 raw or roasted garlic cloves. Mix the garlic with 1 tablespoon of warm water, mashing any large garlic chunks until the paste is smooth. Store in refrigerator up to 1 week.

8 ounces soft silken tofu

3 tablespoons fresh cilantro, minced

3 tablespoons fresh lime juice

1 tablespoon water

½ teaspoon lime zest

½ teaspoon onion powder

¼ teaspoon red pepper sauce

¼ teaspoon kosher salt

⅛ teaspoon black pepper, finely ground

¼ cup canola oil

Cilantro-Lime Tofu Dressing

This dressing adds a kick of Southwest flavor to any salad without adding unwanted fat and calories.

1. Combine tofu, cilantro, lime juice, water, lime zest, onion powder, red pepper sauce, salt, and pepper in a blender. Blend on low until smooth.

2. Keep the blender on low and slowly feed the oil into the mixture. Blend until thoroughly mixed. Pour mixture into a lidded bottle and store in refrigerator. Shake well before use. Discard dressing after one week.

PER SERVING

Calories:......25	Sodium:........8 mg
Fat:..........2.5 g	Fiber:..........0 g
Protein:........0.5 g	Carbohydrate:...0 g

Taste of Tofu

Tofu is a light and almost flavorless substance made of bean curd. The upside to the light taste is that it takes on the flavors of anything with which it's mixed. It's important to use a soft silken tofu for the salad dressing, as it will mix well and provide a creamy texture. Using a hard tofu in the dressing will result in poor mixing and a curded texture.

¼ cup cider vinegar

2 tablespoons fresh lemon juice

1 teaspoon granulated sugar

½ teaspoon salt

½ teaspoon black pepper, ground

1 tablespoon Dijon mustard

⅔ cup extra-virgin olive oil

½ cup light mayonnaise

⅓ cup rice vinegar

¼ cup low-sodium soy sauce

2 tablespoons sesame oil

2 teaspoons sugar

½ teaspoon ginger root, ground

¾ teaspoon garlic powder

1 tablespoon fresh chives, chopped

Cobb Salad Vinaigrette Dressing

Homemade vinaigrettes just taste better than the store-bought varieties. This is the basic version.

Combine the vinegar, lemon juice, sugar, salt, pepper, and mustard in a container or jar with cover and shake vigorously to combine. Add the oil and shake until emulsified. Use immediately or refrigerate overnight. Bring to room temperature before using.

PER SERVING

Calories: 166	Sodium: . . . . . . 148 mg
Fat: 18g	Fiber: . . . . 0 g
Protein: . . . . 0 g	Carbohydrate: . . . 1 g

Asian Ranch Dressing

An Asian combination of flavors fuses with all-American mayonnaise for a twist on the usual ranch dressing.

Combine all ingredients except chives in a blender or food processor until smooth and creamy. Stir in chives by hand. Pour dressing into a bottle and chill in refrigerator until needed.

PER SERVING

Calories: 58	Sodium: . . . . . . 226 mg
Fat: 5g	Fiber: . . . . 0 g
Protein: . . . . 1 g	Carbohydrate: . . . 3 g

4 ounces soft tofu

3 tablespoons lemon juice

1 tablespoon water

1 teaspoon lemon zest

½ teaspoon dried ginger root, ground

¼ teaspoon kosher salt

¼ teaspoon black pepper, finely ground

3 tablespoons extra-virgin olive oil

1 teaspoon poppy seeds

Lemon-Ginger Poppy Seed Dressing

If you prefer a salad dressing with more zing, replace the dried ground ginger with fresh, finely minced ginger root.

1. Combine tofu, lemon juice, water, lemon zest, ginger root, salt, and pepper in a blender. Blend on low until smooth.

2. Slowly feed oil into the blender. Blend on low until emulsified. Pour dressing into a lidded bottle. Add poppy seeds to bottle. Screw on lid and shake well to mix. Store dressing in refrigerator and shake well before using.

PER SERVING

Calories:......29	Sodium: ....1 mg
Fat:...........3 g	Fiber: ....0 g
Protein:........0.5 g	Carbohydrate: ...0.5 g

Using Poppy Seeds

Poppy seeds used in cooking are dried seeds from an Oriental poppy flower that has already bloomed and died. The tiny bluish-black seeds have a nutty flavor that's been appreciated in culinary circles since at least Ancient Greece. Their tiny size and potent taste mean that you only need a little to add color and flavor to a recipe. Remember, it can take hundreds of seeds just to fill 1 teaspoon.

2 tablespoons Mock Sour Cream
(see sidebar)

1 tablespoon low-fat cottage cheese

1 tablespoon light mayonnaise

½ teaspoon lemon juice

½ teaspoon honey

1 tablespoon, plus 2 teaspoons crumbled
blue cheese

Blue Cheese Dressing

This quick dressing has far less fat and calories than regular blue cheese dressing, but still provides that tangy blue cheese flavor.

Put all the ingredients, except the blue cheese, in a blender and process until smooth. Fold in the blue cheese. Scrape dressing into a bottle or bowl. Cover and store in fridge until needed.

PER SERVING

Calories: 29	Sodium: . . . . 95 mg
Fat: . . . . 1.5 g	Fiber: . . . . 0 g
Protein: . . . . 2.5 g	Carbohydrate: . . . 2 g

Mock Sour Cream

In a blender, combine: ⅛ cup nonfat yogurt, ¼ cup nonfat cottage cheese, and ½ teaspoon vinegar. If you prefer a more sour taste, add another ½ teaspoon of vinegar. The type of vinegar you use will affect the taste as well. Apple cider vinegar tends to be more sour than white wine vinegar, for example.

1 cup vegan mayonnaise

¼ cup soy milk

1 teaspoon Dijon mustard

1 tablespoon lemon juice

1 teaspoon onion powder

¾ teaspoon garlic powder

1 tablespoon fresh chives, minced

Dairy-Free Ranch Dressing

An all-American creamy homemade ranch dressing, without the buttermilk. Get those baby carrots ready to dip!

1. Whisk or blend together all ingredients, except chives, until smooth.

2. Stir in chives until well combined. Pour into bottle and chill in fridge until needed.

PER SERVING

Calories: 70		Sodium: . . . . 52 mg	
Fat: . . . . 7 g		Fiber: . . . . 0 g	
Protein: . . . . 0 g		Carbohydrate: . . . 2.5 g	

Vegan Mayonnaise

Vegan mayonnaise is a creamy condiment made without any animal by-products. There are several different ways to create vegan mayonnaise, but most brands use seed oil, nut meat, tofu, or soy milk to create the creamy texture of traditional mayonnaise. Like classic mayonnaise, vegan mayonnaise comes in many varieties, such as Dijon and herb.

¾ cup baby spinach, torn

¼ cup fresh basil, torn

2 garlic cloves, pressed

1 tablespoon walnuts, finely chopped

¼ teaspoon black pepper, ground

⅛ teaspoon kosher salt

3 tablespoons extra-virgin olive oil

2 tablespoons lemon juice

3 tablespoons low-sodium chicken broth

1 tablespoon white wine vinegar

Low-Cal Spinach Pesto Vinaigrette

Play with the baby spinach and basil ratios a little until you discover the perfect balance for your taste preferences.

1. Place spinach, basil, garlic, walnuts, pepper, salt, oil, and 1 tablespoon lemon juice in a processor. Process until silky smooth. Add up to 1 tablespoon extra oil if needed to smooth mixture.

2. Slowly feed remaining 1 tablespoon lemon juice, chicken broth, and vinegar into processor. Process until smooth and fully mixed. Pour mixture into a bottle and store in refrigerator. Shake well before each use.

PER SERVING

Calories: 22	Sodium: . . . . 25 mg
Fat: . . . . 2.5 g	Fiber: . . . . 0 g
Protein: . . . . 0 g	Carbohydrate: . . . 0.5 g

¼ cup miso

2 tablespoons rice wine vinegar

¼ cup soy sauce

2 tablespoons sesame oil

½ cup soy milk

2 tablespoons lime juice

Creamy Miso Sesame Dressing

A creamy and tangy Japanese-inspired salad dressing. A bit of minced fresh ginger would add another layer of flavor if you happened to have some on hand.

Process all ingredients together in a blender or food processor until smooth. Pour into a bottle and chill in refrigerator until needed. Shake well before use.

PER SERVING

Calories:	30	Sodium:	389 mg
Fat:	2 g	Fiber:	0 g
Protein:	1 g	Carbohydrate:	1.5 g

Miso Trivia

Miso is Japanese seasoning made with fermented rice or barley. It's available in a variety of inter-changeable flavors and colors; red, white, and barley miso being the most common. Which type you use is really a personal preference. Asian grocers stock miso at about ⅓ the price of natural-foods stores, so if you're lucky enough to have one in your neighborhood, it's worth a trip.

1 tablespoon ground flaxseeds

2 garlic cloves, minced

2 tablespoons cider vinegar

⅛ teaspoon black pepper, ground

1 small tomato, chopped

¼ teaspoon celery seed

1 tablespoon lemon juice

¼ cup water

Tangy Lemon-Garlic Tomato Dressing

This dressing lives up to its name and the ground flaxseeds hide healthy fiber among the rich flavors. Tastes as good on salads as it does drizzled over meat dishes.

Place all ingredients in blender and blend until smooth.

PER SERVING

Calories: 9	Sodium: . . . . 2 mg
Fat: . . . . 0.5 g	Fiber: . . . . 0.5 g
Protein: . . . . 0.5 g	Carbohydrate: . . . 1 g

Friendly Fat and Fiber

In addition to providing fiber, ground flaxseeds are rich sources of omega-3 and -6 essential fatty acids. The oil is low in saturated fat, and therefore a heart-healthy choice. Just remember that flaxseed oil must be refrigerated; otherwise it goes rancid.

⅔ cup tahini

¼ cup apple cider vinegar

⅓ cup low-sodium soy sauce

2 teaspoons lemon juice

1 garlic clove, minced

¾ teaspoon sugar

⅓ cup olive oil

You Are a Goddess Dressing

Turn this zesty salad dressing into a dip for veggies or a sandwich spread by reducing the amount of liquids.

1. Process all the ingredients, except olive oil, together in a blender or food processor until blended.

2. With the blender or food processor on high speed, slowly add in the olive oil, blending for another full minute, allowing the oil to emulsify.

3. Pour dressing into a bottle and chill in the refrigerator for at least 10 minutes before serving; dressing will thicken as it chills. Shake dressing before use.

PER SERVING

Calories:	69	Sodium:	125 mg
Fat:	6.5 g	Fiber:	0.5 g
Protein:	1.5 g	Carbohydrate:	2 g

In Search of Tahini

Tahini is a sesame seed paste native to Middle Eastern cuisine with a thinner consistency and milder flavor than peanut butter. You'll find a jarred or canned version in the ethnic foods aisle of large grocery stores, or a fresh version chilling next to the hummus if you're lucky. Check the bulk bins at co-ops and natural-foods stores for powdered tahini, which can be rehydrated with a bit of water.

2 ounces soft silken tofu

3 tablespoons water

1 tablespoon spicy brown mustard

2 teaspoons honey

¼ teaspoon mustard seed, ground

⅛ teaspoon kosher salt

⅛ teaspoon red pepper, ground

3 tablespoons olive oil

2 tablespoons white balsamic vinegar

Tangy Honey Mustard Salad Dressing

For the greatest ease, use a small bowl and an immersion hand blender to mix the small amount of dressing together.

1. Add tofu, water, mustard, honey, mustard seed, salt, and pepper to a small blender or food processor. Process until smooth.

2. Add vinegar and oil to dressing. Process until fully mixed. Pour mixture into a bottle and store in refrigerator. Shake well before use and discard after 1 week.

PER SERVING

Calories: 39	Sodium: . . . . 59 mg
Fat: . . . . 3.5 g	Fiber: . . . . 0 g
Protein: . . . . 0.5 g	Carbohydrate: . . . 2 g

⅓ cup canned chickpeas, drained

2 tablespoons white balsamic vinegar

2 tablespoons fresh celery leaves, minced

2 teaspoons water

1 teaspoon flat-leaf parsley, minced

¼ teaspoon dried thyme, crushed

⅛ teaspoon kosher salt

⅛ teaspoon cumin, ground

⅛ teaspoon turmeric, ground

3 tablespoons sunflower seed oil

Chickpea Herb Salad Dressing

This creamy recipe not only adds extra protein to your salads by using chickpeas, it offers far less fat and calories than other dressings.

1. Add chickpeas, vinegar, celery leaves, parsley, thyme, salt, cumin, and turmeric to a blender or food processor. Process until smooth.

2. Add oil to mixture and process until fully mixed. Add water and mix well. Pour dressing into bottle and chill in refrigerator. Shake well before use.

PER SERVING

Calories:......41	Sodium:.......45 mg
Fat:...........3.5 g	Fiber:..........0.5 g
Protein:........0.5 g	Carbohydrate:...2 g

Celery Leaves

Celery leaves are the leaves at the top of each celery stalk and have the same light flavor as the stalks. As long as you can find celery fresh enough to have crisp and springy leaves without slime or cracks, the leaves make a wonderful addition. Simply pull or slice the leaves from the stalk, chop them as needed, and throw into the dish.

CHAPTER 3

Rich Salad Dressings

Garlic Parmesan Salad Dressing
32

Orange Sesame Vinaigrette
33

Classic French Dressing
33

Walnut Honey-Mustard
Vinaigrette
34

Basic Balsamic Vinaigrette
35

Creamy Avocado-Herb Dressing
35

Raspberry and Red Onion
Vinaigrette
36

Roasted Tomato Catalina
Dressing
37

Green Goddess Dressing
38

Creamy Asian Dressing
39

Creamy Feta Salad Dressing
39

Creamy Italian Herb Dressing
40

Italiano Salad Dressing
41

Dijon Vinaigrette
41

Orange Cashew Salad Dressing
42

Honey-Wasabi Vinaigrette
43

Tarragon Salad Dressing
44

Buttermilk Dressing
45

Cashew-Garlic Ranch Dressing
45

Lemon-Almond Dressing
46

Chunky Blue Cheese
Salad Dressing
47

Thai Orange Peanut Dressing
48

¼ cup seasoned rice vinegar

4 large garlic cloves, pressed

1 tablespoon lemon juice

2 tablespoons flat-leaf parsley, chopped

1 tablespoon basil, chopped

1 teaspoon onion powder

½ teaspoon dried rosemary, crushed

½ teaspoon black pepper, finely ground

¼ teaspoon salt

¼ teaspoon cumin, ground

¼ teaspoon dried oregano

¾ cup extra-virgin olive oil

½ cup Parmesan cheese, grated

Garlic Parmesan Salad Dressing

This recipe for garlic lovers tastes great with almost any salad, but truly shines when drizzled over a large bowl of plain iceberg or romaine lettuce.

1. Place everything, except the oil and Parmesan cheese, in a food processor. Process until smooth.

2. Slowly add oil to processor and mix for 30 seconds. Pour Parmesan into the processor and mix for 10 seconds.

3. Pour dressing into a bottle and cover with lid. Shake well before each use and refrigerate to store.

PER SERVING

Calories: 1,677	Sodium: . . . . 1,354 mg
Fat: . . . . 177 g	Fiber: . . . . .0 g
Protein:. . . . . . . 20 g	Carbohydrate: . . .6 g

Why Flat-Leaf Parsley?

Flat-leaf parsley, also known as Italian parsley, has a stronger scent and flavor than other parsley types. There are over thirty different types of parsley, but flat-leaf and curly are the two used most in cooking. Some people prefer curly parsley for its mellow taste, but other ingredients in the recipe tend to overpower its subtle flavor. Thus, curly parsley is most often used as a visually appealing garnish.

INGREDIENTS | SERVES 20

INGREDIENTS | SERVES 20

1 tablespoon orange zest

2 teaspoons lime zest

1 pickled jalapeño pepper, chopped

1 tablespoon pickled jalapeño brine

¼ cup rice wine vinegar

¼ cup orange juice concentrate

1½ teaspoons Dijon mustard

2 tablespoons sesame oil

¼ cup peanut oil

¼ cup olive oil

Salt and pepper, to taste

INGREDIENTS | SERVES 6

1 teaspoon seasoned salt

1 teaspoon lemon pepper

1 teaspoon dry mustard

2 tablespoons fresh lemon juice

2 tablespoons cider vinegar

¾ cup olive oil

Orange Sesame Vinaigrette

This dressing gives a burst of flavor to even the dullest salad.

1. Combine zest, pickled jalapeño, brine, rice vinegar, orange concentrate, Dijon, and sesame oil in a blender.

2. Blend on medium speed, slowly drizzling in the peanut and olive oils. Season to taste with salt and pepper. Pour dressing into a lidded bottle and store in refrigerator. Shake well before using.

PER SERVING

Calories: 51	Sodium: . . . . 0 mg
Fat: . . . . 5 g	Fiber: . . . . 0 g
Protein: . . . . 0 g	Carbohydrate: . . . 0.5 g

Classic French Dressing

A versatile dressing to use over mixed greens topped with rotisserie chicken, on top of green beans, or as a marinade for chicken.

Add all the ingredients in a glass bowl and whisk to combine. Taste and adjust seasoning as desired. Remix just before serving. Refrigerate any unused portion and bring to room temperature before serving.

PER SERVING

Calories: 240	Sodium: . . . . . . 195 mg
Fat: . . . . 27 g	Fiber: . . . . 0 g
Protein: . . . . 0 g	Carbohydrate: . . . 0 g

3 tablespoons walnuts, whole

¼ cup red wine vinegar

1 tablespoon spicy brown mustard

1 tablespoon honey

½ teaspoon kosher salt

½ teaspoon black pepper, ground

¼ teaspoon garlic powder

¼ teaspoon ginger root, ground

⅔ cup olive oil

Walnut Honey-Mustard Vinaigrette

This sweet and tangy salad dressing tastes great with any type of greens, from sweet baby spinach to peppery red mustard leaf.

1. Place walnuts in a chopping bowl. Chop walnuts until they reach a very fine, almost powder-like, consistency.

2. Whisk together the walnuts, vinegar, mustard, honey, salt, pepper, garlic, and ginger together in a small bowl. Mix well.

3. Pour the mixture into a bottle. Add the oil to the bottle and screw the lid on tightly. Shake the mixture very well to combine the oil and vinegar mixture. Store in fridge and shake well before each use.

PER SERVING

Calories:	 1,518	Sodium:	. . . . . 1,183 mg
Fat:	. . . . 160 g	Fiber:	. . . . 1.5 g
Protein:	. . . . 3.4 g	Carbohydrate:	. . 25 g

Working with Walnuts

The easiest way to chop a small amount of walnuts is to use a wooden cutting board, spatula, and knife. Place the nuts in a pile and chop. As the pieces spread out, use the spatula to keep sweeping them back into a pile for chopping. Don't be tempted to place the nuts in a large food processor, as the processor is much more likely to create walnut butter rather than finely chopped nuts.

¼ cup balsamic vinegar

¾ cup olive oil

1 tablespoon Dijon mustard

¼ teaspoon salt

⅛ teaspoon black pepper, ground

½ teaspoon dried basil

½ teaspoon dried parsley

Basic Balsamic Vinaigrette

No need to purchase expensive and sugar-laden salad dressings at the grocery store! This simple vinaigrette will serve you well for a last-minute salad dressing.

Whisk together all ingredients with a fork until well combined.

PER SERVING

Calories:	94	Sodium:	38 mg
Fat:	10 g	Fiber:	0 g
Protein:	0 g	Carbohydrate:	1 g

1 cup avocado, chopped

½ cup mayonnaise

¼ cup water

1 tablespoon lemon juice

1 teaspoon roasted garlic paste

1 teaspoon fresh cilantro, minced

½ teaspoon kosher salt

½ teaspoon fresh parsley, minced

¼ teaspoon dried rosemary, crushed

¼ teaspoon black pepper, finely ground

Creamy Avocado-Herb Dressing

Roasted garlic paste comes in small jars that are usually located near the fresh garlic or spices in grocery stores.

Add ingredients to a food processor or high-powered blender. Process until smooth and pour mixture into a lidded bottle. Chill in fridge and shake well before each use.

PER SERVING

Calories:	967	Sodium:	1,794 mg
Fat:	102 g	Fiber:	11 g
Protein:	3 g	Carbohydrate:	16 g

1 cup fresh raspberries

¼ cup red onion, chopped

¼ cup seasoned rice vinegar

1 teaspoon basil, minced

½ teaspoon kosher salt

¼ teaspoon black pepper, finely ground

¼ teaspoon dried thyme

¼ teaspoon dried parsley

⅛ teaspoon cumin, ground

½ cup extra-virgin olive oil

Raspberry and Red Onion Vinaigrette

Thaw out frozen raspberries if fresh are not available. Use a colander in a bowl for thawing to keep the berries from becoming soggy and watered down.

1. Add raspberries, onion, vinegar, basil, salt, pepper, thyme, parsley, and cumin to a food processor. Process until smooth.

2. Slowly feed the oil into the processor. Process until emulsified. Pour dressing into bottle and twist on lid. Store in fridge and shake well before use.

PER SERVING

Calories: 1,041	Sodium: . . . . . 1,168 mg
Fat: . . . . 109 g	Fiber: . . . . 8.5 g
Protein: . . . . 1 g	Carbohydrate: . . 15 g

Cutting Onions Without Crying

There are a few tricks you can use to cut onions without ending up in tears. Chilling the onion in a freezer for 5–10 minutes before cutting, or cutting the onion in a bowl of cold water, helps weaken and contain the enzymes that cause you to tear up. Using an extremely sharp knife helps prevent crushing the onion, which reduces the amount of tear-inducing enzymes released.

12 plum tomatoes

½ cup extra-virgin olive oil, divided

1 garlic clove, minced

½ teaspoon kosher salt

⅛ teaspoon red pepper, ground

3 tablespoons ketchup

2 tablespoons honey

¼ teaspoon sweet Hungarian paprika

¼ teaspoon mustard seed, ground

¼ teaspoon celery seed

3 tablespoons white wine vinegar

Roasted Tomato Catalina Dressing

The roasted tomatoes in this recipe add a whole new layer of flavor to the tangy dressing and add a hint of smoky sweetness to any salad.

1. Preheat oven to 400°F.

2. Cut the tomatoes in half by length and use a spoon to scoop out the seeds. Place tomatoes on a baking sheet lined with parchment paper. Drizzle 3 tablespoons oil over the tomatoes. Sprinkle with garlic, salt, and pepper.

3. Roast tomatoes for 20 minutes, or until tomatoes concentrate and start to caramelize. Remove from oven and let cool 10 minutes.

4. Place roasted tomatoes, ketchup, honey, paprika, mustard, and celery seed in a food processor. Slowly feed the vinegar as you process. Process until smooth. Slowly feed remaining oil into the processor. Process until emulsified.

5. Pour dressing into a bottle and store in fridge. Shake well before each use.

PER SERVING

Calories:. 1,361	Sodium: . . . . .1,760 mg
Fat:. . . . . 114 g	Fiber: . . . . 13 g
Protein:. . . . . . . 13 g	Carbohydrate: . . 95 g

Storing Roasted Tomatoes

You can store roasted tomatoes in the refrigerator for up to four days if you want to roast one day and make the dressing later. Let the tomatoes cool completely before placing them in a container and storing them in the fridge. You can also freeze the roasted tomatoes for up to six months.

½ cup mayonnaise

¼ cup heavy cream

¼ cup sour cream

1 tablespoon garlic, minced

3 tablespoons fresh parsley, finely chopped

3 tablespoons snipped fresh chives

1 tablespoon fresh tarragon, minced

1 tablespoon fresh lemon juice

1 teaspoon lemon zest

⅛ teaspoon seasoned salt

⅛ teaspoon black pepper, ground

Green Goddess Dressing

Use only fresh herbs for this dressing. It makes a delicious sauce for grilled fish and sturdy greens.

Combine all the ingredients in a nonreactive bowl and whisk until well blended. Taste and adjust seasoning as desired. Pour dressing into lidded container and refrigerate until ready to use. Shake well before using.

PER SERVING

Calories: 178	Sodium: . . . . . . 149 mg
Fat: . . . . 19 g	Fiber: . . . . 0 g
Protein: . . . . 1 g	Carbohydrate: . . . 1.5 g

Herbs and Salads

Fresh herbs add a unique flavor to the traditional salad. A 2-tablespoon serving of basil, chives, or parsley has just a trace of carbs; chervil has 2g of carbs; and fennel has 1g.

¾ cup mayonnaise

¼ cup sour cream

2 tablespoons tamari

1 teaspoon garlic, minced

2 tablespoons rice wine vinegar

1 teaspoon honey

¼ cup scallion, thinly sliced

¼ teaspoon black pepper, ground

⅓ cup feta, crumbled

¼ cup plain yogurt

3 tablespoons milk

1 tablespoon lemon juice

1 tablespoon shallots, minced

½ teaspoon dried parsley

¼ teaspoon kosher salt

⅛ teaspoon white pepper, ground

Creamy Asian Dressing

You can use this as a dressing for chicken salad and add a small amount of water chestnuts, sprouts, and scallions for added crunch.

Combine all the ingredients in a nonreactive bowl and whisk until well blended. Taste and adjust seasoning as desired. Refrigerate until ready to use.

PER SERVING

Calories: 210	Sodium: . . . . . . 518 mg
Fat: . . . . 22 g	Fiber: . . . . 0 g
Protein: . . . . 1 g	Carbohydrate: . . . 2 g

Creamy Feta Salad Dressing

Take a break from blue cheese with this rich and creamy feta dressing that enhances, but never overpowers, any salad.

Add ingredients to a blender. Blend until smooth. Pour mixture into a lidded bottle and store in refrigerator. Shake well before use.

PER SERVING

Calories: 17	Sodium: . . . . 99 mg
Fat: . . . . 1 g	Fiber: . . . . 0 g
Protein: . . . . 1 g	Carbohydrate: . . . 1 g

Creamy Italian Herb Dressing

If you don't care for dried Italian seasonings, spend a few minutes mincing up to 2 tablespoons of fresh herbs to throw into the dressing.

1. Stir together Parmesan, mayonnaise, lemon juice, garlic paste, Italian seasoning, and black pepper in a medium mixing bowl.

2. Whisk oil into bowl and mix until emulsified. Pour dressing into lidded bottle and store in fridge. Shake well before each use.

PER SERVING

Calories:......82	Sodium:.......47 mg
Fat:..........9 g	Fiber:..........0 g
Protein:........1 g	Carbohydrate:...0 g

Types of Olive Oil

Many recipes call for extra-virgin olive oil, which is made from the first pressing of green olives. Virgin olive oil is also made from the first pressing, but consists of extremely ripe green olives. Pure olive oil is made from the second olive pressing and has far less flavor than the other varieties. Extra light olive oil is a mixture of low quality pressings, and thus the weakest type of the oil.

Italiano Salad Dressing

Inspired by Italian dressing, but in a class of its own, this creamy mixture also tastes great as a dip or as a condiment on a sandwich.

1. Combine ingredients in blender and mix until uniform in color. Stop blender and use a spatula to scrape mixture from sides. Cover blender and blend again to ensure thorough mixing.

2. Scrape mixture into a lidded container and store in refrigerator until needed. Shake well before each use.

PER SERVING

Calories: 81	Sodium: . . . . 75 mg
Fat: . . . . 8.5 g	Fiber: . . . . 0 g
Protein: . . . . 0 g	Carbohydrate: . . . 1 g

Dijon Vinaigrette

Whip up this fresh and tangy dressing whenever you want to give a plain salad a kick of flavor.

Put all the ingredients in a small bowl and use a wire whisk or fork to mix. Drizzle dressing over salad immediately or store in fridge until needed. Shake well before use.

PER SERVING

Calories: 94	Sodium: . . . . . . 295 mg
Fat: . . . . 10 g	Fiber: . . . . 0 g
Protein: . . . . 0 g	Carbohydrate: . . . 0 g

4 tablespoons cashews, soaked

2 tablespoons extra-virgin sesame oil

½ cup orange juice

Orange Cashew Salad Dressing

This is a delicious dressing made with a base of cashews. Olive oil may be used in place of the sesame oil.

Place all the ingredients into a blender and blend until smooth. Continue to blend until the cashews are fully emulsified. Pour dressing into a bottle or directly over salad.

PER SERVING

Calories: 246	Sodium: . . . . 4 mg
Fat: . . . . 22 g	Fiber: . . . . 1 g
Protein: . . . . 3 g	Carbohydrate: . . 12 g

Unrefined Oils

A majority of these recipes use unrefined extra-virgin olive oil because it is readily available. There are other types of unrefined oils that you may use in place of olive oil. A health food store should have a good selection. Be sure to check the label to make sure the oils are cold pressed, raw, and extra virgin. Some raw oils include sesame, sunflower, almond, evening primrose, flax, hemp, poppy seed, and coconut.

⅓ cup rice wine vinegar

2 tablespoons honey

1½ teaspoons wasabi paste

¼ teaspoon garlic salt

⅛ teaspoon white pepper, finely ground

⅛ teaspoon cumin, ground

⅛ teaspoon ginger root, ground

⅔ cup salad oil

Honey-Wasabi Vinaigrette

This hot and sweet salad dressing tastes best when paired with mixed or plain greens. The intense dressing does not pair well with salads that include bold flavors or numerous ingredients.

1. Combine vinegar, honey, wasabi, garlic salt, white pepper, cumin, and ginger in a blender. Blend until fully mixed.

2. Slowly add oil as the blender mixes on low. Blend until emulsified. Pour dressing in a lidded container and chill in refrigerator until needed. Shake well before using.

PER SERVING

Calories: 92	Sodium: . . . . 14 mg
Fat: . . . . 9.5 g	Fiber: . . . . 0 g
Protein: . . . . 0 g	Carbohydrate: . . . 2.5 g

Wasabi Paste

Most wasabi, also known as Japanese horseradish, comes as a prepared paste or as a dry powder. Grating and drying the wasabi helps keep it fresh for a longer period. To turn wasabi powder into paste, just mix even amounts of water and powder. Be careful when buying wasabi though, as cheaper products usually include green dye and white horseradish, but no actual wasabi.

⅓ cup tarragon vinegar

1 garlic clove, minced

4 teaspoons Dijon mustard

1 tablespoon fresh tarragon leaves, minced

1 teaspoon kosher salt

½ teaspoon black pepper, ground

⅔ cup extra-virgin olive oil

Tarragon Salad Dressing

Drizzle a little of this mixture over a salad to use it as a dressing, or pour it over a bowl of veggies and chill for 4 hours to use as a marinade.

1. Add vinegar, garlic, mustard, tarragon, salt, and pepper to a blender. Blend on low for 5 seconds.

2. Slowly feed oil into blender. Blend until emulsified. Pour dressing into a lidded bottle and store in refrigerator. Shake well before use.

PER SERVING

Calories:	83	Sodium:	147 mg
Fat:	9 g	Fiber:	0 g
Protein:	0 g	Carbohydrate:	0.5 g

Tarragon Vinegar for Less

Tarragon vinegar is a popular product at high-end grocers. However, it's cheaper to make the infused vinegar yourself. Heat 8 ounces of white wine vinegar in a saucepan. Add two or three sprigs of fresh tarragon, a pinch of white pepper, and a pinch of salt to the empty vinegar bottle. Pour the vinegar back into the bottle, cover with lid, shake well, and keep in a cool, dark place for at least 4 days before using.

Buttermilk Dressing

This subtle dressing works on any kind of salad, be it fruit, meat, grain, or vegetable based.

The easiest way to make this fat-free dressing is to measure all the ingredients into a jar, and stir with a long spoon to ensure the powders dissolve. Put the lid on the jar and shake it vigorously until it's mixed. Refrigerate any unused portions and shake well before using. May be kept in the refrigerator up to 3 days.

PER SERVING

Calories:	13	Sodium:	62 mg
Fat:	0 g	Fiber:	0 g
Protein:	1 g	Carbohydrate:	2 g

Cashew-Garlic Ranch Dressing

This creamy dressing may not taste like any common ranch, but it has just the right blend of spicy and sweet to be as versatile as any traditional recipe.

Process the cashews and water together in a blender or food processor until creamy. Add the remaining ingredients and mix well. Pour into a bottle or bowl and refrigerate for 30 minutes before use. Shake or stir well before use.

PER SERVING

Calories:	20	Sodium:	31 mg
Fat:	1 g	Fiber:	0 g
Protein:	0.5 g	Carbohydrate:	2 g

¼ cup raw almonds

1 tablespoon lemon juice

¼ cup water

1½ teaspoons honey

¼ teaspoon lemon pepper

½ of a slice (1 inch in diameter) peeled ginger

¼ clove garlic

1½ teaspoons fresh chives, chopped

1½ teaspoons fresh sweet basil, chopped

Lemon-Almond Dressing

Add this dressing to any fruit salad to provide a little zip with the sweet dish. Use it on peppery greens to help sweeten and balance the strong flavors.

Put all the ingredients in a food processor or blender and process until smooth. Scrape ingredients into a bottle and store in refrigerator until needed. Shake before use.

PER SERVING

Calories: 17	Sodium: . . . . 0 mg
Fat: . . . . 1 g	Fiber: . . . . 0 g
Protein: . . . . 0.5 g	Carbohydrate: . . . 1.5 g

Salad: Undressed

Make a quick salad without dressing by mixing chopped celery, onion, and other vegetable choices such as cucumbers or zucchini. Add some of your favorite low-salt seasoning or toss the vegetables with some Bragg's Liquid Aminos or low-sodium soy sauce and serve over salad greens.

¾ cup crumbled blue cheese

4 teaspoons hot water

¼ cup sour cream

⅓ cup buttermilk

2 tablespoons mayonnaise

½ teaspoon fresh chives, minced

½ teaspoon roasted garlic paste

⅛ teaspoon black pepper, ground

Chunky Blue Cheese Salad Dressing

If you prefer creamy dressing, just omit the extra ¼ cup of crumbled blue cheese mixed in at the end.

1. Use a fork to combine ½ cup blue cheese and hot water in a medium mixing bowl. Use the liquid to help soften the cheese.

2. Use an electric mixer on low to stir the sour cream, buttermilk, mayonnaise, chives, garlic paste, and pepper into the dressing. Mix well. Use a spoon to stir remaining blue cheese into mixture, place in lidded bowl, and store in refrigerator until needed. Stir well before use.

PER SERVING

Calories: 62	Sodium: . . . . . . 157 mg
Fat: . . . . 5.5 g	Fiber: . . . . 0 g
Protein: . . . . 2.5 g	Carbohydrate: . . . 1 g

¼ cup peanut butter, room temperature

¼ cup orange juice

2 tablespoons soy sauce

2 tablespoons rice vinegar

2 tablespoons water

½ teaspoon garlic powder

½ teaspoon sugar

¼ teaspoon red chili flakes, crushed

Thai Orange Peanut Dressing

A sweet and spicy take on traditional Thai and Indonesian peanut and satay sauce. Add a bit less liquid to use this salad dressing as a dip for veggies.

Whisk together all ingredients until smooth and creamy, adding more or less liquid to achieve desired consistency. Pour into bottle and chill in refrigerator until needed. Shake well before use.

PER SERVING

Calories:	37	Sodium:	178 mg
Fat:	2.5 g	Fiber:	0 g
Protein:	1.5 g	Carbohydrate:	2 g

Make Your Own Peanut Butter

Try making your own peanut butter for a real treat. Combine 1 cup unsalted peanuts, 1 tablespoon peanut oil, and a pinch of salt in a blender and mix until creamy. If you prefer chunky peanut butter, stir ¼ cup chopped peanuts into the smooth mixture. If you prefer sweet peanut butter, add honey or sugar to taste.

CHAPTER 4

Green Salads

Apple Walnut Spinach Salad
50

Mediterranean Tomato Salad
50

Green Goddess Salad
51

Leafy Zucchini Salad
52

Lettuce Lover's Salad Delight
53

Sweet Spring Baby Salad
54

Spring Greens with Berries
54

Tarragon Arugula-Peanut Salad
55

Crunchy Stir-Fry Salad
56

Cactus Salad
57

Russian Beet and Micro
Greens Salad
58

Kale and Sea Vegetables with
Orange Sesame Dressing
59

Marinated Kale and
Avocado Salad
60

Spiced Collards Salad
61

Pomegranate Green Salad
62

Greens with Jalapeño Dressing
63

Crisp Strawberry Spinach Salad
64

Country Garden Salad
64

Wilted Kale Salad with
Roasted Shallots
65

Marinated Avocado and
Mushroom Salad
66

Tofu Tossed Salad
67

Mushroom Lover's Green Salad
68

2 cups baby spinach leaves, torn

1 cup romaine lettuce, torn

1 cup Washington apple, chopped

½ cup red onion, diced

½ cup cucumber, peeled and diced

⅓ cup walnuts, chopped

⅓ cup Caesar salad dressing

¼ cup mini seasoned croutons

Apple Walnut Spinach Salad

While the sweet taste of Washington apples is a popular match for baby spinach, you can use any sweet apples with this salad, depending on personal preference.

Toss spinach, lettuce, apples, onion, cucumber, and walnuts together in a large salad bowl. Drizzle dressing over salad and toss well to mix and coat. Garnish with croutons and serve immediately.

PER SERVING

Calories:	93	Sodium:	204 mg
Fat:	5 g	Fiber:	1.5 g
Protein:	2 g	Carbohydrate:	9 g

2 cups tomatoes, sliced

1 cup cucumber, peeled and chopped

⅓ cup yellow bell pepper, diced

¼ cup radishes, sliced

¼ cup flat-leaf parsley, chopped

1 garlic clove, finely minced

1 tablespoon lemon juice

3 tablespoons extra-virgin olive oil

2 cups baby spinach leaves, torn

Salt and pepper, to taste

Mediterranean Tomato Salad

Use juicy tomatoes for this recipe, such as Heirloom or Beefsteak. You can substitute orange bell pepper for the yellow if needed.

1. Toss tomatoes, cucumbers, bell pepper, radishes, and parsley together in a large salad bowl.

2. Sprinkle garlic, lemon juice, and oil over salad. Toss to coat. Salt and pepper to taste. Split spinach between four plates and top with salad. Serve immediately.

PER SERVING

Calories:	131	Sodium:	71 mg
Fat:	10 g	Fiber:	2.5 g
Protein:	2.5 g	Carbohydrate:	7 g

1 cup broccoli florets

1 cup cauliflower florets

½ cup English cucumber, peeled and sliced

½ cup celery, chopped

¼ cup balsamic vinaigrette salad dressing

1 tablespoon pesto

2 cups mixed baby greens, torn

Green Goddess Salad

Baby greens, also known as mesclun, add a sweet and delicate touch to help balance the texture of the crispy salad.

1. Place the broccoli and cauliflower florets in a large mixing bowl. Break up any large florets into small, bite-size pieces. Add the cucumber and celery to the bowl. Toss to mix.

2. Whisk the salad dressing and pesto together in a small bowl. Drizzle over salad and toss well to coat completely. Gently toss the baby greens into the salad and serve.

PER SERVING

Calories: 91   Sodium: . . . . . . 176 mg
Fat: . . . . 6.5 g   Fiber: . . . . 2 g
Protein: . . . . 2 g   Carbohydrate: . . . 1.5 g

English Cucumbers

Common cucumbers are thick with waxy dark green skin, large seeds, and heavy amounts of water. English cucumbers are thinner, longer, contain smaller seeds, contain slightly less water, and have a thinner skin than common cucumbers. Since it's the skin and seeds that can make cucumbers taste bitter, the thin skin and small seeds make English cucumbers easier to use and more likely to taste sweet.

1 small zucchini

1 cup arugula leaves, torn

2 cups baby spinach leaves

⅓ cup red bell pepper, sliced

⅓ cup white mushrooms, sliced

¼ cup leeks, diced

2 tablespoons red wine vinegar

1 teaspoon fresh basil, minced

½ teaspoon garlic salt

⅛ teaspoon black pepper, ground

2 tablespoons extra-virgin olive oil

Leafy Zucchini Salad

This recipe has a mix of tantalizing delicate, soft, and crunchy textures that pair well with pasta or chicken entrées.

1. Wash and rinse the zucchini. Trim the ends. Cut the zucchini into enough thin slices to fill 1 cup.

2. Toss the zucchini slices, arugula, baby spinach, bell pepper, mushrooms, and leeks together in a large salad bowl.

3. Whisk together the vinegar, basil, garlic salt, and pepper in a small bowl. Whisk in the olive oil, mixing thoroughly. Drizzle dressing over salad and toss to combine. Serve immediately.

PER SERVING

Calories: 85	Sodium: . . . . . . 173 mg
Fat: . . . . 7 g	Fiber: . . . . 1 g
Protein: . . . . 2 g	Carbohydrate: . . . 3.5 g

Zucchinis Small and Large

Zucchini is a type of summer squash distinct for its dark green rind. The vegetable can grow to an enormous size, well over 3 feet long. However, large zucchinis tend to get a little woody and work best in breads or cakes. Stick with small zucchinis for your salad, as they retain a mild and refreshing flavor.

INGREDIENTS | SERVES 4

2 cups romaine lettuce, chopped

1 cup Bibb lettuce, torn

1 cup endive, chopped

½ cup arugula, torn

½ cup red leaf lettuce, torn

⅓ cup celery, sliced

¼ cup baby carrots, chopped

4 teaspoons seasoned rice vinegar

¼ teaspoon kosher salt

⅛ teaspoon hot paprika

⅛ teaspoon garlic powder

⅛ teaspoon onion powder

3 tablespoons olive oil

¼ cup grape tomatoes, sliced

Lettuce Lover's Salad Delight

This crisp and refreshing recipe works best when served before the meal or the delicate contrasts between greens will end up overpowered by the heavier main dish.

1. Combine romaine, Bibb, endive, arugula, red leaf, celery, and carrots in a large salad bowl. Toss gently to mix.

2. Whisk vinegar, salt, paprika, garlic powder, and onion powder together in a small bowl. Whisk oil into dressing and mix until emulsified.

3. Drizzle dressing over salad. Toss extremely well to coat. Add tomato slices to top of salad as a garnish and serve immediately.

PER SERVING

Calories:. 105	Sodium: . . . . . . 165 mg
Fat:. . . . . 10 g	Fiber: . . . . .2 g
Protein:. . . . . . . .1 g	Carbohydrate: . . .3 g

Lettuce Rejoice

Lettuce, which hails from Mediterranean and Asian areas, is the most popular salad ingredient across the globe. There are mentions of lettuce being eaten as far back as ancient Persia during the sixth century B.C. and ancient Egyptian tombs have carvings of primitive lettuce plants. It was popular enough that even Christopher Columbus carried lettuce seeds to the New World.

Sweet Spring Baby Salad

Any type of baby greens work with this recipe, so pick your favorite mixture from the store or whip up your own at home.

1. Combine the greens, carrots, and chives in a large salad bowl. Drizzle vinegar, sugar, and salt over salad. Toss to coat.

2. Drizzle olive oil over salad and toss to coat. Add croutons to salad and toss to mix. Serve immediately.

PER SERVING

Calories: 94	Sodium: . . . . . . 167 mg
Fat: . . . . 7.5 g	Fiber: . . . . 1.5 g
Protein: . . . . 1 g	Carbohydrate: . . . 6 g

Spring Greens with Berries

The acid in the lime juice breaks down the fat in the olive oil to make a flavorful dressing.

1. Slice the jalapeño pepper and remove the seeds and stem. Mince the pepper flesh.

2. Place the lime juice, olive oil, cumin, and 2 teaspoons of the minced jalapeño pepper in a blender and blend together until smooth.

3. Toss the dressing with the greens, berries, and onions and serve as a side salad.

PER SERVING

Calories: 363	Sodium: . . . . . . 242 mg
Fat: . . . . 28 g	Fiber: . . . . 9.5 g
Protein: . . . . 5.5 g	Carbohydrate: . . 21 g

3 cups arugula, torn

2 cups red leaf lettuce, torn

⅓ cup white onion, sliced

¼ cup red bell pepper, diced

2 tablespoons red wine vinegar

2 teaspoons honey

1 teaspoon spicy brown mustard

¼ teaspoon salt

¼ teaspoon dried tarragon

2 tablespoons sunflower oil

½ cup honey-roasted peanuts

Tarragon Arugula-Peanut Salad

The strong flavor of this salad makes it most suitable as a side to savory beef entrées such as peppered steak or pot roast.

1. Toss the arugula, lettuce, onion, and bell peppers together in a large salad bowl.

2. Whisk the vinegar, honey, mustard, salt, and tarragon together in a small bowl. Whisk oil into bowl and mix until emulsified.

3. Drizzle dressing over salad and toss well to coat. Add peanuts to salad and toss to mix. Serve salad immediately.

PER SERVING

Calories:	173	Sodium:	154 mg
Fat:	14 g	Fiber:	1.5 g
Protein:	5 g	Carbohydrate:	6.5 g

Taste of Tarragon

Tarragon is a delicate greenish-gray herb in the sunflower family with a strong flavor reminiscent of anise. It has two main varieties, French and Russian. The sweeter French tarragon is traditionally used in cooking, as Russian tarragon tends to have a bitter taste. Anise, fennel, or licorice extract can be used as a substitute for tarragon, but they will only add a hint of similar taste, not replicate the flavor.

1½ cups sugar snap peas, trimmed

1 (8-ounce) can water chestnuts, diced

1 cup bok choy, diced

½ cup red bell pepper, julienned

½ cup red onion, sliced

¼ cup carrot, diced

2 tablespoons soy sauce

2 tablespoons seasoned rice vinegar

¼ teaspoon ginger root, ground

¼ teaspoon lemon pepper

3 tablespoons sesame oil

2 tablespoons cashews, chopped

Crunchy Stir-Fry Salad

Go for a fresh and crunchy treat with this green salad that mimics a traditional stir-fry, yet keeps everything raw.

1. Cut the sugar snap peas in half and place in a large salad bowl. Drain water chestnuts. Add water chestnuts, bell pepper, onion, and carrots to bowl.

2. Whisk the soy sauce, vinegar, ginger, and lemon pepper together in a small bowl. Whisk oil into bowl and mix until emulsified. Drizzle dressing over salad and toss well to coat.

3. Cover bowl and place in refrigerator. Let salad marinate for 30 minutes. Mix well, garnish with cashews, and serve.

PER SERVING

Calories: 208	Sodium: . . . . . . 281 mg
Fat: . . . . 12 g	Fiber: . . . . 4 g
Protein: . . . . 3.5 g	Carbohydrate: . . 21 g

2 cups canned cactus strips

1½ cups red tomatoes, chopped

⅓ cup pitted black olives, halved

2 tablespoons fresh cilantro

⅓ cup red radishes, diced

¼ cup olive oil

¼ cup red wine vinegar

1 teaspoon garlic salt

1 teaspoon white pepper, ground

½ teaspoon cayenne pepper

Mixed greens

Cactus Salad

Canned cactus strips are available at most large grocery stores today, although you can substitute any vegetable such as broccoli or cauliflower.

1. Drain off the water from the cactus strips. Combine cactus, tomatoes, olives, cilantro, and radishes in a large mixing bowl.

2. In a small container with a cover, mix the olive oil, vinegar, garlic salt, white pepper, and cayenne pepper; shake well to mix.

3. Pour the dressing over the vegetables and toss until well mixed. Chill for at least 30 minutes before serving. Serve over a bed of mixed greens.

PER SERVING

Calories:. 109	Sodium: . . . . . . 227 mg
Fat:. . . . . 10 g	Fiber: . . . . 1.5 g
Protein:. . . . . . . 1.5 g	Carbohydrate: . . . 4.5 g

What about the Stickers?

For those of us in northern climates, the idea of eating cactus is, well, terrifying. However, it really is quite juicy and flavorful. Many people in the southwestern United States will simply pick their own backyard cactus. The canned variety is much mushier and loses some of its flavor but is a good place to start for those new to this delicacy.

3 large beets, trimmed

3 tablespoons mayonnaise

1 garlic clove, crushed

⅛ teaspoon kosher salt

⅛ teaspoon black pepper, ground

¼ cup prunes, finely chopped

¼ cup walnuts, finely chopped

4 cups mixed micro greens

Russian Beet and Micro Greens Salad

Don't try to peel the beets before cooking, just wash them. Beet skins are tough when raw, but slip right off once the beet has been cooked.

1. Place beets in a large pot of boiling salt water. Bring water back to a boil, cover pot with lid, and reduce heat to low. Simmer beets until tender, about 45 minutes. Drain beets and remove skins. Finely chop beets and place in large mixing bowl.

2. Combine mayonnaise, garlic, salt, and pepper in a small bowl. Add dressing to beets and gently mix to coat. Mix prunes and walnuts into salad.

3. Split micro greens evenly between 4 small salad bowls. Spoon beet salad in the middle of each bowl and serve.

PER SERVING

Calories: 177	Sodium: . . . . . . 195 mg
Fat: . . . . 13 g	Fiber: . . . . 3 g
Protein: . . . . 3 g	Carbohydrate: . . 14 g

¼ cup wakame seaweed

½ cup sea lettuce

3 cups kale

½ teaspoon salt

¼ cup orange juice

6 tablespoons sesame seeds (additional for garnish)

1 tablespoon kelp powder

Kale and Sea Vegetables with Orange Sesame Dressing

This salad is a great appetizer for an Asian-themed meal. It is good served with miso soup and nori rolls.

1. Soak the wakame and sea lettuce in water for 30 minutes. Rinse and discard the soak water.

2. Remove the stems from the kale. Roll up the kale leaves and chop into small pieces.

3. Sprinkle salt onto the kale and massage it by hand to create a wilting effect.

4. Place the orange juice, sesame seeds, and kelp powder into a blender and blend until smooth.

5. Toss the dressing with the kale and sea vegetables in a large bowl until well covered. Sprinkle about 1 teaspoon sesame seeds on top.

PER SERVING

Calories: 90		Sodium: . . . . . . 364 mg
Fat: . . . . 5 g		Fiber: . . . . 3 g
Protein: . . . . 4 g		Carbohydrate: . . . 9 g

Sea Vegetables

Sea vegetables are among the most nutritious and mineral-rich foods on earth. Ocean water contains all the mineral elements known to man. For example, both kelp and dulse are excellent sources of iodine, which is an essential nutrient missing in most diets. Sea vegetables are dried and should be soaked in water to reconstitute before eating.

3 cups kale

1 teaspoon salt

2 tablespoons lemon juice

2 tablespoons olive oil

1 tablespoon soy sauce

1½ cups avocado, diced

1 cup cherry tomatoes, chopped

1 tablespoon dulse flakes

Marinated Kale and Avocado Salad

This delicious salad uses wilted and marinated kale, and it has a good balance of flavors to stimulate the taste buds. If you cannot find dulse flakes, also known as dried sea lettuce flakes, use a pinch of dried parsley instead.

1. Peel the stems off the kale leaves. Roll the leaves and chop into small pieces.

2. Place the chopped kale into a large bowl and sprinkle with salt. Massage the salt into the kale by hand and let it sit for 10 minutes so the kale will become soft and wilt.

3. Pour the lemon juice onto the kale and let it marinate for a few minutes. The acidic lemon juice will further wilt the kale.

4. Pour the olive oil and soy sauce onto the kale and mix well.

5. Top the kale with avocado, chopped cherry tomatoes, and dulse flakes. Enjoy as a side salad with your entrée of choice.

PER SERVING

Calories: 356	Sodium: . . . . .1,667 mg
Fat: . . . . 31 g	Fiber: . . . . 10 g
Protein: . . . . .6 g	Carbohydrate: . . 21 g

Kale

Kale is a vegetable in the cabbage family. It is very strong and hearty and will grow in all soil types and most climates. It is considered a superfood because of the high quantity of concentrated nutrients, including carotenoids and other antioxidants, iron, and calcium.

INGREDIENTS | SERVES 2

3 cups young collard greens

1 teaspoon salt

3 tablespoons lemon juice

½ cup pine nuts

2 tablespoons olive oil

½ teaspoon garlic powder

½ tablespoon fresh basil

½ tablespoon fresh oregano

2 cups tomatoes, diced

¼ cup green onions, diced

1 cup red bell pepper, diced

Spiced Collards Salad

The lemon and olive oil in this recipe help balance the bitter greens and herbs. If you don't have pine nuts, try macadamia nuts or cashews instead.

1. Remove the stems from the collard greens. Roll up the greens and chop them into small pieces.

2. Sprinkle the salt onto the collards. Massage the collards by hand to work the salt into the greens so they begin to wilt.

3. Pour 2 tablespoons lemon juice on greens and mix. Let them sit for 1–2 minutes to wilt.

4. Blend the pine nuts, olive oil, garlic powder, and 1 tablespoon lemon juice until smooth. Put the basil and oregano in the blender and briefly pulse until the herbs are mixed in and still chunky.

5. Add tomato, onion, and red bell pepper to the collard greens. Toss the salad with the blended dressing and serve.

PER SERVING

Calories: 383

Fat: . . . . 32 g

Protein: . . . . . . 12 g

Sodium: . . . . . 1,192 mg

Fiber: . . . . 7 g

Carbohydrate: . . 20 g

Collard Greens

Collard greens and kale are the two most nutrient-rich foods in the leafy green category. They belong in the cruciferous and brassica family, along with cabbage, broccoli, and bok choy. Collard greens are excellent sources of antioxidants; phytochemicals; chlorophyll; vitamins A, C, and K; manganese; folate; calcium; zinc; and a number of other nutrients.

Pomegranate Green Salad

INGREDIENTS | SERVES 4

4 cups romaine lettuce, torn

4 cups butterhead lettuce, torn

1 large pomegranate

½ cup green onions, chopped

1 tablespoon fresh chives, chopped

¼ cup toasted pumpkin seeds

½ cup olive oil

⅓ cup pomegranate juice

1 tablespoon lime juice

1 tablespoon mustard

½ teaspoon salt

⅛ teaspoon white pepper

Pomegranates are in season from October to January. They are sold already ripe; choose fruits that are heavy for their size with no cracks or breaks in the skin.

1. In serving bowl, toss together lettuces. Remove seeds from pomegranate and sprinkle over lettuce. Squeeze the pomegranate shells over the salad to remove juice. Sprinkle with green onions, chives, and pumpkin seeds.

2. In small bowl, combine oil, pomegranate juice, lime juice, mustard, salt, and white pepper and beat with wire whisk to blend. Drizzle over salad, toss, and serve.

PER SERVING

Calories: 355	Sodium: . . . . . . 302 mg
Fat: . . . . 33 g	Fiber: . . . . 2.5 g
Protein: . . . . 6 g	Carbohydrate: . . 15 g

Seed a Pomegranate

To remove pomegranate seeds from the pomegranate, cut the large red fruit in half. Using the back of a knife or a large spoon, tap the rounded side of each half; the seeds will pop out from the cut edge. Squeeze the empty halves to remove the pomegranate juice and discard shell.

4 cups butterhead lettuce

2 cups red leaf lettuce

1 (4-ounce) can jalapeño peppers

½ cup sour cream

2 tablespoons honey

2 tablespoons lime juice

½ teaspoon salt

Greens with Jalapeño Dressing

This dressing also makes a wonderful marinade for chicken or turkey that you cook on the grill. Store covered in the refrigerator up to 4 days.

1. Combine lettuces in serving bowl and set aside. In blender or food processor, combine peppers, sour cream, honey, lime juice, and salt. Blend or process until smooth.

2. Pour half of dressing over lettuce mixture and toss gently. Serve remaining dressing on the side.

PER SERVING

Calories:......76	Sodium:......211 mg
Fat:..........4 g	Fiber:..........1 g
Protein:........1.5 g	Carbohydrate:...9 g

How to Prepare Greens

To prepare greens, fill a sink with cold water and add the greens. Swish the greens through the water and let stand for 2–3 minutes so any grit falls to the bottom of the sink. Remove the greens, separate if necessary, and lay on kitchen towels. Roll up towels and store in refrigerator for 1–2 hours.

4 cups baby spinach

1 cup hulled strawberries, sliced

⅓ cup red onion, chopped

⅓ cup baby carrots, julienned

¼ cup French salad dressing

1 tablespoon roasted sunflower seeds

3 cups red leaf lettuce, torn

1 cup baby spinach, torn

½ cup plum tomato, chopped

½ cup yellow squash, thinly sliced

¼ cup zucchini, thinly sliced

¼ cup carrots, sliced

2 tablespoons yellow onion, diced

⅓ cup Russian salad dressing

Crisp Strawberry Spinach Salad

Hulled strawberries are strawberries with the leaves pulled or cut off. For the greatest ease and best taste, just chop the tops off and cut the hulled strawberries into 1-inch slices.

Combine spinach, strawberries, onion, and carrots in a large salad bowl. Add dressing to salad. Toss well to fully mix and coat. Sprinkle sunflower seeds over salad. Serve immediately.

PER SERVING

Calories:	83	Sodium:	151 mg
Fat:	3 g	Fiber:	2.5 g
Protein:	3 g	Carbohydrate:	9 g

Country Garden Salad

This salad doesn't need any garnishes for color or flavor, but some garlic croutons are always a nice addition.

Toss lettuce, spinach, tomato, squash, zucchini, carrots, and onions in a large salad bowl. Drizzle salad with dressing and toss well to coat and mix.

PER SERVING

Calories:	66	Sodium:	188 mg
Fat:	3 g	Fiber:	1 g
Protein:	1 g	Carbohydrate:	8.5 g

3 large bunches kale

10 cups shallots

⅓ cup olive oil

2 tablespoons balsamic vinegar

¼ teaspoon kosher salt

⅛ teaspoon black pepper, ground

Wilted Kale Salad with Roasted Shallots

If you don't have kale, or you'd just like to try something different, you can substitute escarole or even spinach.

1. Preheat oven to 375°F. Clean and dry the kale. Peel the shallots and leave whole.

2. Toss the shallots in the oil and place in a roasting pan and roast in the oven until fork-tender, about 20 minutes. Remove from oven and slice the shallots in half.

3. While shallots roast, quickly wilt the kale in 2 gallons of boiling water for 1 minute. Remove from heat, drain, and set aside to cool.

4. Serve by mounding the cooked kale in the center of a plate or platter. Top with the shallots, drizzle with the vinegar, and sprinkle with salt and pepper.

PER SERVING

Calories: 212	Sodium: . . . . . . 106 mg	
Fat: . . . . 8 g	Fiber: . . . . 1.5 g	
Protein: . . . . 7 g	Carbohydrate: . . 34 g	

Wilting Greens

Wilting greens is a quick way to soften their texture and bring out their flavor. You can wilt greens by throwing them into any boiling liquid for 1–3 minutes. This lightly cooks the greens while preserving more nutrients than a long cooking process would. For more flavor, try wilting the greens in chicken broth or water with herbs thrown in.

2 medium avocados

1 cup button mushrooms, sliced

¼ cup white onion, thinly sliced

2 teaspoons lemon juice

¼ cup salad oil

¼ cup dry white wine

2 tablespoons vinegar

½ teaspoon sugar

¼ teaspoon salt

¼ teaspoon dried basil, crumbled

Bibb lettuce leaves, for serving

Marinated Avocado and Mushroom Salad

Be sure to let this salad marinate in the fridge for about 3 hours before serving so the flavors can mingle.

1. Cut avocados in half and remove seeds. Peel and slice.

2. In a large bowl, combine avocado, mushrooms, and onion rings. Sprinkle lemon juice over avocado mixture to prevent avocado from turning dark.

3. In a screw-top jar, combine oil, wine, vinegar, sugar, salt, and basil. Shake well and pour over vegetables.

4. Cover salad tightly and chill for at least 3 hours, stirring occasionally.

5. Drain avocado mixture. Serve on chilled salad plates on Bibb lettuce leaves.

PER SERVING

Calories:	253	Sodium:	152 mg
Fat:	25 g	Fiber:	5.5 g
Protein:	2 g	Carbohydrate:	8 g

3 cups red leaf lettuce, torn

1 (5-ounce) container alfalfa sprouts

1 small jicama, peeled and julienned

¼ cup dill pickle, chopped

1 tablespoon fresh cilantro, chopped

1 (6-ounce) jar marinated artichoke hearts, drained

1½ cups zucchini, sliced

3 tablespoons green onions, minced

½ cup button mushrooms, sliced

1 cup ripe tomatoes, sliced

1 (14-ounce) container firm tofu

½ cup Italian salad dressing

Tofu Tossed Salad

This salad is tossed with all kinds of tasty and healthy things. The tofu absorbs the flavors around it, and the alfalfa sprouts and jicama add crunch.

1. In a large bowl, combine lettuce, sprouts, jicama, pickle, cilantro, artichoke hearts, zucchini, green onions, mushrooms, and tomatoes.

2. Drain tofu and cut into small squares. Add to salad.

3. Pour your favorite Italian salad dressing over salad just before serving. Toss well.

PER SERVING

Calories: 305	Sodium: . . . . . . 789 mg
Fat: . . . . 21 g	Fiber: . . . . 5 g
Protein: . . . . 19 g	Carbohydrate: . . 18 g

Tofu Creation

Tofu is made by extracting milk from soybeans and letting it curdle. The curdled soy milk mixture is pressed together to form blocks of protein-rich tofu. The two main types of tofu are firm and silken. Firm tofu is pressed together to make dense blocks that hold their shape when cut. Silken tofu is thick and delicate, breaking down easily to add a creamy texture.

4 teaspoons olive oil

½ cup (1 cap) Portobello mushroom, diced

⅓ cup oyster mushrooms, sliced

⅓ cup cremini mushrooms, sliced

1 garlic clove, pressed

¼ teaspoon fine sugar

⅛ teaspoon kosher salt

⅛ teaspoon dried thyme, crushed

¼ cup button mushrooms, diced

2 cups butterhead lettuce, torn

1 cup endive, chopped

1 cup oak leaf lettuce, torn

¼ cup French salad dressing

1 cup seasoned croutons

Mushroom Lover's Green Salad

Add slices of juicy steak or crisp crumbled bacon to turn this flavorful salad into a filling meal.

1. Wash mushrooms and pat dry with a paper towel. Heat oil in a large frying pan over medium heat. Add Portobello, oyster, and cremini mushrooms to pan. Sprinkle with garlic, sugar, salt, and thyme. Sauté mushrooms until lightly browned, about 3 minutes, and remove pan from heat.

2. Combine button mushrooms, butterhead lettuce, endive, and oak leaf lettuce together in a large salad bowl. Add dressing to salad and toss well to coat.

3. Add sautéed mushrooms, and any drippings, to salad. Toss gently to coat and mix. Add croutons to salad, toss lightly, and serve salad immediately.

PER SERVING

Calories: 171	Sodium: . . . . . . 261 mg
Fat: . . . . 14 g	Fiber: . . . . 1.5 g
Protein: . . . . 2.5 g	Carbohydrate: . . 11 g

Mushroom Varieties

Portobello is a fancy name for mature cremini mushrooms, and both types have a slightly nutty taste. Oyster mushrooms are delicate fluted mushrooms with a subtle flavor. Button mushrooms are technically any young mushroom with the cap closed, but white button mushrooms are usually referred to as just button mushrooms in the culinary world. White mushrooms are simply button mushrooms with the caps fully opened.

CHAPTER 5

Fruit Salads

Minty Blueberry Melon Salad
70

Tropical Orange Salad
70

Middle Eastern Fruit Salad
71

Tangy Ruby Raspberry Salad
72

Tropical Strawberry Kiwi Salad
73

Holiday Dried Fruit and
Apple Salad
74

Melon Pineapple Salad
75

Gorgonzola, Apple, and Apricot
Fruit Salad
75

American Fruit Salad
76

Cottage Cheese and Fruit Salad
77

Sweet and Fruity Salad
77

Tropical Fruit Salad with Pecans
78

Rainbow Fruit Salad
79

Grapefruit-Pomegranate Salad
80

Apple with Mascarpone
81

Papaya and Kiwi Fruit Salad
82

Creamy Fruit Salad
82

Passionate Star and Litchi
Fruit Salad
83

Prosciutto Charoses Salad
84

Sweet and Creamy Peach
Fruit Salad
85

Macadamia Strawberry–Star
Fruit Salad
86

Good Gouda Fruit Salad
86

1½ cups cantaloupe, 1-inch cubes

1 cup seedless watermelon, 1-inch cubes

1 cup green grapes, halved

¾ cup blueberries

1 tablespoon mint leaves, minced

1 teaspoon flat-leaf parsley, minced

1 (11-ounce) can mandarin oranges

1 (8-ounce) can pineapple chunks

½ cup Granny Smith apple, peeled and diced

½ cup papaya, diced

2 tablespoons shredded coconut, unsweetened

½ teaspoon lemon zest

Minty Blueberry Melon Salad

Seedless watermelons can sometimes have small white seeds scattered among the flesh. Use a fork to remove any noticeable seeds from the cubed watermelon before making the salad.

1. Gently toss the cantaloupe, watermelon, blueberries, and grapes together in a large salad bowl.

2. Add mint and parsley to salad. Toss to mix. Serve immediately or chill in fridge for up to 2 hours.

PER SERVING

Calories: 65	Sodium: . . . . 12 mg
Fat: . . . . 0.5 g	Fiber: . . . . 1.5 g
Protein: . . . . 1.5 g	Carbohydrate: . . 16 g

Tropical Orange Salad

Don't replace the tart apples in this recipe with sweet red apples. The tart apples help balance the sweet flavor of the oranges and pineapples.

1. Drain syrup from the oranges and pineapples. Discard the syrup/juices. Add the drained oranges and pineapple to a large mixing bowl.

2. Add the apples, papaya, coconut, and lemon zest to the bowl. Mix gently and serve. Chill leftovers in the fridge for up to 24 hours.

PER SERVING

Calories: 81	Sodium: . . . . 3 mg
Fat: . . . . 1 g	Fiber: . . . . 3 g
Protein: . . . . 1 g	Carbohydrate: . . 19 g

2 cups seedless green grapes, halved

1 cup pitted dried dates, chopped

½ cup dried figs, chopped

½ cup raisins

¼ cup toasted almond slices

¼ cup toasted pine nuts, chopped

½ teaspoon lemon zest

Middle Eastern Fruit Salad

Leave out the grapes and mix the dried fruit together to create an instant salad mix. Pour the mixed fruit in with green grapes whenever you want a tangy fruit salad.

1. Mix grapes, dates, figs, raisins, almonds, and pine nuts together in a large salad bowl.

2. Garnish with lemon zest and serve. Chill leftovers in fridge for up to 72 hours.

PER SERVING

Calories:	152	Sodium:	2.3 mg
Fat:	4 g	Fiber:	3 g
Protein:	3 g	Carbohydrate:	31 g

Dealing with Dried Fruit

Dried fruit can be difficult to prepare. If the fruit is too hard and pieces are sticking together, you can soak the fruit in hot water for a few minutes to help soften each piece and break up clumps. If the fruit is sticking to your knife when you chop, rinse the knife with hot water occasionally to help prevent sticky bits from adhering to the metal.

2 large Ruby Red grapefruits

2 cups fresh raspberries

1 cup peach, diced

1 cup nectarine, diced

3 tablespoons granulated sugar

Tangy Ruby Raspberry Salad

The amount of sugar you want to use in this recipe depends on your sweet tooth. Anywhere from 1 teaspoon to ¼ cup works.

1. Use a sharp knife to remove peel and pith (white stuff) from each grapefruit. Remove seeds and slice membrane from around each segment. Slice each segment in half. You should end up with around 3 cups of prepared grapefruit. Discard peels, pith, seeds, and membranes.

2. Combine grapefruit, raspberries, peaches, and nectarines in a large mixing bowl. Sprinkle 2 tablespoons sugar over salad and toss well to coat. Sprinkle the remaining 1-tablespoon sugar over the salad as a garnish and serve immediately.

PER SERVING

Calories: 153   Sodium: . . . . 1 mg
Fat: . . . . 1 g   Fiber: . . . . 7.5 g
Protein: . . . . 3g   Carbohydrate: . . 38 g

Grapefruit Royalty

The Ruby Red grapefruit was the first grapefruit to receive a U.S. patent and is the most popular variety of grapefruit sold. The pink- to red-fleshed grapefruits range from sweet to slightly bitter and tend to have fewer seeds than other grapefruit varieties.

INGREDIENTS | SERVES 6

1 (8-ounce) can pineapple chunks

2 cups strawberries, chopped

1 cup kiwi, peeled and sliced

½ cup mango, diced

4 teaspoons fresh lime juice

¼ teaspoon lime zest

¼ teaspoon kosher salt

¼ cup shredded coconut, unsweetened

Tropical Strawberry Kiwi Salad

Strawberries and kiwis are a classic fruit combination. Make sure to remove all the skin from the kiwi before putting it in the salad or it will ruin the flavor.

1. Drain the juice from the pineapples into a small bowl. Set juice bowl aside and add chunks to a large mixing bowl. Stir strawberries, kiwis, and mango into the pineapple.

2. Stir lime juice, lime zest, and salt into the pineapple juice. Mix well. Drizzle mixture over salad and toss to coat. Sprinkle coconut over salad and toss to mix. Serve immediately.

PER SERVING

Calories:	78	Sodium:	100 mg
Fat:	1.5 g	Fiber:	3 g
Protein:	1.5 g	Carbohydrate:	17 g

2 cups fresh yellow apple, chopped

2 cups fresh red apple, chopped

¼ cup dried apricots, diced

¼ cup unsweetened dried cranberries, diced

¼ cup raisins, chopped

¼ cup dried cherries, diced

½ cup walnuts, finely chopped

⅓ cup orange juice

½ teaspoon orange zest

½ teaspoon rum extract

¼ teaspoon ground allspice

¼ teaspoon ground cinnamon

Holiday Dried Fruit and Apple Salad

Fresh apples, which are available in grocery stores year-round, provide a delicate base for the mix of dried fruits in this sweet winter recipe.

1. Combine yellow apples, red apples, dried apricots, dried cranberries, raisins, dried cherries, and walnuts in a large mixing bowl. Toss gently to mix.

2. Stir orange juice, orange zest, rum extract, allspice, and cinnamon together in a small bowl. Mix well. Drizzle over salad and toss well to coat. Serve immediately or cover and chill up to 2 hours before serving.

PER SERVING

Calories: 119	Sodium: . . . . 2 mg
Fat: . . . . 5 g	Fiber: . . . . 2.5 g
Protein: . . . . 1.5 g	Carbohydrate: . . 19 g

Orange Zest

Orange zest can be found in the spice section of any grocery store. However, packaged orange zest pales next to fresh zest. To zest an orange, wash the skin well first. Go over the rind lightly with a zester, but make sure you only scrape the orange part of the rind. If you zest to the bitter white pith it will ruin the flavor of the zest.

1 medium cantaloupe

1 medium honeydew melon

1 medium ripe pineapple

½ cup lemon yogurt

¼ cup pineapple-orange juice

2 tablespoons chopped mint

¼ cup honey

1 cup crisp red apple, chopped with skin intact

1 cup apricots, diced

½ cup plums, sliced

½ cup firm green pear, chopped with skin intact

¼ cup walnuts, chopped

1 tablespoon lemon juice

1 teaspoon fine sugar

½ cup crumbled Gorgonzola cheese

1/16 teaspoon poppy seeds

Melon Pineapple Salad

This fresh salad can be made with almost any fruit that's in season or any flavor of yogurt.

1. Cut cantaloupe and honeydew melons in half, remove seeds, and cut into balls with a melon baller, or cut into cubes. Place in a serving bowl. Remove leaves from pineapple and cut off skin. Remove center core and slice. Add to melon.

2. In bowl, combine remaining ingredients and mix well. Pour over fruits and toss to coat. Cover bowl and place in refrigerator. Chill for at least 4 hours before serving. Mix gently before serving.

PER SERVING

Calories: 95	Sodium: . . . . 27 mg
Fat: . . . . 0.5 g	Fiber: . . . . 1.5 g
Protein: . . . . 2 g	Carbohydrate: . . 24 g

Gorgonzola, Apple, and Apricot Fruit Salad

Gorgonzola cheese has a bite that contrasts wonderfully with the sweet flavors in this mixed fruit salad.

1. Combine chopped apple, apricot, plum, pear, and walnuts in a large mixing bowl. Toss to mix.

2. Drizzle lemon juice and sugar over salad. Toss gently to coat fully. Add Gorgonzola to salad and toss to mix. Garnish with a pinch of poppy seeds and serve immediately.

PER SERVING

Calories: 105	Sodium: . . . . . . 134 mg
Fat: . . . . 6 g	Fiber: . . . . 2 g
Protein: . . . . 3 g	Carbohydrate: . . 10 g

½ cup cantaloupe, cubed

½ cup honeydew melon, cubed

½ cup watermelon, cubed

½ cup red grapes

½ cup strawberries, quartered

American Fruit Salad

This classic fruit salad is the perfect accompaniment to breakfast, granola, yogurt, eggs, brunch dishes, sandwiches, and lunches.

1. Toss all the fruits together gently in a large bowl.

2. Chill fruit salad before serving.

3. Serve the salad family-style or divide it among four small plates.

PER SERVING

Calories:	38	Sodium:	8 mg
Fat:	0 g	Fiber:	1 g
Protein:	1 g	Carbohydrate:	9.5 g

Grape Types

Grapes are broken into two major categories; wine grapes and table grapes. Wine grapes are red and green grapes with high sugar content for wine purposes. Table grapes are red and green grapes with a lighter and slightly less sweet flavor than wine grapes, making them popular for culinary purposes.

Cottage Cheese and Fruit Salad

This simple salad makes an easy side dish for 4, or a quick midday meal for 2.

Combine all ingredients in a medium mixing bowl. Add salt and pepper to taste. Cover bowl with plastic wrap and chill until ready to serve.

PER SERVING

Calories: 102	Sodium: . . . . . . 462 mg
Fat: . . . . 1 g	Fiber: . . . . 0.5 g
Protein: . . . . 14 g	Carbohydrate: . . . 8.5 g

Sweet and Fruity Salad

Always rinse fresh produce under cool water. This will help remove things you don't want to eat such as pesticides, fertilizers, and bacteria.

Combine all ingredients in a bowl and enjoy.

PER SERVING

Calories: 135	Sodium: . . . . 18 mg
Fat: . . . . 1 g	Fiber: . . . . 5 g
Protein: . . . . 3 g	Carbohydrate: . . 33 g

INGREDIENTS | SERVES 4

2 papayas

1 cup canned pineapple chunks, drained

1 cup canned litchis, drained

1 cup bananas, thinly sliced

¼ cup tropical fruit punch

1 teaspoon granulated sugar

½ cup pecan pieces

Tropical Fruit Salad with Pecans

A rich source of vitamin C and several B vitamins, papayas are available year round in many supermarkets. Canned litchis can be found in the canned fruit section, or at ethnic supermarkets.

1. Cut the papayas in half and use a spoon to remove the seeds. Remove the peel from each half of the papaya with a paring knife. Lay the papayas flat, scooped side downward, and cut crosswise into thin strips.

2. Combine the papaya, pineapple, litchis, and banana in a large salad bowl.

3. In a small bowl, stir together the fruit punch and sugar. Sprinkle the juice over the top of the fruit and toss gently. Garnish with the pecans.

4. Serve immediately, or cover and place in refrigerator to chill until serving time.

PER SERVING

Calories: 228	Sodium: . . . . 7 mg
Fat: . . . . 10 g	Fiber: . . . . 5.5 g
Protein: . . . . 2.5 g	Carbohydrate: . . 36 g

How to Pick a Papaya

When choosing a papaya, look for one that is neither too firm nor too soft, but yields to gentle pressure. The skin should be smooth and firm, and the color mainly yellow. Avoid papayas that have a wrinkled skin or a strong smell.

1 large mango, peeled and diced

2 cups fresh blueberries

1 cup bananas, sliced

2 cups fresh strawberries, halved

2 cups seedless grapes

1 cup nectarines, unpeeled, sliced

½ cup kiwi fruit, peeled, sliced

⅓ cup unsweetened orange juice

2 tablespoons lemon juice

1½ tablespoons honey

¼ teaspoon ginger, ground

⅛ teaspoon nutmeg, ground

Rainbow Fruit Salad

You can't go wrong with this salad—it's juicy, fresh, naturally low in fat and sodium, and cholesterol free. Enjoy it as a salad or as a dessert.

1. Gently toss mango, blueberries, bananas, strawberries, grapes, nectarines, and kiwi together in a large mixing bowl.

2. Stir orange juice, lemon juice, honey, ginger, and nutmeg together in a small bowl and mix well.

3. Chill fruit until needed, up to 3 hours. Just before serving, pour honey-orange sauce over fruit and toss gently to coat.

PER SERVING

Calories:	83	Sodium:	2 mg
Fat:	0.5 g	Fiber:	3 g
Protein:	1.5 g	Carbohydrate:	21 g

Grapefruit-Pomegranate Salad

This is a refreshing alternative to dressings normally found with greens and fruit.

1. Peel the grapefruit with a knife, completely removing all the pith (the white layer under the skin). Cut out each section with the knife, again ensuring that no pith remains. Cut away membrane from each section and place sections in a large mixing bowl. Throw peel, pith, and membrane away.

2. Peel the pomegranate carefully with a paring knife; carefully remove berries/seeds. Place seeds in bowl with grapefruit.

3. Toss greens and stock together in a large mixing bowl. To serve, mound the greens on serving plates and arrange the grapefruit sections and pomegranate on top. Shave Parmesan with a vegetable peeler to form curls and add to each plate.

PER SERVING

Calories: 89	Sodium: . . . . . . 112 mg
Fat: . . . . 2 g	Fiber: . . . . 2.5 g
Protein: . . . . 4.5 g	Carbohydrate: . . 15 g

Playing with Pomegranates

There is no easy way to remove the seeds from a pomegranate, but the effort is worth the taste. The quickest method is to cut the fruit open and place the innards in a bowl of cold water. As you pick the white flesh from the seeds, the flesh floats to the top. Discard the flesh and eat the seeds, as the flesh is bitter.

3 Granny Smith apples

1 tablespoon lemon juice

⅓ cup mascarpone cheese

⅓ cup nonfat plain yogurt

¼ cup dried currants or golden raisins

¼ cup almonds, slivered

Apple with Mascarpone

Any tart, in-season apple may be used in this recipe; try Macoun or Fuji apples.

1. Core and slice the apples, then place them in a large mixing bowl. Mix the lemon juice with enough ice-cold water to cover the apples.

2. Using an electric mixer, mix together the mascarpone and yogurt. Place the mixture in a pastry bag with a tip, and pipe the mixture onto a serving plate.

3. Strain the apples and fan them along the edge of the plate. Sprinkle with currants and scatter almonds over the top.

PER SERVING

Calories: 101	Sodium: . . . . 29 mg
Fat: . . . . 3 g	Fiber: . . . . 2 g
Protein: . . . . 3 g	Carbohydrate: . . 17 g

Mascarpone Magic

Mascarpone is a rich and creamy Italian cheese made with triple-cream from cow's milk. The consistency of the mild cheese is like a mix of cream cheese and yogurt. It's a popular dessert ingredient, especially for tiramisu and lady fingers. If you cannot find mascarpone at your local grocery store, look for it at cheese, gourmet, or Italian grocers.

1 (15-ounce) can papaya chunks, drained

1 cup kiwi, peeled and chopped

⅔ cup banana, sliced

¼ cup toasted pine nuts, chopped

3 tablespoons guava juice

½ cup plain yogurt

¼ teaspoon cinnamon

2 teaspoons honey

1 half section of cantaloupe or other melon

¼ cup fresh blueberries

Papaya and Kiwi Fruit Salad

Breakfast, lunch, or dinner, this salad is refreshing with any meal. Use fresh papaya if available, and throw some fresh guava into the salad if it's an option.

Add papaya, kiwi, banana, and pine nuts to a large mixing bowl. Toss gently to mix. Drizzle with guava juice and toss to mix. Serve immediately or cover and chill up to 1 hour before serving.

PER SERVING

Calories: 75	Sodium: . . . . .2.5 mg
Fat: . . . . 2.5 g	Fiber: . . . . .2.5 g
Protein: . . . . 2 g	Carbohydrate: . . 14 g

Creamy Fruit Salad

Don't feel like cooking? Serve this salad for a convenient summer meal.

Stir yogurt, cinnamon, and honey together in a small bowl until smooth and thoroughly mixed. Remove seeds from the middle of the melon. Spoon yogurt mixture into the middle of the cantaloupe. Garnish with blueberries.

PER SERVING

Calories: 254	Sodium: . . . . . .152 mg
Fat: . . . . 1 g	Fiber: . . . . .4 g
Protein: . . . . . . 11 g	Carbohydrate: . . 55 g

1 (14-ounce) can litchis, drained

1 cup mango, chopped

1 cup seedless green grapes, halved

2 tablespoons passion fruit juice concentrate

1 tablespoon lime juice

1 star fruit, small

Passionate Star and Litchi Fruit Salad

Fresh litchi fruit is hard to find outside of Asian or specialty markets, so stick with canned litchis to save both time and money.

1. Toss litchis, mango, and grapes together in a large mixing bowl. Sprinkle salad with passion fruit and lime juice. Toss gently to mix and coat.

2. Gently wash and dry star fruit. Slice across to make ½-inch thick star slices. Gently toss slices into salad, reserving a few as garnish. Garnish salad and serve immediately.

PER SERVING

Calories:	78	Sodium:	2 mg
Fat:	0.5 g	Fiber:	2 g
Protein:	1 g	Carbohydrate:	20 g

Looking for Litchis

If you don't reside in a warm climate, don't waste too much time looking for fresh litchis. Litchis are delicate fruits with prickly skin, juicy white flesh, and large seeds. The highly perishable fruit damage and spoil easily, making them hard and/or expensive to ship long distances. Most grocers only carry canned litchis, which have the skins and pits removed.

Prosciutto Charoses Salad

INGREDIENTS | SERVES 6

2 cups Washington apple, shredded

3 tablespoons sweet red wine

1 tablespoon honey

¼ teaspoon cinnamon, ground

4 ounces sliced prosciutto, diced

¾ cup walnuts, finely chopped

Though noticeably non-kosher, this sweet and salty recipe adds a tasty new twist to the traditional Jewish charoses recipe.

1. Place the shredded apple in a mixing bowl. Lightly pat the apple with a paper towel to remove excess liquid.

2. Stir the wine, honey, and cinnamon together in a small bowl. Pour over apples and mix thoroughly.

3. Add walnuts and prosciutto to the bowl. Mix well. Serve salad immediately or chill up to 1 hour before serving. Mix well before serving.

PER SERVING

Calories:	162	Sodium:	262 mg
Fat:	12 g	Fiber:	2 g
Protein:	5.5 g	Carbohydrate:	11 g

Cha-Cha Charoses

Charoses is a Jewish recipe served during Passover Seder. The shredded apple and dressing creates a sticky salad with an almost paste-like consistency that represents the straw-free mortar ancient Jewish slaves used for construction in Egypt. Adding prosciutto to the charoses balances the sweet flavors with the salty pork. However, as pork is definitely non-kosher, never serve this dish at Passover or to anyone who follows kosher laws.

2½ cups peach, diced

1 cup nectarine, diced

½ cup toasted almond slices

⅓ cup cream cheese, softened

3 tablespoons milk

2 teaspoons water

¼ teaspoon vanilla extract

Sweet and Creamy Peach Fruit Salad

This light salad takes peaches and cream to a whole new level and can serve as a breakfast entrée, side dish, or dessert.

1. Combine peaches, nectarines, and almond slices in a large mixing bowl.

2. Mix cream cheese, milk, water, and vanilla together in a small bowl. Mix thoroughly.

3. Pour the cream cheese mixture over fruit and mix well. Serve immediately or chill up to 1 hour before serving.

PER SERVING

Calories: 195	Sodium: . . . . 64 mg
Fat: . . . . 13 g	Fiber: . . . . 4 g
Protein: . . . . 6 g	Carbohydrate: . . 18 g

Peachy-Keen Peaches

Peaches hail from China, but are grown across the globe. There are two main types of peaches, clingstone and freestone. Clingstone peaches have flesh that clings to the pit and are almost exclusively used for canning. Freestone peaches have flesh that separates from the pit with ease and are the main type sold at grocers. Look for freestone peaches with a warm yellow hue at the top to indicate ripeness.

Macadamia Strawberry–Star Fruit Salad

This fruit salad makes a perfect side for a tropical-themed entrée, such as coconut shrimp.

Toss ingredients together in a large mixing bowl. Garnish with a sprinkle of sugar and serve.

INGREDIENTS | SERVES 6

2 cups strawberries, sliced

1 star fruit, sliced

½ cup macadamia nuts, chopped

½ cup mango, diced

½ teaspoon granulated sugar

PER SERVING

Calories:.....125		Sodium: ....2 mg	
Fat:...........9 g		Fiber:..........3.5 g	
Protein:........2 g		Carbohydrate: ..15 g	

Good Gouda Fruit Salad

Gouda adds an undercurrent of creamy and smoky depth to this sweet fruit salad.

Toss the ingredients together in a mixing bowl. Serve immediately.

INGREDIENTS | SERVES 4

2 cups strawberries, sliced

1 cup green pear, thinly sliced

1 cup seedless green grapes, halved

½ cup nectarine, diced

½ cup smoked Gouda, sliced

PER SERVING

Calories:.....160		Sodium: ......178 mg	
Fat:...........6 g		Fiber:..........4 g	
Protein:........7 g		Carbohydrate: ..22 g	

CHAPTER 6

Potato Salads

Pesto and New Potato Salad
88

Creamy Blue Cheese
Potato Salad
89

Herbed Potato Salad
90

Mediterranean Potato Salad
91

Potato and Chickpea
Curry Salad
92

Easy Caesar Potato Salad
93

Creamy Horsey Potato Salad
94

Swiss Apple Potato Salad
95

Quick Low-Fat Potato Salad
95

Minty Lemongrass
Potato Salad
96

Countryside Potato Salad
97

Smoky Cheddar
Potato Salad
98

Mexican Potato Salad
99

Tex-Mex Potato Salad
100

Black Forest Potato Salad
101

Sausage and Sauerkraut
Potato Salad
102

New Potato Salad
103

Hot German Dijon Potato Salad
104

Lemon Cumin Potato Salad
105

Fresh Summer Potato Salad
106

Roasted Ham and Sweet
Potato Salad
107

Asian Pineapple and Sweet
Potato Salad
108

Pesto and New Potato Salad

A simple side dish if served hot, or potato salad if served cold, these creamy pesto potatoes are a lively and creative way to use an elegant ingredient.

1. Whisk together pesto and mayonnaise, and toss with potatoes and remaining ingredients.

2. Season generously with salt and pepper, to taste. Serve immediately or cover and chill until serving time.

PER SERVING

Calories: 429	Sodium: . . . . . . 433 mg
Fat: . . . . 26 g	Fiber: . . . . 4.5 g
Protein: . . . . 6.5 g	Carbohydrate: . . 46 g

Pesto Beyond Pasta

Pesto is a simple sauce, consisting of basil, pine nuts, garlic, olive oil, and Parmesan cheese. Toss it with pasta, create a pesto pizza, serve it with whole-grain crackers as an appetizer, or use it as a sandwich spread. To turn it into a creamy veggie dip, combine one cup pesto with a container of nondairy sour cream.

INGREDIENTS | SERVES 8

2 pounds new potatoes

1 teaspoon kosher salt

½ cup blue cheese salad dressing

4 ounces sliced prosciutto, diced

¼ cup walnuts, finely chopped

¼ cup green onions, diced

2 tablespoons flat-leaf parsley, chopped

½ cup blue cheese, crumbled

1 tablespoon sun-dried tomatoes, diced

Creamy Blue Cheese Potato Salad

This salad adds a touch of indulgence to any meal, regardless if you serve it with steaks or hot dogs.

1. Quarter the scrubbed potatoes. Place potatoes and salt in a large saucepan. Cover potatoes with water and bring to a simmer over medium-low heat. Simmer until potatoes are tender enough to poke through with a fork, about 10 minutes.

2. Turn off stove burner and drain the water from the potatoes. Place the drained potatoes back on the warm burner for 1 minute, stirring gently, to remove excess water. Place the saucepan on a cool burner to let the potatoes cool down for 5 minutes.

3. Add the dressing, prosciutto, walnuts, green onions, and parsley to the cooled potatoes. Gently stir until fully mixed. Sprinkle the cheese over the salad and stir until just mixed.

4. Garnish with sun-dried tomatoes and serve. Chill leftovers in a covered container for up to 3 days.

PER SERVING

Calories: 265	Sodium: . . . . . . 759 mg
Fat: . . . . 16 g	Fiber: . . . . .2.5 g
Protein:. . . . . . . 9 g	Carbohydrate: . . 24 g

Blue Cheese

Blue cheese is a considered a hard cheese with a sharp and bold tangy flavor. It can be made with cow, sheep, or goat's milk, but what makes the cheese distinct is the addition of penicillium mold. The mold's reaction to oxygen results in blue-green veins in the white cheese. Popular varieties of blue cheese include Gorgonzola and Stilton.

2½ pounds small new or red potatoes

6 slices bacon

1 tablespoon olive oil

3 large shallots, peeled, finely minced

3 tablespoons extra-virgin olive oil

2½ tablespoons red wine vinegar

½ teaspoon granulated sugar

2 tablespoons fresh dill, chopped

1 teaspoon mustard seed, ground

Salt and pepper, to taste

Herbed Potato Salad

This recipe offsets the starch of the potatoes with the sharpness of red wine vinegar, flavored beautifully with bacon, shallots, and herbs.

1. Place the potatoes in a large saucepan with just enough salted water to cover. Bring the water to a boil. Reduce the heat and simmer, uncovered, until the potatoes are tender (about 20 minutes). Cool and cut into quarters.

2. While the potatoes are cooking, heat a large frying pan on medium-high and cook the bacon until crispy. Remove the bacon, drain on paper towels, and finely chop.

3. Clean out the pan and add 1 tablespoon olive oil. Add the shallots and sauté on medium-high heat until they are softened (3–4 minutes). In a small bowl, whisk together the extra-virgin olive oil, red wine vinegar, sugar, chopped fresh dill, and mustard seed until well blended.

4. Transfer the potatoes to a large bowl. Toss with the cooked shallot, bacon, and the salad dressing. Season with salt and pepper to taste. Serve warm.

PER SERVING

Calories: 316	Sodium: . . . . . . 205 mg
Fat: . . . . 15 g	Fiber: . . . . 4 g
Protein: . . . . 8 g	Carbohydrate: . . 38 g

2 pounds assorted potatoes, cooked and cooled

1 bunch scallions, thinly sliced

1 cup grape tomatoes

2 hard-boiled eggs, quartered

1 cup flat-leaf parsley, chopped

¾ cup pitted niçoise olives

3 tablespoons soy "bacon" bits

2 tablespoons mayonnaise

2 tablespoons buttermilk

1 tablespoon olive oil

1 teaspoon smoked paprika

¼ teaspoon kosher salt

⅛ teaspoon black pepper, ground

Mediterranean Potato Salad

This creamy recipe pairs well with any meat entrée. If you cannot find niçoise olives, use small black olives instead.

1. Cut the potatoes up until they are of a uniform size. Put them into a salad bowl and add the scallions, grape tomatoes, eggs, parsley, olives, and "bacon" bits.

2. Mix together the mayonnaise, buttermilk, olive oil, smoked paprika, salt, and pepper in a small bowl. Whisk together until well mixed. Dress the salad, tossing gently to coat all the ingredients. Serve.

PER SERVING

Calories:.....400	Sodium:......430 mg
Fat:..........16 g	Fiber:..........7 g
Protein:.......11 g	Carbohydrate:..54 g

Potato Assortments

Take advantage of the many different sizes of potatoes stocked in major supermarkets and at farmers' markets. You will probably find the fingerlings in assorted colors, as well as potatoes as small as a thimble and others tinged purple or blue. Mix and match, for the most interesting potato salad.

1 teaspoon olive oil

1 cup yellow onion, sliced

1 rounded cup chickpeas

1½ tablespoons curry powder

1 small garlic clove, minced

1 bay leaf

4 cups vegetable stock

2 cups baked potatoes, cubed

¾ cup celery, cut into small dice

1½ cups cherry tomatoes, cut into halves

Salt and pepper, to taste

Potato and Chickpea Curry Salad

This is yet another perfect example of something that tastes wonderful and is good for you, too!

1. Heat the oil on medium in a stockpot. Sauté the onion for 2 minutes, then add the chickpeas, curry, garlic, and bay leaf.

2. Add the stock and simmer for 2 hours. Strain, discard the stock, and allow the peas to cool.

3. In large bowl, mix together the chickpeas, potatoes, celery, and tomatoes. Season with salt and pepper to taste. Serve with your favorite soup or sandwich.

PER SERVING

Calories: 252	Sodium: . . . . . . 299 mg
Fat: . . . . 3 g	Fiber: . . . . 8 g
Protein: . . . . . . 12 g	Carbohydrate: . . 45 g

Dry or Canned Chickpeas?

You can use either dry or canned chickpeas. If using dry chickpeas, don't forget to soak them overnight. Or you could use canned chickpeas without having to worry about a loss of flavor.

INGREDIENTS | SERVES 8

3 pounds red potatoes

⅔ cup celery, sliced

½ cup red onion, diced

2 tablespoons capers, minced

½ cup Caesar salad dressing

2 tablespoons grated Parmesan cheese

Easy Caesar Potato Salad

Caesar salad dressing adds a rich flavor to this simple potato salad.

1. Scrub potatoes and place in a large pot. Cover with water and bring to a rolling boil. Reduce to simmer and cook potatoes until tender, about 15 minutes. Drain water from potatoes, place back in pot and let cool for 10 minutes.

2. Cut cooled potatoes into quarters and place in a large mixing bowl. Add celery, onions, and capers to bowl. Drizzle dressing over salad and mix well. Garnish with Parmesan. Serve immediately or cover and chill in refrigerator for up to 24 hours.

PER SERVING

Calories:.....236	Sodium: ......257 mg
Fat:...........9 g	Fiber:..........3.5 g
Protein:........4.5 g	Carbohydrate: ..35 g

Why Is It Called Caesar?

Caesar salad has nothing to do with the Emperor Caesar or ancient Rome. The exact origin of the salad is debatable, but the most popular theory is that the Italian chef Cesare Cardini created it for his restaurant in Tijuana, Mexico, during the 1920s.

2 pounds Red Bliss potatoes

⅓ cup white onion, chopped

⅓ cup celery, chopped

⅔ cup sour cream

¼ cup Italian vinaigrette salad dressing

1 tablespoon prepared horseradish

½ teaspoon kosher salt

1 teaspoon fresh parsley, minced

Creamy Horsey Potato Salad

This recipe tastes great as a side dish for a picnic with roast beef sandwiches or fried chicken.

1. Wash, scrub, and dry potatoes. Peel skins and chop into 1-inch cubes. Place potatoes in a large saucepan and cover with cold water. Bring water to a boil over high heat. Reduce heat to low and simmer potatoes until tender, about 10 minutes. Drain potatoes and place back in saucepan to cool.

2. Place cooled potatoes in a large mixing bowl. Gently stir onion and celery into bowl.

3. Stir Italian dressing, sour cream, horseradish, and salt together in a small bowl. Gently fold dressing into potatoes.

4. Cover bowl with lid and place in refrigerator. Chill salad for 2 hours. Garnish salad with a sprinkle of parsley and serve.

PER SERVING

Calories: 219	Sodium: . . . . . . 190 mg
Fat: . . . . 8 g	Fiber: . . . . 3 g
Protein: . . . . 4 g	Carbohydrate: . . 33 g

Being Prepared with Horseradish

Prepared horseradish is grated horseradish root preserved in liquid. Regular prepared horseradish is mixed with vinegar and is white in color. Red prepared horseradish is mixed with beet juice, and therefore is red in color. Both types have a milder flavor than fresh horseradish and a creamier consistency, which makes them useful for mixing into dressings and sauces.

Swiss Apple Potato Salad

This potato salad has a hint of sweet and a hint of tang that pairs well with any picnic entrée.

1. Scrub, peel, and chop potatoes into 1-inch cubes. Place in pot and cover with water. Bring to a rolling boil and reduce to simmer. Cook until tender, about 12 minutes. Drain water from potatoes and place back in pot. Let cool for 15 minutes.

2. Stir salad dressing, shallots, and vinegar together in a small bowl. Place potatoes in a large mixing bowl and gently stir in dressing. Stir in apples and cheese. Serve immediately or chill in refrigerator.

PER SERVING

Calories: 214	Sodium: . . . . . . 137 mg
Fat: . . . . 9 g	Fiber: . . . . 3 g
Protein: . . . . 7 g	Carbohydrate: . . 27 mg

Quick Low-Fat Potato Salad

Don't let the low calories fool you, this potato salad can hold its own. The drawback is that it doesn't keep as long as mayonnaise-based potato salads.

1. Boil, skin, and cut the potatoes into chunks.

2. Whisk yogurt, celery seed, mustard, and white pepper together in a large mixing bowl. Add the potatoes and toss them gently to coat. Place the onion rings on top and sprinkle with parsley and paprika. Serve immediately.

PER SERVING

Calories: 120	Sodium: . . . . 28 mg
Fat: . . . . 0 g	Fiber: . . . . 2 g
Protein: . . . . 4 g	Carbohydrate: . . 19 g

INGREDIENTS | SERVES 6

2 pounds red new potatoes

¼ cup green onion, diced

2 tablespoons seasoned rice vinegar

2 tablespoons sesame oil

1½ teaspoons fresh lemongrass, minced

½ teaspoon garlic paste

¼ teaspoon kosher salt

¼ teaspoon red pepper sauce

1 tablespoon fresh mint, finely minced

½ teaspoon toasted sesame seeds

Minty Lemongrass Potato Salad

If you don't have seasoned rice vinegar, use regular rice vinegar and a pinch of sugar instead.

1. Place scrubbed potatoes in a large pot, cover with water, and add a pinch of salt. Bring water to a rolling boil and reduce to a simmer. Cook potatoes until tender, about 10 minutes.

2. Drain water from potatoes and place back in pot. Cook potatoes over low heat for 1 minute, stirring constantly, to help dry them out. Remove potatoes from heat and let cool for 10 minutes.

3. Cut cooled potatoes into quarters and place in a large mixing bowl. Add onions to bowl.

4. Whisk vinegar, oil, lemongrass, garlic, salt, and red pepper sauce together in a small bowl. Pour dressing over potatoes and toss gently to coat.

5. Add mint to potatoes and toss gently to mix. Garnish salad with toasted sesame seeds. Serve salad immediately or cover bowl with lid and chill up to 24 hours before serving.

PER SERVING

Calories: 173	Sodium: . . . . 6 mg
Fat: . . . . 5 g	Fiber: . . . . 3 mg
Protein: . . . . 3 g	Carbohydrate: . . 30 g

Using Fresh Lemongrass

When buying fresh lemongrass, look for stalks that are moist and springy. To prepare, peel the stiff outer layer from each stalk and discard. Use the side of a knife to press the soft inner layer of stalk to release the juices. Finely mince the pressed stalk with a sharp knife and measure out as needed.

2 pounds russet potatoes

1 (15-ounce) can yellow sweet corn, drained

1 cup smoked honey ham, cubed

½ cup Roma tomatoes, chopped

¼ cup red bell pepper, diced

¼ cup radish, shredded

½ cup mayonnaise

2 tablespoons fresh chives, minced

1 tablespoon fresh parsley, minced

1 tablespoon white balsamic vinegar

½ teaspoon celery seed

¼ teaspoon mustard seed, ground

¼ teaspoon kosher salt

Countryside Potato Salad

This hearty recipe works as an entrée or side dish. If you don't care for radishes, add a little white onion instead.

1. Scrub, peel, and chop potatoes into bite-size pieces. Place potatoes in a large pot filled with water. Bring to a boil, reduce heat to simmer, and cook potatoes until tender, about 10 minutes. Drain water from potatoes and place back in pan to cool. Let potatoes cool for 5 minutes.

2. Place cooled potatoes in a large mixing bowl. Add corn, ham, tomatoes, bell pepper, and radishes to potatoes.

3. Stir mayonnaise, chives, parsley, vinegar, celery seed, mustard seed, salt, and pepper together in a small bowl. Pour into salad and mix well. Cover bowl with plastic wrap and chill in refrigerator for 30 minutes.

PER SERVING

Calories: 281	Sodium: . . . . . . 537 mg
Fat: . . . . 14 g	Fiber: . . . . 2.5 g
Protein: . . . . 9 g	Carbohydrate: . . 31 g

3 pounds Yukon Gold potatoes

8 ounces Polska kielbasa smoked sausage

¼ cup mayonnaise

2 tablespoons water

2 teaspoons Dijon mustard

1 teaspoon hickory liquid smoke

¼ teaspoon black pepper, finely ground

1 cup sharp Cheddar cheese, shredded

3 tablespoons flat-leaf parsley, chopped

Smoky Cheddar Potato Salad

Make sure to use smoked sausage, which doesn't need cooking, for this recipe. If you prefer a different sausage, cook it well and pat away the excess grease before adding it to the salad.

1. Scrub, peel, and dice potatoes into 1-inch cubes. Place potatoes in a large pot and cover with water. Bring water to a rolling boil over high heat. Reduce heat to simmer and cook potatoes until tender, about 15 minutes.

2. Drain water from potatoes and place back in pot. Place potatoes over low heat and cook for 2 minutes, stirring frequently, to remove excess water. Let potatoes cool to room temperature, about 10 minutes.

3. Meanwhile, dice sausage and place in a large mixing bowl. Add cooled potatoes to bowl.

4. Stir mayonnaise, water, mustard, liquid smoke, and black pepper together in a small bowl. Pour dressing over potatoes and mix gently to coat. Stir cheese and parsley into salad. Serve immediately.

PER SERVING

Calories: 330
Fat: . . . . 16 g
Protein:. . . . . . . 11 g

Sodium: . . . . . . 490 mg
Fiber: . . . . 3.5 g
Carbohydrate: . . 35 g

Smoke in a Bottle

Liquid smoke adds a smoked flavor to anything. Most liquid smoke products are created by filtering hickory smoke through water. The water captures the smoky essence, and then is filtered to remove any sooty bits. Remember that a little goes a long way.

1 pound small red potatoes

¼ cup pitted black olives, sliced

½ cup green onions, sliced

1 tablespoon fresh cilantro, minced

¼ cup tomato salsa

1 tablespoon olive oil

2 tablespoons lime juice

½ teaspoon salt

½ teaspoon ground black pepper

¾ cup beefsteak tomato, chopped

Mexican Potato Salad

Use this as a side dish to complement a spicy fish or poultry meal.

1. Clean and quarter the potatoes. Boil in 1 quart of water until tender but not mushy, about 8–10 minutes. (They may also be cooked in the microwave.) Drain and set aside.

2. Combine olives, onions, cilantro, salsa, oil, lime juice, salt, and pepper in a small saucepan. Cook uncovered on low heat for 5 minutes, stirring occasionally.

3. Pour the sauce over the potatoes and toss gently to mix. Store in a covered bowl in the refrigerator for 8–12 hours before serving. Gently toss tomatoes into salad just before serving.

PER SERVING

Calories:......77	Sodium: ......211 mg
Fat:..........2.5 g	Fiber:..........1.5 g
Protein:........1.5 g	Carbohydrate:..13 g

4 pounds Yukon Gold potatoes

1 cup red onion, chopped

4 garlic cloves, chopped

3 tablespoons olive oil

1 (1-ounce) package taco seasoning

1 cup plain yogurt

½ cup mayonnaise

½ cup salsa

2 cups frozen corn, thawed and drained

¾ cup red bell pepper, chopped

¾ cup green bell pepper, chopped

1 jalapeño chile, seeded and minced

½ cup queso blanco, crumbled

Tex-Mex Potato Salad

This updated potato salad has a lot of colorful vegetables. You could make it a main dish by adding some chopped ham, grilled chicken, or cooked shrimp. Serve it with lettuce in a tostada shell for a nice presentation.

1. Preheat oven to 400°F. Scrub potatoes and cut into cubes. Place in large baking pan along with red onion and garlic. Drizzle with olive oil; toss using hands, coating vegetables with oil. Bake at 400°F for 50–65 minutes, turning once with spatula, until potatoes are tender and crisp.

2. Meanwhile, in large bowl combine taco seasoning, yogurt, mayonnaise, and salsa, and mix well. Add corn, bell peppers, and jalapeño and mix well. When potatoes are done, stir into mayonnaise mixture along with cheese, turning gently to coat.

3. Cover salad and refrigerate for at least 3 hours until chilled. Or you can serve the salad immediately.

PER SERVING

Calories: 447	Sodium: . . . . . . 263 mg
Fat: . . . . 20 g	Fiber: . . . . 6.5 g
Protein: . . . . 10 g	Carbohydrate: . . 61 g

Potato Substitutions

Yukon Gold potatoes are a distinct variety of buttery-tasting potato with a yellow tint. You can substitute russet potatoes for the Yukon Gold potatoes in this recipe. Don't substitute red potatoes; they are waxy and won't keep their shape after baking.

4 medium red potatoes

4 slices bacon, chopped

2 tablespoons white onions, chopped

Vegetable oil

2 tablespoons cider vinegar

1 tablespoon sugar

½ teaspoon dry mustard

½ teaspoon salt

⅛ teaspoon pepper

Black Forest Potato Salad

This tasty recipe is surprisingly light for a potato and bacon salad, making it an ideal side dish for heavier entrées, such as fried chicken or cheeseburgers.

1. Scrub the potatoes well and boil or steam, whole and unpeeled. When done, drain well, let cool, and slice thinly.

2. Meanwhile, sauté the bacon and onion over medium heat until the bacon is done; remove and reserve the drippings, adding enough vegetable oil to make 2 tablespoons.

3. Return the bacon and onion to the skillet and add the vinegar, sugar, mustard, salt, and pepper. Mix well and bring to a boil.

4. Add the potatoes and toss gently. Serve warm.

PER SERVING

Calories:	134	Sodium:	329 mg
Fat:	4 g	Fiber:	2 g
Protein:	4.5 g	Carbohydrate:	20 g

Chopping Bacon

The key to chopping raw bacon without making a mess is to use chilled meat and a wet knife blade. Chilling the bacon well ensures the fat is solidified and easy to cut. When the bacon is too warm, the fat becomes slimy and difficult to slice. The wet knife blade helps prevent fat and meat from sticking as you cut.

2 pounds Yukon Gold potatoes

8 ounces smoked turkey kielbasa sausage, diced

½ cup sauerkraut

2 tablespoons sauerkraut juice, reserved

3 tablespoons mayonnaise

1 teaspoon honey mustard

1 teaspoon fresh dill, minced

3 tablespoons olive oil

½ cup celery, diced

3 tablespoons green onions, sliced

Sausage and Sauerkraut Potato Salad

Using turkey sausage instead of beef or pork makes the salad healthier and the mellow flavor helps balance out the strong sauerkraut.

1. Scrub potatoes and place in a pot of boiling water. Cook potatoes until just tender, drain, and place back in pot. Cook potatoes over low heat for 2 minutes, stirring constantly, to dry them out. Remove potatoes from heat and let cool for 10 minutes.

2. Add sausage to a large frying pan over medium heat. Cook sausage, stirring frequently, for 5 minutes, or until warm and lightly browned. Remove pan from heat.

3. Chop cooled potatoes into bite-size cubes and place in a large mixing bowl. Drain sauerkraut and reserve 2 tablespoons of the juice. Chop the sauerkraut into small pieces and add to potatoes.

4. Whisk reserved juice, mayonnaise, honey mustard, and dill together in a small bowl. Whisk oil into bowl and mix until emulsified. Drizzle dressing over potatoes. Toss gently to coat and mix fully. Add celery, onions, and sausage to potatoes. Toss gently to coat and mix fully. Serve immediately.

PER SERVING

Calories: 248	Sodium: . . . . . . 403 mg
Fat: . . . . 14 g	Fiber: . . . . 2.5 g
Protein: . . . . 6 g	Carbohydrate: . . 24 g

4 pounds new potatoes

½ cup red bell pepper, chopped

½ cup green bell pepper, chopped

¼ cup celery, chopped

¼ cup red onion, chopped

¼ cup fresh chives, chopped

2 tablespoons fresh parsley, minced

¼ cup olive oil

2 tablespoons red wine vinegar

1 teaspoon dried thyme

Salt and pepper, to taste

New Potato Salad

Off for a summer picnic? This is a great potato salad to tote along because it doesn't contain any mayonnaise. Try chilling it prior to taking it on a picnic and packing it in a cooler.

1. Scrub potatoes. Cook in salted water for 20 minutes until potatoes are tender yet still firm. Drain and cool at room temperature. Cut into bite-sized pieces.

2. In a large bowl combine potatoes, peppers, celery, onion, and herbs.

3. Combine oil, vinegar, thyme, salt, and pepper in a jar with screw top. Shake until blended. Pour over potato mixture.

4. Toss gently until all the vegetables are thoroughly coated. Serve at room temperature.

PER SERVING

Calories: 211	Sodium: . . . . 8 mg
Fat: . . . . 5 g	Fiber: . . . . 4 g
Protein: . . . . 4 g	Carbohydrate: . . 37 g

Keep the Skins on Potatoes!

When you peel potatoes, you peel away most of the nutrients! Rather than peeling them, keep the skins on. Scrub them really well with a vegetable brush. The flavor of the potatoes is even better with their jackets left on!

4 large potatoes, precooked and cooled

½ cup yellow onion, thinly sliced

2 tablespoons olive oil

⅓ cup water

⅓ cup apple cider vinegar

1 tablespoon Dijon mustard

1 tablespoon flour

1 teaspoon granulated sugar

3 tablespoons scallions, chopped

3 tablespoons vegan bacon bits

Salt and pepper, to taste

Hot German Dijon Potato Salad

Tangy deli-style German potato salad requires potatoes that are thinly sliced and not overcooked. This vegan version is just as good—if not better— than any other recipe you'll find.

1. Slice potatoes into thin coins and set aside.

2. In a large skillet, heat onions in olive oil over medium heat and cook until just barely soft, about 2–3 minutes.

3. Reduce heat and add water, vinegar, mustard, flour, and sugar, stirring to combine. Bring to a simmer and cook until thickened, about 1–2 minutes.

4. Reduce heat and stir in potatoes, scallions, and bacon bits. Season with salt and pepper to taste.

PER SERVING

Calories: 223	Sodium: . . . . . . 102 mg
Fat: . . . . 8 g	Fiber: . . . . 3 g
Protein: . . . . 4.5 g	Carbohydrate: . . 31 g

Perfect Potatoes

To prepare your potatoes for a potato salad, give them a quick scrub. Peeling is an aesthetic preference entirely up to you. Either way, chop them into chunks (or thin coins, for a German-style salad), then simmer just until soft, about 15 minutes or less. Drain and rinse your potatoes immediately under cold water to stop them from cooking further and getting too soft.

⅔ cup yellow onion, diced

2 tablespoons olive oil

1½ teaspoons cumin

4 large cooked potatoes, chopped

3 tablespoons lemon juice

2 teaspoons Dijon mustard

1 scallion, chopped

¼ teaspoon cayenne pepper

2 tablespoons fresh cilantro, chopped

Lemon Cumin Potato Salad

A mayonnaise-free potato salad with exotic flavors, this one is delicious either hot or cold.

1. Heat onions in olive oil for 2–3 minutes until soft. Add cumin and potatoes, and cook for 1 minute, stirring well to combine. Remove from heat.

2. Whisk together the lemon juice and Dijon mustard and pour over potatoes, tossing gently to coat. Add scallions, cayenne pepper, and cilantro and combine well.

3. Chill before serving.

PER SERVING

Calories:.....187	Sodium:........8 mg
Fat:...........7 g	Fiber:..........3 g
Protein:........3 g	Carbohydrate:..27 g

The Family Recipe Goes Vegan

Traditional American potato salads are easy to veganize, so if you've got a family favorite, take a look at the ingredients. Substitute vegan mayonnaise or sour cream for regular, omit the eggs, and use mock meats in place of the bacon bits or other meats.

5 pounds small red potatoes

12 eggs

1 cup green onions, chopped

1 teaspoon mustard

¼ cup half-and-half

¾ cup mayonnaise

¼ teaspoon black pepper, ground

¼ teaspoon kosher salt

Fresh Summer Potato Salad

The eggs, half-and-half, and mayonnaise make this salad extra creamy and rich. Serve as a side, or heap it onto bread to make filling sandwiches.

1. Scrub and cut the potatoes in half, boil about 10–15 minutes until soft, testing by piercing them with a fork. Drain and "fluff" them in a colander. (Shake the potatoes up and down a bit in the colander, until they detach from the colander and the outside layer of the potatoes appears fluffy.) Slice the potatoes into bite-size pieces and set aside.

2. Hard-boil the eggs, then cool and slice them. Add the sliced eggs and the chopped onions to the potatoes.

3. Mix the mustard, half-and-half, mayonnaise, pepper, and salt together in a medium bowl; add to the potato mixture. Add extra mayonnaise if the salad appears too dry. Serve immediately.

PER SERVING

Calories: 639	Sodium: . . . . . . 410 mg
Fat: . . . . 34 g	Fiber: . . . . 8 g
Protein: . . . . 20 g	Carbohydrate: . . 64 g

Summer Potato Salad

This potato salad is best in summer with fresh garden potatoes and green onions. The secret here is the use of a rich mayonnaise and fresh cream or half-and-half for the dressing. This recipe is not low calorie or low fat, but it is simply the best potato salad you will ever eat. A little fresh red pepper can also be added to enhance both the color and the texture.

2 pounds sweet potatoes

¼ cup olive oil

¼ teaspoon garlic salt

⅛ teaspoon black pepper, finely ground

⅛ teaspoon ginger root, ground

¼ cup red wine vinaigrette dressing

1 cup honey ham, cubed

½ cup red apple, diced

¼ cup red onion, diced

Roasted Ham and Sweet Potato Salad

Any kind of sweet ham works for the salad, so feel free to use maple, honey, or Black Forest ham.

1. Preheat oven to 425°F. Wash, peel, and chop potatoes into 1-inch cubes. Place cubes in a large bowl. Add oil, garlic salt, pepper, and ginger to bowl. Toss to coat. Place cubes on nonstick baking sheets.

2. Bake potatoes for 10 minutes, remove pan from oven, and turn potatoes over. Bake potatoes until golden and crispy, about 10 more minutes. Remove sheet from oven and place potatoes in a large bowl to cool for 10 minutes.

3. Pour vinaigrette over cooled potatoes and toss to coat. Cut ham into ½-inch cubes. Add ham, apple, and onion to salad. Toss gently to mix. Garnish with raisins, cranberries, or pecans. Serve immediately.

PER SERVING

Calories: 250	Sodium: . . . . . . 412 mg
Fat: . . . . 10 g	Fiber: . . . . 5 g
Protein: . . . . 7.5 g	Carbohydrate: . . 33 g

Fresh-Cracked Black Pepper

Like many seeds, peppercorn's best flavor remains locked inside until it is smashed. Once crushed, the flavor starts to seep away from the spice. This is why fresh-cracked black pepper always tastes richer than pre-packed pre-ground pepper.

2 pounds sweet potatoes, peeled and cubed

1 (15-ounce) can pineapple chunks

2 tablespoons olive oil

2 tablespoons soy sauce

2 teaspoons rice wine vinegar

⅛ teaspoon red pepper, ground

1 (8-ounce) can diced water chestnuts, drained

⅓ cup red onion, diced

¼ cup green onion, sliced

Asian Pineapple and Sweet Potato Salad

Serve this rich salad as a side dish for a spicy entrée. The sweet pineapple and sweet potato will help balance out the fiery meal.

1. Add sweet potatoes to a large pan of boiling water and cook until tender, about 10 minutes. Drain potatoes, place in a large mixing bowl, and let cool for 5 minutes.

2. Drain pineapple juice into a small bowl. Stir oil, soy sauce, vinegar, and red pepper into bowl. Mix until emulsified. Pour dressing over potatoes and toss to coat. Add drained pineapples, water chestnuts, red onion, and green onion to bowl. Toss to mix and coat. Serve immediately.

PER SERVING

Calories: 175	Sodium: . . . . . . 297 mg
Fat: . . . . 3.5 g	Fiber: . . . . 5 g
Protein: . . . . 3 g	Carbohydrate: . . 34 g

CHAPTER 7

Pasta Salads

Blackened Corn and
Sweet Shallot Pasta Salad
110

Italian Chef's Pasta Salad
111

Tomato and Artichoke-Feta
Pasta Salad
112

Creamy Salsa and Chorizo
Pasta Salad
113

Garden Glory Pasta Salad
114

Colorful Pasta Salad
114

Pasta Salad with Hot Peppers
and Sweet Red Pepper Dressing
115

Broccoli and Pasta Salad
116

Pasta Salad with Shrimp and
Snow Pea Pods
117

Spinach and Orzo Pasta Salad
118

Pickle Lover's Egg Pasta Salad
118

Tabbouleh Pasta Salad
119

Portobello Penne Pasta Salad
120

Tex-Mex Pasta Salad
121

Greek Pasta Salad
122

Tuna Macaroni Salad
122

Deli-Style Macaroni Salad
123

Bacon and Tomato Pasta Salad
124

Pesto Pasta Salad
125

Asiago Cucumber and Olive
Pasta Salad
126

3 tablespoons red wine vinegar

2 teaspoons fine granulated sugar

¼ teaspoon garlic powder

¼ teaspoon dried thyme, crushed

⅛ teaspoon cumin, ground

¼ cup vegetable oil

½ cup shallots, sliced

8 ounces penne pasta, uncooked

1 (15-ounce) can sweet corn, drained

3 tablespoons pitted black olives, diced

2 tablespoons celery leaves, minced

Blackened Corn and Sweet Shallot Pasta Salad

Fine granulated sugar is like regular granulated sugar, except it's broken into smaller pieces to make it dissolve quickly in liquid.

1. Whisk vinegar, sugar, garlic powder, thyme, and cumin together in a small bowl. Whisk oil into bowl. Add shallots to bowl and toss to mix. Cover bowl and place in refrigerator. Let shallots marinate for at least 30 minutes.

2. Cook pasta according to package instructions. Drain, rinse, and throw pasta in a large mixing bowl. Add marinated shallots and dressing to the pasta. Toss well to coat.

3. Place corn in a skillet over medium-high heat. Cook corn, stirring frequently, about 5 minutes until the edges of the kernels start to blacken. Add corn to pasta and toss gently to mix.

4. Gently stir olives and celery leaves into salad. Toss well to mix and coat. Serve immediately.

PER SERVING

Calories: 284	Sodium: . . . . 41 mg
Fat: . . . . 12 g	Fiber: . . . . 3 g
Protein: . . . . 6.5 g	Carbohydrate: . . 43 g

Blackening Corn

Fresh or canned, whole corn kernels contain ample water, which makes them easy to cook without oil or butter. Throwing the kernels in a hot skillet makes the moisture inside heat up and release to help keep the skin from sticking to the pan. Stirring the corn frequently lets you develop a light burn on the outer skin without drying out or scorching the meat.

2 cups rotini tri-colored pasta, uncooked

½ cup Italian vinaigrette salad dressing

3 tablespoons mayonnaise

1 teaspoon roasted garlic paste

½ teaspoon anchovy paste

½ cup button mushrooms, sliced thin

½ cup provolone cheese, shredded

½ cup artichoke hearts, chopped

¼ cup pepperoni slices, diced

¼ cup salami, diced

¼ cup sun-dried tomatoes, chopped

Italian Chef's Pasta Salad

Rotini is corkscrew-shaped pasta popular for the way its tightly spiraled edges create pockets that hold pools of sauce/dressing around the noodle.

1. Cook pasta according to package instructions. Drain water from cooked pasta and rinse well in cold water. Pour drained pasta into a large mixing bowl.

2. Stir the salad dressing, mayonnaise, garlic paste, and anchovy paste together in a small bowl. Mix well. Stir the dressing into the pasta. Mix well.

3. Add mushrooms, cheese, artichokes, pepperoni, salami, and sun-dried tomatoes to the pasta. Toss well to mix and coat. Cover bowl and chill salad for 1–12 hours before serving. Mix well before serving.

PER SERVING

Calories: 244	Sodium: . . . . . . 715 mg
Fat: . . . . 17 g	Fiber: . . . . 1.5 g
Protein: . . . . 8 g	Carbohydrate: . . 15 g

8 ounces corkscrew pasta

1 (6-ounce) jar marinated artichoke hearts

1 cup plum tomatoes, chopped

¼ cup kalamata olives, sliced

2 tablespoons fresh basil, chopped

⅓ cup Italian vinaigrette salad dressing

3 tablespoons lemon juice

1 garlic clove, crushed and minced

¼ teaspoon white pepper, ground

1 cup feta cheese, crumbled

Tomato and Artichoke-Feta Pasta Salad

Be careful serving this recipe with wine, as the marinated artichokes can make both red and white wines taste a little off.

1. Cook pasta according to package directions. Drain pasta, rinse with cold water, and pour into a large mixing bowl.

2. Drain and dice the artichoke hearts. Add the artichoke hearts, tomatoes, olives, and basil to the pasta. Mix well.

3. Whisk together the salad dressing, lemon juice, garlic, and white pepper in a small bowl. Mix well. Drizzle dressing over pasta and toss to coat.

4. Cover and chill in refrigerator for 1–24 hours. Toss in crumbled feta before serving.

PER SERVING

Calories: 428	Sodium: . . . . . . 980 mg
Fat: . . . . 19 g	Fiber: . . . . 5 g
Protein: . . . . 14 g	Carbohydrate: . . 53 g

Plum Good Tomatoes

Plum tomatoes are small, round, and usually available throughout the year. They contain less juice than the average tomato, which means they have a stronger, more concentrated flavor. The strong flavor and firm flesh make raw plum tomatoes ideal for salads and sandwiches. They also work well for quick sauces when you don't have time to let the liquid boil away.

8 ounces bow-tie pasta, uncooked

8 ounces Mexican chorizo sausage

⅓ cup spicy salsa

⅓ cup cream cheese, softened

1 (15-ounce) can pinto beans

1 cup celery, chopped

⅓ cup red bell pepper, diced

⅓ cup orange bell pepper, diced

Creamy Salsa and Chorizo Pasta Salad

Mexican chorizo is a variety of spicy and fresh pork sausage. Don't confuse Mexican chorizo, which needs to be cooked, with Spanish chorizo, which is cured and ready to eat.

1. Cook pasta according to package instructions. Drain cooked pasta and rinse with cold water.

2. Meanwhile, remove the casing from the chorizo and crumble sausage into a small skillet over medium heat. Brown sausage for about 6 minutes and drain any excess grease. Add chorizo to pasta.

3. Stir salsa and cream cheese together in a medium mixing bowl. Mix well. Stir into pasta and mix well.

4. Drain and rinse the pinto beans. Stir the beans, celery, red bell pepper, and orange bell pepper into the pasta. Mix well and serve.

PER SERVING

Calories: 210	Sodium: . . . . . . 384 mg
Fat: . . . . 10 g	Fiber: . . . . 3 g
Protein: . . . . 9.5 g	Carbohydrate: . . 21 g

Spectacular Salsa

Nothing beats fresh homemade salsa, especially since it's so easy to make. Drain half the liquid from a 14.5-ounce can of diced tomatoes with chilies. Add the remaining contents to a bowl with some chopped onion and cilantro. Stir in a little minced garlic and red pepper sauce. Cover the bowl and let the salsa marinate in the fridge at least 1 hour.

8 ounces macaroni noodles, uncooked

½ cup Thousand Island salad dressing

½ cup broccoli florets

½ cup cauliflower florets

½ cup red onion, chopped

¼ cup carrots, shredded

¼ cup red cabbage, shredded

1 tablespoon radish, shredded

3 cups fusilli vegetable pasta

½ cup low-fat mayonnaise

½ cup plain yogurt

1 tablespoon Dijon honey mustard

1 cup green seedless grapes

Garden Glory Pasta Salad

This mellow pasta salad makes a healthy and refreshing side for burgers and hot dogs at summer barbecues.

1. Cook noodles according to package instructions. Drain water from noodles and rinse with cold water. Pour the noodles into a large mixing bowl. Stir the salad dressing into the noodles.

2. Break the broccoli and cauliflower florets into bite-size pieces. Stir the broccoli, cauliflower, onions, carrots, and cabbage into the pasta. Mix well. Garnish with shredded radish and serve.

PER SERVING

Calories: 165	Sodium: . . . . . . 141 mg
Fat: . . . . 6 g	Fiber: . . . . 1.5 g
Protein: . . . . 4 g	Carbohydrate: . . 24 g

Colorful Pasta Salad

Fusilli vegetable pasta adds color and flavor to this simple salad. To speed up the preparation time even further, use leftover cooked pasta.

1. Cook the pasta according to the package directions, or until it is tender but still firm. Drain and place pasta in a large mixing bowl.

2. In a medium mixing bowl, stir together the mayonnaise, yogurt, and honey mustard.

3. Add grapes to the cooked pasta. Pour dressing over salad and toss gently to mix.

PER SERVING

Calories: 128	Sodium: . . . . 60 mg
Fat: . . . . 5.5 g	Fiber: . . . . 1 g
Protein: . . . . 3 g	Carbohydrate: . . 16 g

¼ cup olive oil

4 cloves garlic

1 red onion, finely chopped

4 jalapeño peppers, minced

2 chipotle peppers, minced

½ cup red wine vinegar

¼ cup mayonnaise

Salt and freshly ground pepper, to taste

12 ounces small whole wheat pasta, cooked

4 cups bitter greens

Pasta Salad with Hot Peppers and Sweet Red Pepper Dressing

Watercress and arugula are delicious bitter greens that pair well with hot peppers.

1. Heat the olive oil in a large sauté pan. Add the garlic, onion, and peppers. Cook until just slightly softened. Remove pan from heat.

2. Stir vinegar, mayonnaise, salt, and pepper into pan.

3. Add the whole-wheat pasta and mix well. Place the greens on a serving platter and put the pasta salad on top.

PER SERVING

Calories: 370	Sodium: . . . . . . 399 mg
Fat: . . . . 26 g	Fiber: . . . . 3 g
Protein: . . . . 6 g	Carbohydrate: . . 26 g

Picking Peppers

Jalapeño and chipotle peppers are in the same genus as sweet bell peppers, despite the differences in taste and temperament! Look for peppers that are smooth, dry, and firm. If they feel light, leave them; they're probably dried out. Store fresh peppers loose in the refrigerator. Use them within a week.

1 lemon

2 tablespoons Pinot Grigio vinegar

½ cup olive oil

1 teaspoon toasted sesame seed oil

1 teaspoon soy sauce

1 teaspoon red pepper flakes

1 teaspoon Splenda

⅔ cup mayonnaise

1 pound of broccoli florets, rinsed and blanched

1 pound small whole wheat pasta, cooked

Broccoli and Pasta Salad

If you dress the pasta and broccoli while still hot or warm, they will take on a great deal of flavor from the dressing. Whole-grain pasta is better than regular because it's a complex carb.

1. Juice the lemon into a small bowl. Grate the zest from the lemon into the bowl.

2. Whisk the lemon juice, zest, vinegar, oils, soy sauce, spices, Splenda, and mayonnaise in a serving bowl. Stir in the broccoli and pasta. Cover bowl and place in refrigerator. Chill salad for at least 30 minutes. Mix well and serve.

PER SERVING

Calories:	641	Sodium:	220 mg
Fat:	40 g	Fiber:	8 g
Protein:	12 g	Carbohydrate:	63 g

Blanched Vegetables

Dropping your green veggies in boiling water for a minute or two doesn't overcook them. If you shock them in icy water afterward, they will retain their beautiful color. Blanch 'em and shock 'em for vegetables that look as good as they taste.

½ cup olive oil

4 cloves garlic, chopped

1 pound raw, cleaned shrimp

1 pound snow pea pods, washed and trimmed

1 pound curly pasta, cooked

⅔ cup mayonnaise

1 teaspoon mustard

¼ cup lime juice

¼ teaspoon kosher salt

⅛ teaspoon black pepper, ground

2 teaspoons capers

4 sprigs fresh dill to garnish

Pasta Salad with Shrimp and Snow Pea Pods

This dish can be served hot, warm, or chilled. Shrimp supplies both protein and fat, and pasta provides carbs.

1. Heat the oil in a large pot over medium heat. Sauté the garlic for about 3 minutes. Add the shrimp and toss until pink.

2. Stir in the pea pods, pasta, mayonnaise, mustard, salt, pepper, juice, and capers. Serve, sprinkling dill over the top.

PER SERVING

Calories: 676	Sodium: . . . . . . 372 mg
Fat: . . . . 39 g	Fiber: . . . . 5 g
Protein: . . . . 22 g	Carbohydrate: . . 63 g

Snow Pea Pods

Snow pea pods are commonly used in Asian cooking. Blanch the pea pods briefly in boiling water to help them retain their vivid green color. Don't have snow peas? That's okay. Use green beans instead.

Spinach and Orzo Pasta Salad

Orzo, a rice-shaped pasta, adds a delicate texture and flavor to the salad. For a nuttier taste, lightly sauté the orzo in a little butter before cooking.

1. Cook orzo according to package directions. While the pasta is cooking, wash the spinach and leave it in the colander so it has time to dry.

2. Stir cooked orzo and pine nuts together in a bowl. Add dressing to bowl and mix. Stir dried spinach and pear into the bowl. Mix well and serve.

PER SERVING

Calories:	162	Sodium:	101 mg
Fat:	6.5 g	Fiber:	2.5 g
Protein:	5 g	Carbohydrate:	22 g

Pickle Lover's Egg Pasta Salad

This recipe has the perfect blend of tangy and creamy to end up the first empty bowl at a potluck.

1. Cook pasta al dente according to packaging. Drain, rinse, drain well, and pour pasta into a bowl.

2. Add pickle relish and Thousand Island dressing to pasta. Stir gently and mix well. Fold celery, radish, and carrots into salad. Serve immediately or cover and chill up to 12 hours before serving. Crumble egg slices and fold into salad just before serving.

PER SERVING

Calories:	217	Sodium:	395 mg
Fat:	8.5 g	Fiber:	2 g
Protein:	7 g	Carbohydrate:	29 g

1 cup bulgur wheat

8 ounces uncooked bow-tie pasta

1¼ cups green onion, diced

1 cup flat-leaf parsley, finely chopped

½ cup fresh mint leaves, finely torn

½ cup cucumber, peeled and diced

¼ cup fresh lemon juice

½ cup olive oil

Salt and pepper, to taste

Tabbouleh Pasta Salad

Bulgur wheat may also be called bulgar, bulghur, and burghul wheat.

1. Place bulgur wheat in a large bowl. Cover with cold water and soak for 1 hour. To drain, put wheat in center of fine cotton towel and close the towel around the wheat to form a tight bag. Squeeze the wheat with your hands to remove excess water.

2. Meanwhile, cook pasta according to package instructions. Drain pasta and place in a large mixing bowl. Stir drained wheat, onion, parsley, mint, and cucumbers into bowl.

3. Add lemon juice and oil to bowl. Mix ingredients together with clean hands, as a spoon will not mix thoroughly enough. Salt and pepper to taste. Serve immediately or chill until needed.

PER SERVING

Calories: 162	Sodium: . . . . 1.5 mg
Fat: . . . . 9 g	Fiber: . . . . 2 g
Protein: . . . . 3 g	Carbohydrate: . . 18 g

What Is Tabbouleh?

Tabbouleh is a Levantine, or eastern Arabic, salad made with bulgur wheat. Bulgur wheat is parboiled wheat that is then dried and broken into small pieces. Tabbouleh recipes usually call for the soaked wheat to be mixed with fresh green onions, parsley, and mint in a lemon juice and olive oil dressing. The salad also often contains ripe tomatoes and/or cucumbers.

2 cups penne pasta, uncooked

4 Portobello mushroom caps

¼ cup red wine vinegar

6 tablespoons extra-virgin olive oil

1 teaspoon Worcestershire sauce

¼ teaspoon kosher salt

¼ teaspoon lemon pepper

⅛ teaspoon Hungarian paprika, sweet

⅛ teaspoon dried dill

⅓ cup celery, diced

1 tablespoon flat-leaf parsley, minced

2 tablespoons shallots, diced

1 garlic clove, finely minced

Portobello Penne Pasta Salad

This hearty salad works as a side dish or as an entrée. Substitute vegetarian Worcestershire sauce for regular to keep the salad free of animal products.

1. Cook pasta according to package instructions. Drain and rinse pasta. Add to a large mixing bowl. While the pasta is cooking, slice mushroom caps into strips about ½-inch wide and 3-inches long. Set mushrooms aside.

2. Whisk vinegar, Worcestershire sauce, 4 tablespoons oil, salt, lemon pepper, paprika, and dill together in a small bowl. Whisk until emulsified. Pour mixture over cooked pasta and toss to coat. Add celery and parsley to pasta.

3. Heat remaining 2 tablespoons oil in a large skillet over medium-high. Add sliced mushrooms, shallots, and garlic to skillet. Sauté for 4 minutes. Remove skillet from heat. Pour skillet contents over the pasta. Toss well to mix and coat.

4. Let salad cool for 5 minutes. Cover bowl with lid and place cooled salad in refrigerator. Let salad marinate for 30 minutes. Toss well before serving.

PER SERVING

Calories: 151	Sodium: . . . . 82 mg
Fat: . . . . 11 g	Fiber: . . . . 1 g
Protein: . . . . 3 g	Carbohydrate: . . 15 g

Pass the Penne

Penne is cylinder-shaped Italian pasta made to hold the sauce both on top and inside the noodle. This means it's particularly important to cook the pasta al dente, or until thoroughly cooked but still firm.

½ cup mayonnaise

1 cup plain yogurt

¼ cup milk

1 cup chunky salsa

2 teaspoons chile paste

¾ cup green bell pepper, chopped

¾ cup red bell pepper, chopped

1 jalapeño pepper, seeded and minced

1 (12-ounce) can chunk chicken, drained

1 cup crumbled queso fresco

2 cups frozen corn

1 cup frozen baby peas

1 (16-ounce) package gemelli pasta

Tex-Mex Pasta Salad

Pasta salads are a great choice during the summer months. Make the salad in the morning or evening, then let it marinate until serving time. If you cannot find gemelli pasta, any other medium-size twisted pasta will work.

1. In large bowl, combine mayonnaise, yogurt, milk, salsa, and chile paste and mix well. Stir in bell peppers, jalapeño pepper, chicken, and queso fresco and mix well. Place corn and peas on top of salad mixture.

2. Cook pasta according to package directions, drain, and stir into salad mixture while hot. Stir gently to coat all ingredients with dressing, cover, and refrigerate for 1–2 hours to blend flavors.

PER SERVING

Calories: 486	Sodium: . . . . . . 370 mg
Fat: . . . . 18 g	Fiber: . . . . 4.5 g
Protein: . . . . 25 g	Carbohydrate: . . 60 g

Queso What-o?

Queso fresco, which is Spanish for fresh cheese, is an extremely popular kind of Mexican white cheese. The cheese has a mild flavor with a little bite and a semi-soft, crumbly texture. If you cannot find queso fresco, you can use a mild feta cheese. If you're really in a bind, you can use a little Monterey jack, but it will change the flavor and texture of the dish.

Greek Pasta Salad

INGREDIENTS | SERVES 4

1 tablespoon lemon juice

3 tablespoons olive oil

1 teaspoon dried oregano

1 teaspoon Dijon mustard

1 garlic clove, minced

2 cups cooked pasta

1 cup blanched almonds, slivered

1 cup cucumber, sliced

1 cup fresh tomato, diced

½ cup red onion, chopped

½ cup Greek olives

2 ounces feta cheese, crumbled

1½ cups romaine lettuce leaves

Serve this salad alone, with crusty chunks of bread, or as a side for a lamb dish.

1. In a large salad bowl, whisk the lemon juice together with the olive oil, oregano, mustard, and garlic. Cover and refrigerate for 1 hour, or up to 12 hours.

2. Immediately before serving, toss the pasta with the almonds, cucumbers, tomatoes, red onions, olives, and feta cheese. Serve over the lettuce.

PER SERVING

Calories:.....443	Sodium: ......564 mg
Fat:..........35 g	Fiber:..........4.5 g
Protein:.......10 g	Carbohydrate:..27 g

Tuna Macaroni Salad

INGREDIENTS | SERVES 10

1 cup mayonnaise

½ cup yellow onion, chopped

1 teaspoon salt

½ teaspoon black pepper, ground

8 ounces wagon wheel macaroni

4 (6-ounce) cans tuna, drained

2 cups carrot, shredded

2 cups celery, thinly sliced

4 hard-boiled eggs, chopped

The leftovers of this traditional comfort recipe works as a snack, meal, or filling for a sandwich.

1. In a small bowl, combine the mayonnaise, onion, salt, and pepper.

2. Prepare the macaroni according to package instructions; drain and cool.

3. Stir half the mayonnaise into the macaroni, then add the remaining ingredients along with the remaining mayonnaise, combining well. Serve immediately or cover and chill in refrigerator.

PER SERVING

Calories:.....249	Sodium: ......444 mg
Fat:..........19 g	Fiber:..........1.5 g
Protein:........9 g	Carbohydrate:..11 g

3 cups cooked macaroni

¼ cup carrot, diced small

½ cup green peas

½ cup yellow corn

⅓ cup celery, diced

½ cup vegan mayonnaise

1½ tablespoons prepared mustard

2 tablespoons white or apple cider vinegar

2 teaspoons sugar

2 tablespoons pickle relish

1 tablespoon chopped fresh dill

Salt and pepper, to taste

Deli-Style Macaroni Salad

A classic creamy pasta salad with vegan mayonnaise. Add a can of kidney beans or chickpeas for a protein boost.

1. Combine the macaroni, carrot, peas, corn, and celery in a large bowl.

2. In a separate small bowl, whisk together the mayonnaise, mustard, vinegar, sugar, and relish. Combine with macaroni.

3. Stir in the fresh dill and season with salt and pepper, to taste.

4. Chill for at least 2 hours before serving, to allow flavors to combine and to soften veggies. Mix gently before serving.

PER SERVING

Calories: 237	Sodium: . . . . . . 172 mg
Fat: . . . . 5 g	Fiber: . . . . 3 g
Protein: . . . . 6 g	Carbohydrate: . . 41 g

Pasta Salad Secrets

One secret to making flavorful vegan pasta salads is to use heavily salted water when boiling the pasta. So go ahead, dump in a full tablespoon (or even two!) of salt to the cooking water.

1 cup white (plain) cheese-filled tortellini

1 cup green (spinach) cheese-filled tortellini

½ cup Italian salad dressing

1 cup cut green beans

1 tablespoon red onion, chopped

6 slices bacon, cooked and crumbled

1 cup Roma tomatoes, seeded and chopped

¼ cup ranch salad dressing

1 tablespoon fresh parsley, chopped

Salt and pepper, to taste

Bacon and Tomato Pasta Salad

Use refrigerated tortellini to ensure the freshest taste possible. Filled tortellini in cans tends to have too many preservatives to taste handmade.

1. Cook the pasta al dente according to package directions. Drain pasta. While it is still warm, toss in a deep bowl with ¼ cup Italian salad dressing. Allow to cool at room temperature 30 minutes, stirring occasionally.

2. Meanwhile, blanch the beans, then place in a bowl with the onion and remaining ¼ cup Italian dressing; stir to coat. Marinate about 30 minutes at room temperature, stirring occasionally.

3. Cover both bowls and refrigerate. Allow the pasta and the vegetables to marinate separately at least 4 hours or overnight.

4. When ready to serve, add the beans and dressing to the pasta, along with the tomato and bacon. Add the ranch dressing and parsley, and toss. Add salt and pepper to taste. Serve immediately.

PER SERVING

Calories:.....278	Sodium:......749 mg
Fat:..........17 g	Fiber:..........2 g
Protein:.......10 g	Carbohydrate:..23 g

Fresh Pasta

Fresh pasta needs only a minute or two of cooking, just to heat through. Nowadays, you can buy freshly made pasta (usually refrigerated) in the supermarket, and although it's more expensive than the boxed variety, think of it as a special treat.

INGREDIENTS | SERVES 6

1 (9-ounce) package pesto-filled tortellini

¾ cup Italian vinaigrette salad dressing

1 medium cucumber

¾ cup carrot, shredded

¼ cup red onion, chopped

¼ cup mozzarella, shredded

¼ cup Parmesan cheese, grated

1 tablespoon fresh parsley, chopped

Salt and pepper, to taste

Pesto Pasta Salad

Add seared and sliced chicken, steak, or salmon to turn the pasta salad into a full meal.

1. Cook the pasta al dente according to package directions. Drain pasta.

2. While it is still warm, toss in a deep bowl with about ¼ cup salad dressing. Allow to cool at room temperature 30 minutes, stirring occasionally.

3. Meanwhile, partially peel the cucumber by removing ¼-inch strips of skin ¼-inch apart. Quarter the cucumber lengthwise, and slice. Combine the cucumber with the carrot and onion in a deep narrow bowl or container.

4. Add about ½ cup dressing and stir to coat. Allow to marinate about 30 minutes at room temperature, stirring occasionally. Cover both bowls and refrigerate. Allow the pasta and the vegetables to marinate separately for at least 4 hours or overnight.

5. When ready to serve, add the vegetables and their dressing to the pasta and toss with the cheese and parsley. Season with salt and pepper to taste.

PER SERVING

Calories: 295
Fat: . . . . 16 g
Protein: . . . . 9.5 g

Sodium: . . . . . . 600 mg
Fiber: . . . . 2 g
Carbohydrate: . . 28 g

12 ounces tri-colored bow-tie pasta, uncooked

3 tablespoons red wine vinegar

2 teaspoons granulated sugar

1 teaspoon roasted garlic paste

¼ teaspoon red pepper, ground

⅛ teaspoon kosher salt

⅛ teaspoon white pepper, finely ground

⅓ cup extra-virgin olive oil

1 cup cucumber, peeled and sliced

½ cup pitted Manzanilla olives, chopped

⅓ cup button mushrooms, diced

⅓ cup Asiago cheese, shredded

Asiago Cucumber and Olive Pasta Salad

Asiago is a hard and sharp Italian cheese often used in the same way as Parmesan cheese. If you cannot find Asiago, use shredded Parmigiano-Reggiano or Romano cheese.

1. Cook pasta according to package directions. Drain, rinse, and place pasta in a large mixing bowl. While pasta cooks, peel the cucumber and cut it into quartered slices.

2. Whisk vinegar, sugar, garlic paste, red pepper, salt, and white pepper together in a medium mixing bowl. Mix well, making sure the sugar dissolves completely. Whisk oil into bowl and mix until emulsified. Pour mixture over cooked pasta and toss to mix.

3. Add cucumbers, olives, mushrooms, and Asiago cheese to the pasta. Toss gently, but thoroughly, to mix and coat. Serve immediately or cover and chill in refrigerator for up to 2 hours before serving.

PER SERVING

Calories:.....297	Sodium:......300 mg
Fat:..........16 g	Fiber:..........2 g
Protein:........7 g	Carbohydrate:..35 g

Manzanilla Olives

Manzanilla olives, also known as Spanish olives, are medium-sized green-brown olives soaked in brine to keep the flesh firm. The brined olives are usually pitted and stuffed with pimento, garlic, and/or peppers. Their sharp and smoky flavor makes them popular as appetizers and drink garnishes.

CHAPTER 8

Bean Salads

Southwest Black Bean Salad
128

Four-Bean Salad
129

Sweet Lime Three-Bean Salad
130

Sweet Bacon Bean Salad
131

Cuban Three-Bean Salad
132

Marinated Pea and Bean Salad
133

Lemon-Parmesan
Four-Bean Salad
134

White and Black Bean Salad
135

Italian Double-Tomato
Bean Salad
136

Tex-Mex Bean Salad
137

Cannellini Bean Salad
138

Asian Green and
Yellow Bean Salad
139

Green Bean Almondine Salad
140

Aunt Gloria's Italian
Green Bean Salad
141

Citrus Green-Bean Salad
142

Easy Four-Bean Salad
142

Spicy Southwestern
Two-Bean Salad
143

Cucumber-Parsley
Edamame Bean Salad
144

Kidney Bean and Chickpea Salad
145

Traditional Three-Bean Salad
146

Palm Heart and Herb Bean Salad
147

Pearl Onion and
Artichoke Bean Salad
148

INGREDIENTS | SERVES 12

1 (15-ounce) can black beans

1 (15-ounce) can pinto beans

⅓ cup Catalina salad dressing

3 tablespoons olive oil

2 tablespoons fresh cilantro, finely chopped

1 tablespoon green onion, finely chopped

1 tablespoon lime juice

½ teaspoon cayenne pepper, ground

1 (14.5-ounce) can diced tomatoes with green chilies

⅓ cup red bell pepper, diced

⅓ cup yellow bell pepper, diced

⅓ cup red onion, diced

Southwest Black Bean Salad

Pair this recipe with tortilla chips to turn it into a dip or serve it over a bed of iceberg lettuce to turn it into a lunchtime entrée.

1. Drain and rinse the black beans and pinto beans. Place beans in a large mixing bowl.

2. Whisk the salad dressing, olive oil, cilantro, green onion, lime juice, and cayenne pepper together in a medium mixing bowl. Whisk for at least 30 seconds, or until the oil is fully mixed in.

3. Pour the dressing over the beans and mix well. Stir the tomatoes, red bell pepper, green bell pepper, and onion into the salad. Chill for 1–6 hours before serving. Mix well before serving.

PER SERVING

Calories: 156	Sodium: . . . . . . 415 mg
Fat: . . . . 9 g	Fiber: . . . . 4 g
Protein: . . . . 4.5 g	Carbohydrate: . . 16 g

Soaking Beans

If you prefer fresh beans over canned, you need to soak them first to soften each bean and help remove sugars that cause gas. Pick through the dried beans before soaking to remove any gravel or dirt. Place beans in a large bowl and add 3 cups water for every 1 cup of beans. Cover the bowl, place it in the refrigerator and let the beans soak for 8 hours.

INGREDIENTS | SERVES 8

2 cups frozen green beans

2 cups frozen wax beans

1 (15-ounce) can chickpeas, drained and rinsed

1 (15-ounce) can kidney beans, drained and rinsed

½ cup olive oil

¼ cup lemon juice

¼ cup sugar

½ teaspoon celery seed

¼ teaspoon salt

⅛ teaspoon white pepper

Four-Bean Salad

This salad can be served as a vegetarian main course by serving it over mixed salad greens. You could add some chopped toasted walnuts, too, for flavor and crunch.

1. Prepare green beans and wax beans as packages direct. Drain well and place warmed beans in serving bowl along with drained chickpeas and kidney beans.

2. In small bowl, combine olive oil, lemon juice, sugar, celery seed, salt, and pepper and mix well with wire whisk. Drizzle over vegetables and stir to coat.

3. Cover salad and refrigerate at least 4 hours, stirring occasionally, before serving.

PER SERVING

Calories: . . . . . 433　　Sodium: . . . . . . 397 mg
Fat: . . . . 16 g　　Fiber: . . . . 18 g
Protein: . . . . . . 17 g　　Carbohydrate: . . 59 g

1 (15-ounce) can kidney beans

1 (15-ounce) can pinto beans

1 (15-ounce) can black-eyed peas

¾ cup celery, chopped

¼ cup Spanish peanuts, finely chopped

2 tablespoons shallots, diced

⅓ cup lime juice

¼ cup rice vinegar

¼ cup granulated sugar

2 teaspoons fresh parsley, minced

½ teaspoon kosher salt

½ teaspoon chipotle pepper, ground

⅛ teaspoon cumin, ground

3 tablespoons salad oil

Sweet Lime Three-Bean Salad

If you prefer your bean salad on the dry side, drain the dressing from the bowl after the salad has had time to marinate.

1. Drain and rinse the kidney beans, pinto beans, and black-eyed peas. Place beans in a large mixing bowl. Stir celery, peanuts, and shallots into the bowl.

2. Whisk lime juice, vinegar, sugar, parsley, salt, chipotle pepper, and cumin together in a small bowl. Mix until sugar dissolves completely.

3. Pour dressing over beans and mix well. Drizzle oil over salad and mix well. Cover bowl with lid and place in refrigerator. Let salad marinate for 1–12 hours. Mix well before serving.

PER SERVING

Calories: 185	Sodium: . . . . . . 379 mg
Fat: . . . . 7 g	Fiber: . . . . 4 g
Protein: . . . . 7.5 g	Carbohydrate: . . 26 g

Coaxing Juice from a Lime

Squeezing fresh lime juice is an easy way to give a kick of flavor to any dish. Press the whole lime with your hand and roll it across the counter to help loosen the juice. Cut the lime in half by width and twist it over the cone of a hand juicer. Once juiced, you can throw the skin away or carefully grate off the lime zest to use in another dish.

½ pound bacon

1 (15-ounce) can northern white beans

1 (15-ounce) can cannellini beans

1 (15-ounce) can red kidney beans

1 (15-ounce) can pinto beans

½ cup white onion, diced

½ cup Catalina salad dressing

3 tablespoons apple cider vinegar

3 tablespoons ketchup

2 tablespoons dark molasses

2 teaspoons Worcestershire sauce

½ teaspoon chili powder

¼ teaspoon cumin, ground

¼ teaspoon garlic salt

¼ teaspoon dried thyme

Sweet Bacon Bean Salad

Cannellini beans are Italian white kidney beans. You can use white navy beans instead of the northern or cannellini beans if preferred.

1. Fry bacon until crispy. Remove bacon from pan and pat away excess grease with a paper towel. Discard drippings. Crumble bacon into a large mixing bowl.

2. Drain and rinse white, cannellini, kidney, and pinto beans. Add beans and onion to bacon.

3. Combine remaining ingredients together in a medium bowl. Mix well. Stir dressing into salad. Mix well.

4. Cover bowl with plastic wrap and place in refrigerator. Chill salad for at least 2 hours before serving. Mix well before serving.

PER SERVING

Calories:	212	Sodium:	437 mg
Fat:	8.5 g	Fiber:	5.5 g
Protein:	11 g	Carbohydrate:	24 g

1 fresh jalapeño pepper

⅓ cup extra-virgin olive oil

¼ cup fresh cilantro, chopped

¼ cup lime juice

2 garlic cloves, finely minced

½ teaspoon lime zest

¼ teaspoon onion salt

⅛ teaspoon black pepper, finely ground

1 (15-ounce) can black beans

1 (15-ounce) can garbanzo beans

1 (15-ounce) can kidney beans

1 cup heirloom yellow pear tomato, chopped

¾ cup celery, sliced

¼ cup red onion, diced

Cuban Three-Bean Salad

This spicy bean salad tastes great served alone or heaped over a piece of grilled chicken.

1. Remove the seeds from the jalapeño and chop the flesh into very fine pieces. Stir the jalapeño, oil, cilantro, lime juice, garlic, lime zest, onion salt, and black pepper together in a large mixing bowl.

2. Drain and rinse the black beans, garbanzo beans, and kidney beans. Stir the beans into the bowl.

3. Add tomato, celery, and onion to the beans. Stir gently to mix. Cover bowl with plastic wrap and place in refrigerator. Chill salad for at least 4 hours before serving. Gently mix before serving.

PER SERVING

Calories: 160	Sodium: . . . . . . 341 mg
Fat: . . . . 7 g	Fiber: . . . . 5 g
Protein: . . . . 5.5 g	Carbohydrate: . . 20 g

Components of Cuban Cuisine

Cuban cuisine is a mix of African, Spanish, and Caribbean cultures with a hint of South American influence. Cuban dishes are often made with the freshest possible ingredients, even if the recipe calls for sweet fruit or spicy peppers. The food is known for always being flavorful, and you can rest assured that no Cuban meal will ever taste bland or plain.

¾ cup granulated sugar

¼ cup salad oil

½ cup vinegar

1 tablespoon water

1 (8-ounce) can baby peas, drained

1 (15-ounce) can French cut green beans, drained

1 cup celery, diced

1 (6-ounce) jar pimentos

¾ cup green onions, diced

¼ cup carrot, thinly sliced

Marinated Pea and Bean Salad

This salad requires at least 12 hours to marinate fully before serving, so make it the night before to give it plenty of time to soak up the flavors in the dressing.

1. Whisk together the sugar, oil, vinegar, and water in a large mixing bowl. Mix until sugar fully dissolves.

2. Add peas, green beans, celery, pimentos, green onions, and carrots to bowl. Mix well to coat thoroughly. Cover bowl with plastic wrap and place salad in refrigerator. Let the salad marinate overnight, or at least for 12 hours.

3. Mix salad well after marinating. Drain dressing from salad and discard. Serve salad immediately after draining.

PER SERVING

Calories: 174	Sodium: . . . . 28 mg
Fat: . . . . 7 g	Fiber: . . . . 3 g
Protein: . . . . 2 g	Carbohydrate: . . 26 g

1 (15-ounce) can French-cut green beans

1 (15-ounce) can cannellini beans

1 (15-ounce) can wax beans

1 (15-ounce) can garbanzo beans

¼ cup lemon juice

2 tablespoons apple cider vinegar

1 tablespoon maple syrup

½ teaspoon kosher salt

½ teaspoon lemon zest

¼ teaspoon black pepper, finely ground

3 tablespoons extra-virgin olive oil

3 ounces Parmigiano-Reggiano

Lemon-Parmesan Four-Bean Salad

This salad is easy to mix and match with different beans. You can add sugar snaps, yellow beans, kidney beans, or whatever else you have on hand without ruining the flavor.

1. Drain and rinse the green, cannellini, wax, and garbanzo beans. Cut the green beans and wax beans in half by width. Place beans in a large mixing bowl.

2. Combine lemon juice, vinegar, syrup, salt, zest, and pepper in a small bowl. Mix well. Add oil to bowl and mix until emulsified.

3. Drizzle dressing over beans and mix well. Cover bowl and place in refrigerator. Let beans marinate for 1 hour. Remove bowl from fridge and mix well. Grate Parmigiano-Reggiano into the bowl and toss to mix. Serve immediately.

PER SERVING

Calories: 268		Sodium: . . . . . . 808 mg
Fat: . . . . 6.5 g		Fiber: . . . . 12 g
Protein: . . . . 14 g		Carbohydrate: . . 39 g

Parmesan and Parmigiano-Reggiano

Generally, cheap Parmesan is a powdery, grated cheese substance flavored to mimic Parmigiano-Reggiano. Parmigiano-Reggiano is the real thing, a hard and sharp-flavored cheese sold in wedges or shredded into little slivers. While cheap Parmesan may taste fine over pasta sauces, there is a vast flavor and texture difference between the fake and real stuff. For the best results, never substitute cheap Parmesan for Parmigiano-Reggiano.

1 cup red onions, finely chopped

2 cloves garlic, minced

2 tablespoons olive oil

⅓ cup red wine vinegar

¼ cup red bell pepper, seeded and chopped

¼ cup green bell pepper, seeded and chopped

2 tablespoons fresh parsley, minced

2 tablespoons granulated sugar

¼ teaspoon sea salt

¼ teaspoon black pepper, finely ground

1 (15-ounce) can Great Northern beans, rinsed and drained

1 (15-ounce) can black beans, rinsed and drained

Salt and pepper, to taste

White and Black Bean Salad

Reserve a few red and green bell pepper rings to use as a colorful garnish for this filling bean salad.

1. In a nonstick skillet over medium heat, sauté the onions and garlic in the oil for 4–5 minutes until the onions are just beginning to soften. Remove from the heat and allow to cool until warm.

2. Stir the vinegar, peppers, parsley, and sugar into the onions and garlic.

3. Combine beans in a large mixing bowl. Pour onion mixture over beans and mix well. Season with salt and pepper, if desired, and garnish with pepper rings. Serve immediately or cover and chill in refrigerator for up to 3 hours before serving.

PER SERVING

Calories: 177	Sodium: . . . . 79 mg
Fat: . . . . 3.5 g	Fiber: . . . . 5.5 g
Protein: . . . . 7.5 g	Carbohydrate: . . 27 g

1 (15-ounce) can cannellini beans

1 (15-ounce) can wax beans

1 (15-ounce) can garbanzo beans

¼ cup sun-dried tomatoes, julienned

2 tablespoons flat-leaf parsley, minced

1 tablespoon fresh basil, minced

⅓ cup apple cider vinegar

⅓ cup extra-virgin olive oil

¼ cup granulated sugar

2 garlic cloves, pressed

1 teaspoon kosher salt

¼ teaspoon black pepper, ground

1 cup plum tomato, chopped

¼ cup toasted pine nuts, chopped

Italian Double-Tomato Bean Salad

This large salad is ideal for potlucks and parties. Serve the salad over a bed of greens to turn it from a side dish to entrée.

1. Drain and rinse the beans. Combine beans, sun-dried tomatoes, parsley, and basil in a large mixing bowl.

2. Whisk vinegar, oil, sugar, garlic, salt, and pepper together in a medium bowl. Whisk until emulsified. Pour dressing over salad and mix well.

3. Cover salad and place in refrigerator. Let salad marinate for 2–4 hours. Remove salad from refrigerator and mix well. Stir plum tomatoes and pine nuts into salad. Serve immediately.

PER SERVING

Calories: 288	Sodium: . . . . . . 137 mg
Fat: . . . . 8.5 g	Fiber: . . . . 12 g
Protein: . . . . 12 g	Carbohydrate: . . 42 g

Rules of Sun-Dried Tomatoes

Using sun-dried tomatoes can ruin a recipe if you don't know what you're doing. Plain sun-dried tomatoes can be very dry and leathery, making them suitable for soups and stews, but not for raw dishes. Salads use sun-dried tomatoes marinated in oil and herbs. This helps keep the tomatoes a little moister, so that they're easy to chew, filled with flavor, and require no cooking.

1 pound green beans

1 (15-ounce) can black-eyed peas

1 (15-ounce) can pinto beans, rinsed

½ cup sweet onion, minced

½ cup green onions, chopped

2 cups ham, chopped

½ cup olive oil

¼ cup lime juice

2 tablespoons lemon juice

3 tablespoons sugar

1 jalapeño, seeded and minced

½ teaspoon salt

⅛ teaspoon cayenne pepper

½ teaspoon cumin

6–8 romaine lettuce leaves

Tex-Mex Bean Salad

Three-bean salad typically has a sweet-and-sour dressing coating green beans and wax beans. This recipe adds ham, pinto beans, black-eyed peas, and the spice of minced jalapeño peppers.

1. Trim green beans and steam over boiling water for 8–12 minutes until crisp-tender. Remove and place in serving bowl. Rinse and drain black-eyed peas and pinto beans and add to bowl along with sweet onion, green onions, and ham.

2. In small bowl, combine olive oil, lime and lemon juices, sugar, jalapeño, salt, cayenne pepper, and cumin and mix with wire whisk until blended. Pour over bean mixture, stir gently, cover, and refrigerate for at least 2 hours to blend flavors. Serve on lettuce leaves.

PER SERVING

Calories: 297	Sodium: . . . . . . 778 mg
Fat: . . . . 16 g	Fiber: . . . . 7.5 g
Protein: . . . . . . 12 g	Carbohydrate: . . 28 g

3 sprigs fresh thyme

3 cups cooked cannellini beans

2 tablespoons shallot, minced

⅓ cup lemon juice

2 teaspoons lemon zest

⅓ cup extra-virgin olive oil

¼ teaspoon black pepper, ground

Cannellini Bean Salad

If you use canned beans for this recipe, be sure to drain the beans, rinse them, and dry them thoroughly before mixing with the other ingredients.

1. Clean the thyme and remove the leaves (discard the stems). Thoroughly drain and dry the beans.

2. Mix together the shallots, thyme, oil, lemon juice, lemon zest, and black pepper.

3. Add the beans to the oil mixture, and combine thoroughly. Serve immediately.

PER SERVING

Calories: 267   Sodium: . . . . 10 mg
Fat: . . . . 7.5 g   Fiber: . . . . 9 g
Protein: . . . . 14 g   Carbohydrate: . . 37 g

Thyme Time

There are around 100 types of thyme, but garden or common thyme is what you use for cooking. You want to purchase thyme sprigs with a rich green color and perky leaves to guarantee freshness. If you're using the thyme directly in the recipe, it's important to remove the leaves and discard the stem.

1 (15-ounce) can yellow wax beans

1 (15-ounce) can green beans

3 tablespoons rice wine vinegar

2 tablespoons teriyaki sauce

1 teaspoon hoisin sauce

3 tablespoons sesame oil

1 (8-ounce) can diced water chestnuts, drained

¼ cup orange bell pepper, diced

Asian Green and Yellow Bean Salad

Hoisin sauce is a sweet and spicy Chinese condiment. The exact recipe can change, but the sauce generally consists of soybeans, sugar, vinegar, garlic, and spices.

1. Drain, rinse, and place beans in a large mixing bowl. Whisk rice wine vinegar, teriyaki sauce, hoisin sauce, and oil together in a small bowl. Add sauce mixture, water chestnuts, and bell peppers to beans. Toss well to coat.

2. Cover bowl and chill in refrigerator for at least 30 minutes. After chilling, toss salad to mix, garnish with toasted sesame seeds if desired, and serve.

PER SERVING

Calories:	247	Sodium:	191 mg
Fat:	6.5 g	Fiber:	14 g
Protein:	12 g	Carbohydrate:	37 g

Green Bean Almondine Salad

This simple and healthy salad pairs well with almost any beef, pork, chicken, or fish entrée.

1. Wash and trim green beans. Place beans in pan filled with 1 inch of boiling water. Cover and steam for 2 minutes. Drain and rinse beans with cold water for at least 10 seconds. Place beans in a large salad bowl.

2. Drizzle beans with oil and lemon juice. Mix well. Gently toss Parmesan, almonds, onions, and tomatoes into the beans. Salt and pepper to taste. Serve immediately.

PER SERVING

Calories: 148	Sodium: . . . . 30 mg
Fat: . . . . 10 g	Fiber: . . . . 4.5 g
Protein: . . . . 4 g	Carbohydrate: . . 12 g

2 pounds red potatoes

5 cups Italian flat green beans

1½ cups red onions, finely sliced

⅔ cup extra-virgin olive oil

⅓ cup red wine vinegar

1 tablespoon dried oregano

¼ teaspoon black pepper, ground

Aunt Gloria's Italian Green Bean Salad

This simple dish is great to take on picnics. It can be served chilled, slightly warm, or at room temperature.

1. Place the potatoes in a large pot and add enough water to cover. Simmer the potatoes until just fork-tender (do not overcook them). Drain well and dry in hot (400°F) oven for 2 minutes and let cool.

2. Fill a large pot with about 1 inch of water and bring to a simmer. Add the beans, and cook for 4 minutes until just tender but still crisp. Drain well, shock in ice-cold water to stop cooking process, drain again, and let cool.

3. Peel and large-dice the potatoes. Toss together all the ingredients in a large bowl, mixing well to distribute the spices and oil evenly. Serve immediately or cover and chill in refrigerator until needed.

PER SERVING

Calories: 224	Sodium: . . . . 8 mg
Fat: . . . . 15 g	Fiber: . . . . 4 g
Protein: . . . . 3 g	Carbohydrate: . . 20 g

Red Onions

Red onions are sweeter than white or yellow, but the taste is still very strong. If you are eating them raw, on sandwiches for example, the taste will be mellower if you soak the slices in cold water for 10 minutes, then drain and pat dry before using.

5 cups fresh green beans

½ cup hazelnuts

⅓ cup fresh scallions, sliced

½ cup Asiago cheese, grated

½ cup extra-virgin olive oil

¾ cup orange juice

¼ teaspoon black pepper, ground

1 (16-ounce) can garbanzo beans

1 (16-ounce) can red kidney beans

1 (16-ounce) can white kidney beans

1 (16-ounce) can black beans

½ cup white onion, diced

½ cup green bell pepper, diced

1 cup Italian salad dressing

¼ teaspoon salt

¼ teaspoon black pepper, ground

1 tablespoon fresh parsley, diced

Citrus Green-Bean Salad

The Italian cooking term al dente, which normally refers to pasta, can also be used when cooking vegetables for salads. The green beans in this recipe should be cooked until just al dente, or until there is a bit of a crunch when you bite into them.

1. Clean and cut off the ends of the green beans. Crush the hazelnuts.

2. Blanch the green beans and shock in ice water.

3. Mix together all the ingredients, and serve.

PER SERVING

Calories: 215	Sodium: . . . . 80 mg
Fat: . . . . 16 g	Fiber: . . . . 3 g
Protein: . . . . 5 g	Carbohydrate: . . 15 g

Easy Four-Bean Salad

This quick recipe is perfect for when you want to impress everyone at a potluck without having to spend too much time in the kitchen.

1. Drain the beans and rinse well. In a bowl, combine the beans, onion, pepper, and salad dressing, mixing well.

2. Season with salt and pepper, and sprinkle with parsley. Cover and refrigerate for at least 2 hours before serving. Mix gently before serving.

PER SERVING

Calories: 240	Sodium: . . . . . . 785 mg
Fat: . . . . 8.5 g	Fiber: . . . . 8 g
Protein: . . . . 9 g	Carbohydrate: . . 34 g

1 (15-ounce) can black beans, drained and rinsed

1 (15-ounce) can black-eyed peas, drained and rinsed

⅔ cup yellow bell pepper, chopped

1 cup beefsteak tomato, diced

⅔ cup sweet corn

½ cup red onion, diced

⅓ cup olive oil

¼ cup lime juice

½ teaspoon chili powder

½ teaspoon garlic powder

¼ teaspoon cayenne pepper

½ teaspoon salt

¼ cup fresh cilantro, chopped

¾ cup avocado, diced

Spicy Southwestern Two-Bean Salad

This cold bean salad with Tex-Mex flavors is even better the next day—if it lasts that long!

1. In a large bowl, combine the black beans, black-eyed peas, bell pepper, tomato, corn, and onion.

2. In a separate small bowl, whisk together the olive oil, lime juice, chili powder, garlic powder, cayenne, and salt.

3. Pour dressing over bean mixture, tossing to coat. Stir in fresh cilantro.

4. Cover and chill for at least 1 hour before serving to allow flavors to mingle.

5. Add avocado and gently toss again just before serving.

PER SERVING

Calories: 292	Sodium: . . . . . . 419 mg
Fat: . . . . 17 g	Fiber: . . . . 9.5 g
Protein: . . . . 8.5 g	Carbohydrate: . . 31 g

Make It a Pasta Salad

Omit the avocado, and add some cooked whole wheat pasta and extra dressing to turn it into a high-protein Tex-Mex pasta salad!

1 (16-ounce) package shelled edamame soybeans

1 (15-ounce) can garbanzo beans, drained

1 cup grape tomatoes, chopped

¾ cup English cucumber, thinly sliced

¼ cup fresh parsley, chopped

¼ cup yellow bell pepper, diced

⅓ cup balsamic vinaigrette salad dressing

2 garlic cloves, pressed

2 teaspoons honey

½ teaspoon black pepper, ground

Cucumber-Parsley Edamame Bean Salad

Serve this salad the same day as it's made to ensure the tomatoes and cucumbers still have a little crisp in them.

1. Prepare edamame according to package instructions. Drain cooked beans, rinse with cold water, and drain well. Place beans in a large mixing bowl. Add garbanzo beans, tomato, cucumber, parsley, and bell pepper to bowl. Toss gently to mix.

2. Whisk salad dressing, garlic, honey, and pepper together in a small bowl. Pour dressing over salad and toss to coat. Serve immediately or cover and chill up to 4 hours before serving.

PER SERVING

Calories: 205	Sodium: . . . . . . 177 mg
Fat: . . . . 6.5 g	Fiber: . . . . 5 g
Protein: . . . . 13 g	Carbohydrate: . . 26 g

Eating Edamame

Edamame beans are basically young soybeans picked before the bean has time to harden from maturity. The fat, green, oval beans come in long pods that are not particularly tasty, so you want to buy shucked beans for the greatest ease. For the best taste, look for frozen edamame beans as opposed to canned.

¼ cup olive oil

¼ cup red wine vinegar

½ teaspoon sweet Hungarian paprika

2 tablespoons lemon juice

1 (14-ounce) can chickpeas, drained

1 (14-ounce) can kidney beans, drained

½ cup sliced black olives

1 (8-ounce) can yellow corn, drained

½ cup red onion, chopped

1 tablespoon fresh parsley, chopped

Salt and pepper, to taste

Kidney Bean and Chickpea Salad

This marinated two-bean salad is perfect for summer picnics or as a side for outdoor barbecues or potlucks.

1. In a small bowl, whisk together olive oil, vinegar, paprika, and lemon juice.

2. In a large bowl, combine the chickpeas, beans, olives, corn, red onion, and parsley. Pour the olive oil dressing over the bean mixture and toss well to combine.

3. Season generously with salt and pepper, to taste.

4. Cover and chill for at least 1 hour before serving to allow flavors to mingle. Gently mix before serving.

PER SERVING

Calories:	236	Sodium:	477 mg
Fat:	12 g	Fiber:	5 g
Protein:	6.5 g	Carbohydrate:	26 g

1 (16-ounce) can French-cut green beans, drained

1 (16-ounce) can yellow (wax) beans, drained

1 (16-ounce) can red kidney beans, drained

1 large white onion

½ cup sugar

⅔ cup white wine vinegar

⅓ cup vegetable oil

½ teaspoon salt

⅛ teaspoon black pepper, ground

Traditional Three-Bean Salad

One of the most important ingredients in a traditional bean salad is the sugar, as it not only sweetens everything up, it helps bond the different flavors together.

1. Slice the onion thinly, then cut the slices in quarters.

2. In a small bowl, whisk together the sugar, vinegar, oil, and salt and pepper.

3. In a large bowl, combine the beans, onions, and dressing. Mix well. Chill at least 4 hours or overnight, stirring occasionally. If desired, the salad can be drained before serving.

PER SERVING

Calories: 365	Sodium: . . . . . . 320 mg
Fat: . . . . 11 g	Fiber: . . . . 16 g
Protein: . . . . 14 g	Carbohydrate: . . 55 g

Waxy Beans

Yellow wax beans are a type of snap bean. They're picked young, but tend to be thinner and longer than green beans. They taste like a mellow version of common sugar and snap bean flavor. Wax beans also come in the less common purple variety. If you can find purple wax beans, they taste similar to yellow and provide a wonderful burst of color to any dish.

1 cup dry lentils, rinsed

1 (15-ounce) can chickpeas

1 cup red bell pepper, chopped

¾ cup palm hearts, sliced

⅓ cup daikon radish, diced

2 tablespoons fresh sweet basil, minced

2 teaspoons fresh chives, minced

1 teaspoon fresh thyme, minced

2 tablespoons apple cider vinegar

1 tablespoon apple juice

½ teaspoon fresh ginger root, finely grated

⅛ teaspoon kosher salt

⅛ teaspoon sweet Hungarian paprika

3 tablespoons sesame oil

Palm Heart and Herb Bean Salad

This flavorful salad is hearty enough to serve as an entrée for a family dinner and sophisticated enough to serve as an appetizer or side dish for a party.

1. Place lentils in a large saucepan and cover with water. Bring water to a rolling boil and reduce heat to low. Cover saucepan with lid, leaving a large crack open on one side. Cook lentils until tender, about 25 minutes. Drain lentils and place in a large mixing bowl.

2. Drain and rinse chickpeas. Add chickpeas, bell pepper, palm hearts, radish, basil, chives, and thyme to lentils. Stir very gently to mix.

3. Whisk vinegar, juice, ginger, salt, and paprika together in a small bowl. Whisk oil into bowl and mix until emulsified. Drizzle dressing over salad. Toss gently, but thoroughly, to mix and coat. Serve warm or cover and chill in refrigerator up to 12 hours before serving.

PER SERVING

Calories:......205	Sodium:......259 mg
Fat:..........6 g	Fiber:.........10 g
Protein:........9.5 g	Carbohydrate:..29 g

Learning about Lentils

Lentils are legumes, just like peas and beans. They come in brown, red, and green, and tend to be small, round, and flat. The small size means dry lentils do not need soaking the way dry beans do, you can just throw them in boiling water and cook until tender. Be careful about how long you cook the lentils though, as they quickly turn to mush if overcooked.

INGREDIENTS | SERVES 8

1 (8-ounce) jar marinated artichoke hearts

1 cup pearl onions, halved

½ cup orange bell pepper, julienned

⅓ cup pitted black olives, sliced

2 cups fresh fava beans, shucked

1 (15-ounce) can northern white beans

2 teaspoons white wine vinegar

1 teaspoon garlic paste

⅛ teaspoon dried oregano, crushed

2 tablespoons olive oil

Pearl Onion and Artichoke Bean Salad

Serve with an antipasto side platter to turn the salad into a full and well-balanced meal.

1. Fill a metal bowl with ice water and set aside. Bring a pot of water to a rolling boil and add fava beans. Bring back to a boil, cook beans for 2 minutes, drain, and add beans to ice water. Let cool for 5 minutes. Drain beans well and place in mixing bowl. Remove shells from beans. Discard shells.

2. Drain and rinse white beans. Add white beans to fava beans. Drain artichoke marinade into a small bowl and set aside. Dice the drained artichoke hearts. Add artichoke hearts, bell pepper, and olives to bowl. Toss gently to mix.

3. Whisk vinegar, garlic paste, and oregano into the reserved marinade. Whisk oil into bowl and mix until emulsified. Pour dressing over salad and toss well to coat. Serve immediately or cover and chill in refrigerator for up to 4 hours before serving.

PER SERVING

Calories: 261	Sodium: . . . . . . 155 mg
Fat: . . . . 7 g	Fiber: . . . . 12 g
Protein: . . . . 14 g	Carbohydrate: . . 38 g

Fava Bean Fears

Fava beans have a wonderful flavor, but most people avoid them because they grow with double shells and take longer to prepare than other beans. You string and shuck the large pod to release the beans. The shucked beans are blanched, drained, and rinsed. You must then remove the shell from each bean before serving. While it may take extra effort, the rich and meaty beans are worth the work.

CHAPTER 9

Poultry/Beef/Pork Salads

Chicken BLT Salad
150

Dijon Apricot Chicken Salad
151

Sugar-Snapped Mandarin
Chicken Salad
152

Turkey and Nectarine Bibb Salad
153

Fall Turkey Sandwich Salad
153

Grilled Teriyaki Steak and
Watercress Salad
154

Creamy Broccoli Bacon Salad
155

Turkey Waldorf Salad
156

Wild Rice Ham Salad
157

Chinese Chicken Salad
158

Golden Raisin Smoked
Turkey Salad
159

Filet Mignon Caesar
160

Sirloin Steak Salad
161

Spinach, Pear, and
Smoked Ham Salad
162

Chinese Barbecued Pork Salad
163

Grapefruit-and-Chicken Salad
164

Curried Chicken and
Mango Salad
165

Beef and Horseradish Salad
166

Pot Roast and Oyster
Mushroom Salad
167

Strawberry Chicken Salad
168

Swiss-Herb Pork Loin Salad
169

Corn and Pepper Salad
with Ham
170

1 pound boneless chicken breast

6 strips bacon

2 cups iceberg lettuce, shredded

1 cup beefsteak tomato, diced

½ cup yellow onion, diced

½ cup ranch salad dressing

⅓ cup seasoned croutons

Chicken BLT Salad

Reminiscent of the popular sandwich, this recipe provides all the flavor of a BLT and an extra punch of vegetables.

1. Cut chicken breasts into 1-inch cubes. Cover skillet with nonstick cooking spray and add chicken. Cook over medium heat for 6–8 minutes until no longer pink. Place chicken in a large bowl and set aside.

2. Cook bacon over medium-high heat until crispy. Crumble bacon into bowl with chicken. Set bowl aside.

3. Toss lettuce, tomato, and onion together in a large salad bowl. Toss the chicken and bacon into the salad. Drizzle dressing over salad and toss gently to mix. Sprinkle croutons over salad and serve immediately.

PER SERVING

Calories: 343	Sodium: . . . . . . 533 mg
Fat: . . . . 23 g	Fiber: . . . . 1 g
Protein: . . . . 26 g	Carbohydrate: . . . 7 g

Make Seasoned Croutons

To make your own seasoned croutons, use a few slices of stale bread. Cut the bread into cubes, place in a large bowl, drizzle with a little olive oil and toss to coat. Sprinkle cubes with a pinch of garlic powder, pepper, and Italian seasonings. Toast bread on a nonstick cookie sheet in an oven set to 250°F. Toast for 5–10 minutes, stirring once, until croutons are dry and golden.

3 tablespoons mayonnaise

1 tablespoon Dijon mustard

2 tablespoons water

1 tablespoon honey

1 pound boneless chicken breasts

2 tablespoons olive oil

¼ teaspoon garlic salt

¼ teaspoon lemon pepper

2 cups bok choy, chopped

1 cup fresh apricot, diced

½ cup leeks, chopped

¼ teaspoon lemon zest

Dijon Apricot Chicken Salad

Chopped bok choy adds a delightful crunch to the salad. Mix in some radicchio with the bok choy if you prefer a little more bite to the flavor.

1. Stir mayonnaise, mustard, water, and honey together in a small bowl. Mix well and set aside.

2. Slice chicken breasts into 1-inch thick strips. Warm oil in a large skillet over medium heat and add chicken. Sprinkle with garlic salt and lemon pepper. Cook chicken about 8 minutes until no longer pink and starting to brown. Remove from heat and place strips in a large salad bowl.

3. Stir mustard dressing into the chicken. Mix well. Add bok choy, apricots, and leeks to salad. Toss to coat. Garnish with lemon zest and serve.

PER SERVING

Calories:.....282	Sodium: ......134 mg
Fat:..........16 g	Fiber:..........2.5 g
Protein:.......22 g	Carbohydrate:.. 14 g

Dijon Demystified

Dijon mustard hails from Dijon, France, and has a stronger flavor than American yellow mustards. Dijon consists of brown or black mustard seeds mixed with wine or vinegar and herbs. The popular mustard comes in many varieties, from mild to spicy, and in many flavors, from champagne to raspberry. Its distinct taste cannot be replaced with yellow mustard, as the two flavors are extremely different.

2 pounds boneless chicken breast

3 tablespoons sesame oil

½ teaspoon garlic powder

½ teaspoon lemon pepper

1 (15-ounce) can mandarin orange segments

1 cup sugar snap peas

2 tablespoons rice vinegar

1 tablespoon soy sauce

¼ teaspoon ginger root, ground

¼ teaspoon lemon zest

2 cups watercress, chopped

½ teaspoon toasted sesame seeds

Sugar-Snapped Mandarin Chicken Salad

This filling entrée salad is perfect for mid-spring to early summer, when fresh sugar snap peas are plentiful in gardens and grocery stores.

1. Cut chicken breasts into finger-sized slices. Warm oil in a large skillet over medium-high heat. Add chicken to the skillet and sprinkle with garlic powder and lemon pepper. Stir-fry chicken for 10 minutes until no longer pink and starting to brown. Remove skillet from heat.

2. Drain syrup from mandarin oranges into a small bowl. Set small bowl aside. Add drained oranges to a large salad bowl. Cut the tips from the sugar snap peas and slice each pea in half. Stir peas into the bowl and mix well.

3. Stir vinegar, soy sauce, ginger, and lemon zest into the small bowl of syrup. Add syrup to cooked chicken and mix well. Add chicken mixture and watercress to the salad. Toss well to mix salad and disperse dressing. Garnish with sesame seeds and serve immediately.

PER SERVING

Calories:	222	Sodium:	155 mg
Fat:	8 g	Fiber:	2 g
Protein:	28 g	Carbohydrate:	10 g

Lucky Oranges

Native to Southeast Asia, mandarin oranges are considered symbols of good luck by the Chinese and often given as presents during New Year celebrations. The most distinct quality of the oranges is the way the outer peel separates from the ripe fruit with ease.

INGREDIENTS | SERVES 2

8 ounces peppered turkey lunchmeat, sliced

½ cup Swiss cheese, shredded

1 cup nectarine, sliced

2 cups Bibb lettuce, lightly packed

2 tablespoons balsamic vinaigrette salad dressing

Turkey and Nectarine Bibb Salad

If Bibb lettuce is not available, try this recipe with Boston lettuce or baby spinach leaves instead.

1. Dice the sliced turkey into bite-size strips. Toss the turkey, cheese, nectarine slices, and Bibb lettuce together in a large salad bowl.

2. Drizzle dressing over salad and toss well to coat. Serve immediately.

PER SERVING

Calories: 295	Sodium: . . . . . 1,191 mg
Fat: . . . . 12 g	Fiber: . . . . 2 g
Protein: . . . . 30 g	Carbohydrate: . . 18 g

INGREDIENTS | SERVES 4

1 (10-ounce) can turkey in water

¼ cup honey mustard salad dressing

1 tablespoon mayonnaise

¾ cup celery, chopped

½ cup white onion, chopped

½ cup walnuts, chopped

¼ cup dried cranberries, unsweetened

½ cup Italian seasoned croutons, dry

4 cups crisp lettuce, shredded

Fall Turkey Sandwich Salad

This recipe puts the turkey sandwich in the salad while adding a little fall flavor.

1. Drain water from turkey and place meat in a large mixing bowl. Stir dressing and mayonnaise into bowl. Mix well.

2. Stir celery, onions, walnuts, and cranberries into bowl. Serve immediately or chill up to 24 hours before serving. Stir croutons into salad just before serving. Serve salad on a bed of shredded lettuce.

PER SERVING

Calories: 280	Sodium: . . . . . . 215 mg
Fat: . . . . 14 g	Fiber: . . . . 2.5 g
Protein: . . . . 20 g	Carbohydrate: . . 22 g

1½ pounds beef tenderloin

1 cup teriyaki marinade

3 cups watercress, torn

½ cup rice noodles, crunchy

¼ cup green onion, chopped

¼ cup radicchio, shredded

2 tablespoons lemon ginger salad dressing

1 teaspoon toasted sesame seeds

Grilled Teriyaki Steak and Watercress Salad

You can use a cheaper cut of meat if needed, just marinate it a little longer than you would the beef tenderloin to ensure a tender texture.

1. Place the beef in a shallow baking dish and cover with the marinade. Flip the meat over in the dish a few times to coat. Cover with plastic wrap and place in fridge for 1–3 hours.

2. Preheat the grill to medium-high. Remove meat from fridge and discard marinade. Place meat on grill and cook until medium to well-done, about 7 minutes per side. Remove meat from grill and let rest on a plate for 10 minutes before cutting.

3. Meanwhile, toss the watercress, rice noodles, green onions, and radicchio together in a bowl. Drizzle dressing over salad and toss well to coat.

4. Cut the steak, against the grain, into 1-inch thick slices. Split the salad between four bowls and top with steak slices. Garnish each bowl with a pinch of sesame seeds and serve.

PER SERVING

Calories: 548	Sodium: . . . . 1,892 mg
Fat: . . . . 37 g	Fiber: . . . . 1 g
Protein: . . . . 35 g	Carbohydrate: . . 18 g

Giving Meat a Rest

Allowing cooked meat time to rest before cutting is a vital technique for great taste. If you cut the meat while it's still piping hot, the juices are at their most liquid and will drip out of the flesh, robbing the cut of flavor and moisture. By allowing time to cool down, you help retain the juices and the flavor of the meat.

INGREDIENTS | SERVES 6

1 pound sliced bacon

1 pound broccoli

1 cup sunflower seeds, lightly salted

½ cup raisins

¼ cup yellow onion, finely chopped

1 cup mayonnaise

2 tablespoons white wine vinegar

¼ cup granulated sugar

1 teaspoon shallots, grated

Creamy Broccoli Bacon Salad

This recipe works with any kind of bacon, be it plain, peppered, hickory, or applewood. If you don't have any shallots on hand, grate some white onion into the dressing instead.

1. Cook the bacon until crispy and pat away excess fat with a paper towel. Crumble the bacon into a large mixing bowl.

2. Wash the broccoli well. Chop tops and stems into bite-size pieces. Add broccoli, sunflower seeds, raisins, and onions to the bacon. Mix well. Chill mixture in refrigerator until needed.

3. Combine mayonnaise, vinegar, sugar, and shallots in a medium mixing bowl. Mix well. Add dressing just before serving and mix well to coat. Serve immediately.

PER SERVING

Calories: 692
Fat: . . . . 51 g
Protein: . . . . 28 g
Sodium: . . . . . 1,107 mg
Fiber: . . . . 5 g
Carbohydrate: . . 36 g

3 Granny Smith apples

1 cup golden raisins

1 cup toasted walnuts, chopped

2 cups cooked turkey breast, chopped

1½ cups mayonnaise

¼ teaspoon allspice

⅛ teaspoon white pepper

Turkey Waldorf Salad

Waldorf salad is traditionally made of chopped apples and walnuts in a creamy dressing. Adding turkey to this salad elevates it to a main dish delight.

1. Core apples and coarsely chop. Combine in medium bowl with raisins, walnuts, and turkey.

2. In small bowl, combine mayonnaise, allspice, and pepper and blend well. Spoon over turkey mixture and toss to coat.

3. Cover and refrigerate for 10–15 minutes to blend flavors. Store leftovers in refrigerator.

PER SERVING

Calories: 636
Fat: . . . . 54 g
Protein: . . . . 13 g

Sodium: . . . . . . 364 mg
Fiber: . . . . 4 g
Carbohydrate: . . 33 g

Toasting Walnuts

Toasting walnuts concentrates and brings out the flavor. To toast them, spread on a shallow baking sheet and bake in a 350°F oven for 10–15 minutes, stirring twice during baking time. Or microwave the nuts by placing them in a single layer on microwave-safe plate and heating them at 100 percent power for 2–4 minutes, until fragrant.

½ cup wild rice

1 cup brown rice

¾ cup mayonnaise

3 tablespoons mustard

¼ cup olive oil

¼ cup Parmesan cheese, grated

1 green bell pepper, chopped

1 cup ham, diced

1 cup celery, chopped

1 cup Swiss cheese, diced

Wild Rice Ham Salad

To make this salad stretch even further, serve it on top of mixed torn salad greens. For a splurge, use double the wild rice and cut the brown rice in half.

1. In small saucepan, combine wild rice with 1 cup water. Bring to a boil, reduce heat, cover, and simmer for 40–45 minutes until rice is tender. Meanwhile, in medium saucepan, combine brown rice with 2 cups water. Bring to a boil, reduce heat, cover, and simmer for 30–35 minutes until rice is tender.

2. In large bowl, combine mayonnaise, mustard, olive oil, and Parmesan cheese and mix well.

3. When rice is cooked, drain if necessary and add to mayonnaise mixture along with remaining ingredients. Stir well to coat. Serve immediately, or cover and chill before serving.

PER SERVING

Calories: 561	Sodium: . . . . . . 521 mg
Fat: . . . . 38 g	Fiber: . . . . 2 g
Protein: . . . . 14 g	Carbohydrate: . . 21 g

¼ cup bean sprouts

⅓ cup rice vinegar

¼ cup peanut oil

1 tablespoon soy sauce

3 tablespoons hoisin sauce

1 tablespoon minced fresh ginger

¾ pound cooked skinless chicken, diced

2 cups Napa cabbage, shredded

¼ cup scallions, sliced

¼ cup sliced water chestnuts, drained

½ cup unsalted dry-roasted peanuts, chopped

Chinese Chicken Salad

This is a hearty salad and an excellent use for leftover chicken. Serve on a bed of baby greens with a drizzle of the extra dressing on the side.

1. Place the bean sprouts in a bowl of ice water to cover. Soak for 3–5 minutes.

2. Combine the vinegar, oil, soy sauce, hoisin, and ginger in a large bowl and whisk to combine. Remove ½ cup dressing from the bowl and set aside.

3. Add the chicken, cabbage, scallions, and water chestnuts to the large bowl and mix to combine. Add more dressing as needed to achieve desired consistency.

4. Transfer the bean sprouts to paper towels to drain. To serve, divide the chicken salad among 4 salad plates. Garnish with bean sprouts and chopped peanuts. Serve any extra dressing on the side.

PER SERVING

Calories: 325	Sodium: . . . . . . 431 mg
Fat: . . . . 22 g	Fiber: . . . . 2 g
Protein: . . . . 21 g	Carbohydrate: . . 11 g

Salad Additions

Consider adding a tablespoon of toasted sunflower seeds on top of your salad in place of croutons. One tablespoon of sunflower seeds is worth 1 g of carbohydrates. Roasted pumpkin seeds are worth 2 g of carbohydrates for a 1-tablespoon serving.

4 cups broccoli, chopped

2 cups cauliflower, chopped

⅓ cup shallots, chopped

1⅓ cups golden raisins

1 cup low-fat cottage cheese

¼ cup mayonnaise

¼ cup firm silken tofu

3 tablespoons tarragon vinegar

1 tablespoon balsamic vinegar

¼ cup brown sugar

¼ pound (4-ounces) smoked turkey breast, chopped

4 cups salad greens

Golden Raisin Smoked Turkey Salad

Because of the smoked turkey, this salad is high in sodium. If you're on a sodium-restricted diet, consider substituting regular cooked turkey or chicken breast.

1. Combine the broccoli, cauliflower, and shallots in a large bowl and stir in the raisins.

2. In a blender or food processor, combine the cottage cheese, mayonnaise, tofu, vinegars, brown sugar, and pepper and blend until smooth.

3. Toss the dressing over the broccoli, cauliflower, raisins, shallots, and turkey. Chill until ready to serve. Serve over salad greens.

PER SERVING

Calories: 457

Fat: . . . . 13 g

Protein: . . . . 20 g

Sodium: . . . . . . 721 mg

Fiber: . . . . 7 g

Carbohydrate: . . 72 g

2 (6-ounce each) filet mignons, each wrapped in a strip of bacon

2 strips bacon

½ teaspoon kosher salt

½ teaspoon black pepper, ground

2 cups romaine hearts, chopped

2 tablespoons Parmesan cheese, grated

¼ cup Caesar dressing

6 anchovy fillets, drained and rolled into pinwheels

Filet Mignon Caesar

For ease and convenience, this recipe uses a commercial Caesar dressing. You can substitute your favorite homemade dressing if you desire.

1. Pat the steaks dry with paper towels. Wrap a slice of bacon around each steak. Lightly season the steaks with salt and pepper. Heat an indoor grill pan or a sauté pan over medium-high heat. Cook the steaks and bacon to desired doneness, 4–6 minutes per side for medium-rare. Transfer the filets to a plate and tent with tinfoil to keep warm.

2. Toss together the lettuce, half of the dressing, and the Parmesan cheese. Add additional dressing to achieve desired consistency. To serve, divide the salad between 2 dinner plates. Add a hot filet and 3 of the anchovies to each plate.

PER SERVING

Calories: 722	Sodium: . . . . .1,315 mg
Fat: . . . . 56 g	Fiber: . . . . .1 g
Protein: . . . . . . 50 g	Carbohydrate: . . . 3 g

Bottled Dressings Versus Homemade

There are a number of great bottled dressings available in the refrigerated section of your grocer. Read the labels. Many of the dressings are loaded with unnecessary saturated fats and many are packed with sugars and salt. It's worth experimenting with your own homemade vinaigrettes to come up with your personal healthy favorite.

2 teaspoons olive oil

8 ounces top sirloin, 1-inch thick

¼ teaspoon kosher salt

¼ teaspoon black pepper, ground

¼ cup scallions, sliced

½ cup red pepper, julienned

1 tablespoon soy sauce

1 tablespoon red wine vinegar

1 teaspoon sesame oil

1 teaspoon minced fresh ginger

¼ teaspoon kosher salt

4 cups salad greens

Sirloin Steak Salad

Increase the amount of steak if you have larger appetites at the table. Use a stovetop grill pan for great results for the steak and vegetables.

1. Heat the oil in a large nonstick skillet over medium-high heat. Season the steak with salt and pepper.

2. Place meat, scallions, and red peppers in the hot skillet and cook until the vegetables begin to brown and the steak is medium-rare, about 10 minutes total, turning the steak once and stirring the vegetables occasionally. Transfer cooked meat and vegetables to a plate and tent with tinfoil to keep warm. Let meat rest for 5 minutes to allow the juices to reabsorb.

3. Combine soy sauce, vinegar, sesame oil, ginger, and kosher salt in a salad bowl and whisk to combine. Add the greens and toss with the dressing. Divide between 2 large dinner plates.

4. Slice the meat against the grain into very thin slices. Fan the meat over the salad greens and arrange the cooked scallions and peppers alongside the meat.

PER SERVING

Calories: 369	Sodium: . . . . .1,124 mg
Fat: . . . . .27 g	Fiber: . . . . .2 g
Protein:. . . . . . .26 g	Carbohydrate: . . .5.5 g

Flavored Vinegars

There is a variety of fruit and herb vinegars available, including raspberry, tarragon, dill, hot chili, and other specialty blends. These flavored vinegars are generally used for specific applications.

2 cups baby spinach

2 pears, cored and diced

¼ pound smoked ham, shredded

½ cup mayonnaise

2 tablespoons lemon juice

½ cup toasted pecans, chopped

Spinach, Pear, and Smoked Ham Salad

This salad is naturally just a bit sweet but not overpowering, and the mayonnaise-lemon juice combo is delicious.

1. Arrange the spinach on 4 plates. Sprinkle the diced pears over the spinach and add the ham.

2. Mix the mayonnaise and lemon juice together and drizzle over the salad. Garnish with toasted pecan pieces.

PER SERVING

Calories: 381	Sodium: . . . . . . 516 mg
Fat: . . . . 32 g	Fiber: . . . . 5 g
Protein: . . . . 8 g	Carbohydrate: . . 20 g

⅓ cup honey mustard vinaigrette salad dressing

1 teaspoon Chinese mustard

½ teaspoon toasted sesame seeds

12 ounces Chinese barbecued pork, thinly sliced

1 (8-ounce) can sliced bamboo shoots

1 (8-ounce) can diced water chestnuts, drained

2 cups iceberg lettuce, chopped

1 cup baby escarole leaves, torn

¼ cup red bell pepper, diced

Chinese Barbecued Pork Salad

Chinese barbecued pork, also known as char sui, *is a popular appetizer in many American-Chinese restaurants. The thinly sliced pork is usually served with mustard and sesame seeds.*

1. Whisk dressing, mustard, and sesame seeds together in a medium bowl. Add sliced pork to bowl and toss to coat. Set bowl aside. Drain water from shoots and add to a medium bowl filled with ice water. Soak shoots for 5 minutes to lightly crisp, drain again, and roughly chop with a sharp knife.

2. Combine diced shoots, water chestnuts, iceberg lettuce, escarole leaves, and bell pepper in a large mixing bowl. Toss well to mix. Pour meat and sauce into salad. Toss gently to mix and coat fully. Serve immediately.

PER SERVING

Calories: 245	Sodium: . . . . 64 mg
Fat: . . . . 8.5 g	Fiber: . . . . 3 g
Protein: . . . . 27 g	Carbohydrate: . . 15 g

¼ cup grapefruit juice, no sugar added

1 tablespoon olive oil

½ teaspoon Splenda

1 teaspoon fresh rosemary leaves

⅛ teaspoon kosher salt

⅛ teaspoon black pepper, ground

2 cups mixed baby field greens

1 (8-ounce) boneless, skinless chicken breast, halved lengthwise

1 Ruby Red grapefruit, sectioned

Grapefruit-and-Chicken Salad

If you find the grapefruit too tart for your taste, add more Splenda.

1. Whisk the grapefruit juice, olive oil, Splenda, rosemary, salt, and pepper together in a bowl to make dressing. Arrange the greens on serving plates.

2. Drizzle 2 teaspoons of dressing on the chicken. Grill the chicken over medium heat.

3. Slice the chicken and arrange it over the greens. Add the grapefruit sections and drizzle the rest of the dressing over the dish.

PER SERVING

Calories: 219	Sodium: . . . . . . 166 mg
Fat: . . . . 8 g	Fiber: . . . . 3 g
Protein: . . . . 22 g	Carbohydrate: . . 18 g

Selecting Grapefruit

Don't rely on a grapefruit's color to gauge its ripeness; grapefruit skins can have a greenish tint yet still be perfect on the inside. Pick a grapefruit that feels heavy for its size. The extra weight translates into extra juice. Avoid lumpy fruit; it's usually overripe.

3 cups chicken breast, cooked and cubed

1 cup mango, diced

½ cup celery, sliced

¼ cup green onions, sliced

¼ cup red apple, diced

⅓ cup mayonnaise

2 teaspoons soy sauce

1 teaspoon yellow curry powder, mild

¼ teaspoon ginger root, ground

2 tablespoons hot water

1 teaspoon granulated sugar

1 parsley sprig

Curried Chicken and Mango Salad

Stick with a mild curry for this recipe, as a hot curry will overwhelm the other flavors and taste odd when mixed with the mayonnaise.

1. Combine chicken, mango, celery, onions, and apple in a large mixing bowl.

2. Stir mayonnaise, soy sauce, curry powder, and ginger together in a small bowl. Mix well. Stir water and sugar together in a small bowl. Mix until sugar dissolves completely. Pour sugar water into dressing and mix well.

3. Pour dressing over salad and mix well to coat. Garnish with parsley and serve immediately, or chill for up to 2 hours before serving. Mix well before serving.

PER SERVING

Calories: 208   Sodium: . . . . . . 283 mg
Fat: . . . . 14 g   Fiber: . . . . 1.5 g
Protein: . . . . 12 g   Carbohydrate: . . 10 g

Cooking Chicken

The best way to retain moisture and flavor when cooking chicken is to cook the whole breast, let it cool for 5–10 minutes, and then cut the cooked meat as the recipe requires. However, this technique also takes more time and effort, which is why cubing the chicken before cooking is such a popular practice.

1 cup fresh green beans

1½ cups baby carrots

¾ pound beef sirloin steak, 1-inch thick

¼ cup softened cream cheese

2 tablespoons prepared horseradish sauce

3 tablespoons milk

4 cups Boston lettuce, torn

1 (16-ounce) can julienne-cut beets

Beef and Horseradish Salad

This salad is a meal in itself. Serve with Cherries Jubilee or cherry pie for dessert.

1. Wash the green beans. Remove the ends and strings and cut in half lengthwise. Cook the beans, covered, in boiling water in a medium-sized saucepan for 5 minutes.

2. Add the carrots and cook for 10–15 more minutes or until the vegetables are tender. Drain. Cover and chill the vegetables for 4–24 hours.

3. Remove broiler pan from the oven. Preheat broiler.

4. Place the steak on unheated rack of broiler pan. Broil 3 inches from the heat for 13–15 minutes for medium, turning once.

5. In the meantime, combine the cream cheese, horseradish sauce, and milk in a small container with a cover. Cover and shake until well mixed.

6. Arrange the torn lettuce and beets on plates. Top with steak. Drizzle with dressing.

PER SERVING

Calories: 301	Sodium: . . . . . . 385 mg
Fat: . . . . 12 g	Fiber: . . . . 5 g
Protein: . . . . 30 g	Carbohydrate: . . 18 g

1 pound cooked pot roast

⅔ cup fresh oyster mushrooms, thinly sliced

½ cup leeks, sliced

¼ cup baby yellow squash, diced

2 tablespoons fresh parsley, finely chopped

3 tablespoons sweet red wine

1 garlic clove, pressed

⅛ teaspoon red pepper, ground

⅛ teaspoon kosher salt

2 tablespoons olive oil

4 cups romaine lettuce, torn

2 cups lamb's lettuce

4 rosemary sprigs, small

Pot Roast and Oyster Mushroom Salad

A great way to use up leftover pot roast, this salad is fancy enough to come out of a restaurant, but easy enough to whip together in minutes.

1. Slice 1 pound of chilled meat from a leftover pot roast. Cut the meat into ½-inch-thick, 2-inch-long slices, trimming away as much fat as possible. You should end up with almost 2 cups sliced meat. Place meat in large mixing bowl.

2. Toss mushrooms, leeks, squash, and parsley into the beef. Whisk wine, garlic, pepper, and salt in a small bowl. Whisk oil into bowl and mix until emulsified. Pour over beef and toss well to coat.

3. Serve immediately or cover salad and chill up to 12 hours. To serve, toss romaine and lamb's lettuce together in a large salad bowl. Split salad evenly between 4 plates. Split beef salad between plates and serve over lettuce. Drizzle remaining dressing in the bowl over the salads. Garnish with rosemary sprig and serve immediately.

PER SERVING

Calories: 344	Sodium: . . . . . . 128 mg
Fat: . . . . 23 g	Fiber: . . . . 2 g
Protein: . . . . 27 g	Carbohydrate: . . . 5 g

Oyster Mushrooms Unshelled

Oyster mushrooms, so named for their oyster-shell shape, are fluted mushrooms with long white gills and spores. An oyster mushroom's stem is hard and dry, so always cut the caps away and discard the stems. Buy the lightly flavored mushrooms the same day as you plan to use them, as they're delicate and tend to dehydrate quickly.

1½ pints fresh strawberries

½ cup mayonnaise

2 tablespoons chutney of your choice

1 tablespoon lemon juice

1 teaspoon lemon zest

1 teaspoon salt

1 teaspoon curry powder

2 cups cooked chicken, diced

1 cup celery, sliced

¼ cup red onion, chopped

4 lettuce leaves

Fresh mint sprigs, for garnish

Strawberry Chicken Salad

This is a wonderful luncheon meal or fancy picnic dish.

1. Remove the stems from the strawberries.

2. In a large bowl, stir together the mayonnaise, chutney, lemon juice, zest, salt, and curry powder, mixing well.

3. Add the chicken, celery, and onion. Toss well, cover, and chill.

4. Just before serving, slice 1 pint of strawberries. Add to the chicken mixture and toss gently.

5. Line a platter of individual serving plates with the lettuce leaves. Mound the chicken mixture on the lettuce. Garnish with the whole strawberries and mint. Serve at once.

PER SERVING

Calories: 303	Sodium: . . . . . . 250 mg
Fat: . . . . 22 g	Fiber: . . . . 3.5 g
Protein: . . . . 12 g	Carbohydrate: . . 16 g

Strawberry Garnish

Using a strawberry with the green cap and stem still on, make thin slices nearly up to the cap, being careful not to cut all the way through. Press gently to create a strawberry fan. The color and flavor complement poultry dishes but it looks beautiful with any meal.

¼ teaspoon dried thyme, crushed

¼ teaspoon dried lemongrass, crushed

⅛ teaspoon dried oregano, crushed

⅛ teaspoon salt

⅛ teaspoon black pepper, ground

⅛ teaspoon sweet paprika, ground

1 teaspoon vegetable oil

12 ounces pork loin, trimmed

3 cups romaine lettuce, torn

3 cups mixed baby greens

1 cup Swiss cheese, shredded

¼ cup radish, julienned

¼ cup raspberry vinaigrette salad dressing

2 teaspoons fresh chives, minced

Swiss-Herb Pork Loin Salad

For something extra special, butterfly the loin and rub with herbs before cooking.

1. Preheat oven to 425°F. Combine thyme, lemongrass, oregano, salt, black pepper, and paprika in a small bowl. Rub oil over entire loin and sprinkle with herb mixture. Place loin in roasting pan and roast for 25 minutes, or until internal temperature reaches at least 160°F. Remove loin from oven and let cool for 10 minutes.

2. Toss romaine lettuce, baby greens, Swiss cheese, and radish together in a large salad bowl. Add dressing and toss to coat. Split salad evenly between 4 bowls. Cut pork into ½-inch-thick slices and fan meat over each salad. Garnish each bowl with chives and serve immediately.

PER SERVING

Calories: 331	Sodium: . . . . . . 208 mg
Fat: . . . . 21 g	Fiber: . . . . 1 g
Protein: . . . . 26 g	Carbohydrate: . . . 8 g

1 cup low-fat mayonnaise

¼ cup cider vinegar

2 jalapeño peppers, seeded and minced

Salt and pepper, to taste

4 ears cooked corn, cut from the cob

1 sweet red pepper, cored and chopped

1 green bell pepper, cored and chopped

½ pound country ham, cut in cubes

12 scallions, chopped

1 tart apple, cored and chopped

Corn and Pepper Salad with Ham

When corn is in season, it's a great time to make a delicious corn salad. The addition of red and green peppers and ham to traditional corn salad makes this a perfect entrée for lunch.

1. In a small bowl, make the dressing by mixing the mayonnaise, cider vinegar, jalapeños, salt, and pepper. Set aside.

2. Mix the vegetables, ham, and chopped apple together. Toss gently with dressing and serve.

PER SERVING

Calories: 382	Sodium: . . . . . . 854 mg
Fat: . . . . 16 g	Fiber: . . . . 5.5 g
Protein: . . . . . . 17 g	Carbohydrate: . . 48 g

Grilled Corn

To cook corn on the cob, you can steam it, microwave it, boil it, or grill it. To grill, soak the ears in cold water before grilling (leaving the husks on). Then place the corn on a hot grill and close the lid. Turn the ears every 5 minutes until the husks are charred, then remove from the heat, husk, and serve!

CHAPTER 10

Fish/Seafood Salads

Spicy Shrimp Cocktail Salad
172

Smoked Salmon and
Asparagus Salad
173

Cajun Shrimp and Mango Salad
174

Lemon Roll-Up Fillet Salad
175

Norwegian Salmon Salad
176

Salmon-Spinach Salad
177

Shrimp and Melon Salad
177

Lime-Poached Flounder
178

Hollywood Lobster Salad
179

Salmon Tortellini Salad
180

Couscous Salad with
Fresh-Grilled Tuna
181

Pasta and King Crab Salad
182

Dilled Shrimp and
Watercress Salad
183

Italian Seafood Salad
184

Thailand Seafood Salad
185

Spicy Shrimp Salad
186

Grilled Calamari Salad
187

Cuban Shrimp Salad
188

Rosemary and Orange–Seared
Scallop Salad
189

Grilled Halibut Herb Salad
190

Crab Cake Salad
191

Anchovy and Tomato Salad
192

⅓ cup ketchup

1 tablespoon prepared horseradish

1 teaspoon lemon juice

½ teaspoon Worcestershire sauce

1 pound cooked baby shrimp

2 cups iceberg lettuce, shredded

⅓ cup red onion, chopped

⅓ cup celery, chopped

1 lemon slice

Spicy Shrimp Cocktail Salad

The cocktail sauce in this recipe just crosses the line into the hot category, so you may want to adjust the horseradish according to your preference.

1. Mix ketchup, horseradish, lemon juice, and Worcestershire sauce together in a small bowl. Mix well, cover with plastic wrap, and chill in fridge for at least 15 minutes.

2. Place cooked (and thawed if using frozen) shrimp in a large serving bowl. Drizzle chilled dressing over the shrimp and mix well.

3. Toss the lettuce, onion, and celery into the shrimp. Mix well, garnish with a slice of lemon, and serve.

PER SERVING

Calories: 122	Sodium: . . . . . . 373 mg
Fat: . . . . 2 g	Fiber: . . . . 1 g
Protein: . . . . 18 g	Carbohydrate: . . . 8 g

Cocktail Hour

The first seafood cocktails consisted of spicy tomato sauce and, more often than not, oysters rather than shrimp. Cocktail snacks, including shrimp cocktail, burst onto the scene during the 1920s as Prohibition kicked in. Restaurant and bar owners left with fancy glasses and nothing to fill them with took to serving food, such as fruit and seafood, in the glasses instead.

1 pound asparagus

1 cup cherry tomatoes, quartered

1 cup mixed baby greens, lightly packed

1 tablespoon shallots, minced

1 tablespoon lemon juice

¼ teaspoon fresh dill weed, minced

4 ounces thinly sliced smoked salmon

2 tablespoons crumbled feta cheese

Smoked Salmon and Asparagus Salad

Stick with traditional smoked salmon for this recipe and forgo the temptation to use lox. Lox are salt-cured smoked salmon and taste too salty when added to this dish.

1. Trim the woody bottoms from the asparagus and cut each stalk in half. Add asparagus to a large saucepan filled with 2 inches of lightly salted boiling water. Cook for 2 minutes, drain, and rinse well in cold water. Place asparagus in a large salad bowl.

2. Add the tomatoes, greens, and shallots to the asparagus. Sprinkle with lemon juice and dill. Toss well to coat.

3. Cut the smoked salmon slices into small strips. Add the salmon to the salad and toss to mix. Garnish with a sprinkle of feta and serve.

PER SERVING

Calories:......73	Sodium: ......486 mg
Fat:...........2 g	Fiber:..........3 g
Protein:........7.5 g	Carbohydrate: ...7.5 g

1 pound large shrimp, peeled and deveined

2 teaspoons Cajun seasoning

3 tablespoons butter

2 garlic cloves, finely minced

2 cups mango, peeled and diced

1 cup celery, chopped

4 cups Romaine leaves, torn

1 tablespoon lemon juice

Cajun Shrimp and Mango Salad

The easiest way to peel a mango is to cut away the cheeks, score the flesh, and peel away the skin.

1. Place clean shrimp into a large mixing bowl. Sprinkle with Cajun seasoning and toss to coat.

2. Melt butter in a large skillet over medium heat. Add garlic and shrimp to skillet. Cook, stirring frequently, 3–4 minutes until shrimp just turns pink. Pour contents of skillet into a large mixing bowl.

3. Add the mangoes and celery to the shrimp. Drizzle lemon juice over salad. Toss to mix and coat. Split the romaine lettuce between 4 plates. Split the shrimp between the plates and serve over lettuce.

PER SERVING

Calories:	233	Sodium:	240 mg
Fat:	11 g	Fiber:	3 g
Protein:	19 g	Carbohydrate:	17 g

Cajun Creations

If you don't have a favorite Cajun spice mix, it's easy to whip up your own. Mix 2 teaspoons each salt, garlic powder, and sweet paprika with 1 teaspoon each of cayenne pepper, black pepper, onion powder, dried parsley, and dried basil. Add a pinch of dried thyme and cumin. Crush the spices together with a mortar and pestle. Place the mixture in a lidded bottle and store until needed.

⅓ cup butter

⅓ cup lemon juice

1 teaspoon red pepper sauce

2 teaspoons chicken bouillon

1 cup white rice, cooked

1½ cups broccoli, chopped

1 cup mild Cheddar cheese, shredded

8 (4-ounce) fish fillets

8 cups romaine lettuce, chopped

¼ teaspoon sweet Hungarian paprika

Lemon Roll-Up Fillet Salad

You want to use plain and thin fish fillets for this recipe. Stick with lighter flavored fish, such as cod, tilapia, or flounder.

1. Preheat oven to 375°F.

2. Melt butter in a small saucepan over medium heat. Add lemon, pepper sauce, and bouillon to pan. Heat for 2 minutes, stirring frequently, until the bouillon dissolves.

3. Combine rice, broccoli, and cheese in a large bowl. Divide mixture between fillets, rolling it inside each fillet. Place fillets in an 8 × 8-inch baking dish and cover with lemon mixture. Bake fillets for 25 minutes.

4. Let fillets cool, cover dish with plastic wrap, and place in fridge. Let fillets chill for 12 hours. Cut chilled fillet rolls into medallions and serve over lettuce. Garnish with a sprinkle of paprika and serve.

PER SERVING

Calories: 290	Sodium: . . . . . . 241 mg
Fat: . . . . 18 g	Fiber: . . . . 1.5 g
Protein: . . . . . . 22 g	Carbohydrate: . . . 9 g

2 Seville oranges, large

½ fennel bulb

⅓ cup carrot, grated

⅔ cup plum tomatoes, diced

3 tablespoons extra-virgin olive oil

3 tablespoons red wine vinegar

2 tablespoons orange juice

¼ teaspoon red pepper flakes

1 (8-ounce) fillet Norwegian salmon, cooked

2 tablespoons fresh dill, chopped

Norwegian Salmon Salad

Not only is Norwegian salmon famous for its rich taste and texture, it is high in heart-healthy omega-3 fatty acids.

1. Peel and cut the white pith from the oranges. Cut the oranges into sections and remove membrane, reserving 2 tablespoons of the juice. Thinly slice the fennel bulb. Place oranges, fennel, carrot, and tomatoes in a large salad bowl.

2. In a small bowl, whisk together the olive oil, red wine vinegar, orange juice, and red pepper flakes.

3. Cut the salmon into chunks. Arrange the salmon in a salad bowl with the tomatoes, oranges, fennel, and grated carrot. Drizzle the dressing over top. Refrigerate until ready to serve. Garnish with the fresh dill before serving.

PER SERVING

Calories:	209	Sodium:	45 mg
Fat:	13 g	Fiber:	3 g
Protein:	10 g	Carbohydrate:	15 g

Hearty Fare

Fermented fish, sour milk cheese, and cured leg of mutton probably do not sound gourmet. Norway had no history of aristocratic classes to help raise the culinary bar, as did France. Norway's cuisine was rooted in using fresh ingredients such as cod, mutton, and cabbage. What makes some of today's Norwegian cuisine "gourmet" is the adoption of foreign, usually French, culinary practices, used to highlight their native culinary resources.

Salmon-Spinach Salad

This salad makes perfect use of leftover salmon! Salmon will only remain good in the fridge for 2 days, so make sure you find a good use for it quickly!

Combine ingredients in a bowl and enjoy.

PER SERVING

Calories:..... 259		Sodium: .... 94 mg	
Fat:.......... 9 g		Fiber: .... 3 g	
Protein:....... 24 g		Carbohydrate: .. 20 g	

Shrimp and Melon Salad

Executive Chef Jacques Poulin of Auberge au Lion D'or in Québec suggests you garnish his recipe with Boston hearth lettuce and a sprig of fresh baby dill.

1. In a medium-sized bowl stir together lemon juice, minced baby dill, mayonnaise, and wine. Add melon and shrimp. Cover bowl with plastic wrap and refrigerate for at least 1 hour.

2. To serve, scoop a generous portion of shrimp and melon salad onto Boston hearth lettuce on a large pasta plate.

PER SERVING

Calories:..... 347		Sodium: ...... 311 mg	
Fat:.......... 24 g		Fiber: .... 1.5 g	
Protein:....... 18 g		Carbohydrate: .. 14 g	

¾ cup leek, sliced

¼ cup cilantro, leaves separated from stems

1½ pounds flounder fillets

1¾ cups fish stock

2 tablespoons fresh lime juice

½ teaspoon fresh lime zest

¼ teaspoon kosher salt

¼ teaspoon black pepper, ground

1 cup yellow onion, shredded

⅔ cup carrots, shredded

⅔ cup celery, shredded

2 tablespoons extra-virgin olive oil

Lime-Poached Flounder

Lime brings out the delicate flavor of the fish and complements the zip of the cilantro.

1. Place the leek slices and cilantro stems (reserve the leaves) in a large skillet, then lay the flounder on top.

2. Add the stock, lime juice, lime zest, salt, and pepper. Bring to simmer, cover, and cook for 7–10 minutes, until the flounder is thoroughly cooked. Remove from heat. Strain off and discard the liquid.

3. To serve, lay the shredded onions, carrots, and celery in separate strips on serving plates. Top with flounder, drizzle with the extra-virgin olive oil, and sprinkle with the reserved cilantro leaves.

PER SERVING

Calories:	150	Sodium:	293 mg
Fat:	6 g	Fiber:	1 g
Protein:	18 g	Carbohydrate:	3.5 g

Using Frozen Fish

Don't fret if you do not have fresh fish available in your area. Using a quality fish frozen at sea is perfectly fine. In fact, sometimes the frozen fish is fresher than the fresh!

¾ pound lobster meat, cooked and torn into chunks

4 tablespoons extra-virgin olive oil

1 teaspoon lemon juice

3 tablespoons chopped chives

⅓ cup fat-free Miracle Whip salad dressing

1 head Boston lettuce

Hollywood Lobster Salad

You can use any kind of salad greens for this bed of lobster salad, but the Boston lettuce gives the dish a soft taste and texture.

1. Gently fold all ingredients except the lettuce together.

2. Cover and refrigerate until chilled.

3. Arrange salad on a bed of salad greens and serve immediately.

PER SERVING

Calories:	205	Sodium:	410 mg
Fat:	15 g	Fiber:	1 g
Protein:	13 g	Carbohydrate:	5 g

Cooking Lobster

Stick with lobster tails, they're easy to prepare and cook. The easiest method is baking. Cut the top of the shell from each tail and use a knife to loosen the meat, but do not remove it. Wrap the tails in foil with a pinch of lemon juice. Bake 4-ounce to 6-ounce tails at 450°F for about 20 minutes. Let tails cool, remove foil, and remove the meat from the shell.

8 ounces frozen or fresh cheese tortellini

2 (6-ounce) cans salmon

½ cup carrots, peeled and sliced

1 cup zucchini, sliced

⅓ cup red bell pepper, julienned

1 cup plain low-fat yogurt

¼ cup Parmesan cheese, grated

¼ cup fresh parsley, chopped

1 tablespoon low-fat milk

1 teaspoon dried oregano

Salmon Tortellini Salad

Serve with fresh fruit and a green salad. If you're lucky enough to have fresh salmon, grill it lightly, let it cool, and flake it with a fork.

1. Cook the tortellini according to package directions. Drain, rinse under cold water, and drain again. Drain the salmon and flake with a fork.

2. In medium-sized bowl, gently toss together the pasta, carrots, zucchini, and bell pepper. Add the salmon and mix.

3. In a small bowl, stir together the yogurt, cheese, parsley, milk, and oregano until well mixed. Add to the pasta mixture and toss gently to coat evenly.

4. Cover and refrigerate for several hours before serving.

PER SERVING

Calories:......447	Sodium: ......458 mg
Fat:..........14 g	Fiber:..........2 g
Protein:.......44 g	Carbohydrate:..35 g

1 tablespoon olive oil

2 tablespoons fresh orange zest

1 tablespoon ginger root, minced

1½ pounds tuna (sushi grade)

½ cup leek, thinly sliced

2½ cups vegetable or fish stock

1¼ cups uncooked Moroccan couscous

1 teaspoon extra-virgin olive oil

Couscous Salad with Fresh-Grilled Tuna

Moroccan couscous can be purchased in a specialty or gourmet food store.

1. Heat grill (or use a broiler) to medium-high heat.

2. Mix together half the olive oil with half the zest and half the ginger in a bowl; rub on the tuna. Grill (or broil) the tuna medium-rare (about 3–4 minutes per side) or to desired doneness.

3. While the tuna cooks, heat the remaining olive oil in a small saucepan on medium heat; quick-sauté the leeks for 1 minute. Add the stock and the remaining ginger and zest; bring to simmer. Add the couscous, cover, and cook for 5 minutes. Remove from heat.

4. Fluff the couscous with a fork, then spoon into mounds on serving plates. Thinly slice the tuna and fan it over the couscous, then drizzle with the extra-virgin olive oil.

PER SERVING

Calories: 237	Sodium: . . . . . . 208 mg
Fat: . . . . 5 g	Fiber: . . . . 2 g
Protein: . . . . 37 g	Carbohydrate: . . . 8.5 g

Sushi-Grade Fish

Sushi-grade fish is the finest you can buy. But if it smells too "fishy" do not get it! Fish should have relatively no odor when fresh. When you're using sushi-grade fish in this recipe, try it on the rare side for an incredible increase in flavor.

12 ounces uncooked farfalle pasta

6 tablespoons olive oil

3 tablespoons lemon juice

2 cloves garlic, minced

¼ teaspoon kosher salt

¼ teaspoon black pepper, ground

1 cup fresh king crab, cooked

4 scallions, cooked and sliced

⅔ cup radishes, chopped

2 tablespoons fresh parsley, chopped

Pasta and King Crab Salad

You needn't stick with king crab. Feel free to substitute your favorite seafood.

1. Cook farfalle pasta in water until al dente, as directed by packaging, then drain. Add pasta to a large mixing bowl.

2. Combine olive oil, lemon juice, garlic, salt, and pepper in a small bowl. Pour the olive oil mixture over the pasta and mix. Let pasta stand for 5 minutes.

3. Mix together the crab, scallions, radishes, and parsley in a medium bowl. Add the crab mixture to the salad, toss again, and serve.

PER SERVING

Calories: 431	Sodium: . . . . . 1,184 mg
Fat: . . . . 16 g	Fiber: . . . . 2.5 g
Protein: . . . . 30 g	Carbohydrate: . . 43 g

1 pound medium shrimp, cleaned and cooked

½ cup leeks, sliced

3 tablespoons seasoned rice vinegar

2 teaspoons fresh dill, minced

1 teaspoon honey mustard

¼ teaspoon kosher salt

⅛ teaspoon dried rosemary, crushed

5 tablespoons extra-virgin olive oil

2 cups watercress, torn

1 cup Bibb lettuce, torn

1 cup red leaf lettuce, torn

Dilled Shrimp and Watercress Salad

Prepare shrimp at least 1 hour before serving to give them time to marinate in the dill dressing.

1. Combine shrimp and leeks in a large mixing bowl.

2. Whisk vinegar, dill, mustard, salt, and rosemary together in a small bowl. Whisk oil into dressing and mix until emulsified. Pour dressing over shrimp and toss well to coat thoroughly. Cover bowl and place in refrigerator. Chill for at least 1 hour.

3. Toss watercress and Bibb, and red leaf lettuces together in a large bowl. Split the lettuce evenly between 4 plates. Remove shrimp from refrigerator. Toss gently to mix shrimp and dressing again. Split the shrimp salad between 4 plates and serve over greens. Drizzle remaining dressing over each plate.

PER SERVING

Calories: 252	Sodium: . . . . . . 280 mg
Fat: . . . . 19 g	Fiber: . . . . 1 g
Protein: . . . . 18 g	Carbohydrate: . . . 3 g

Boiling Shrimp

If you prefer fresh shrimp, boiling is the easiest way to cook them. Remove the shell and scrape away the vein on each shrimp. Add shrimp to a pot of boiling water, cover, and reduce heat to low. Shrimp are done as soon as they turn pink, about 3 minutes for medium shrimp and 8 minutes for jumbo. Quickly drain the cooked shrimp, rinse them in cold water, and place them in a bowl.

¼ cup water

¼ cup dry white wine

1 teaspoon lemon juice

16 medium shrimp, peeled and deveined

16 medium sea scallops

½ pound fillet of bluefish, skinless

1 pound crab legs, cut in 2-inch lengths, cracked

½ pound mussels, scrubbed

1 cup Italian dressing

2 teaspoons capers

Black pepper, to taste

1 cup fresh Italian flat-leaf parsley, pulled from stems

½ teaspoon coriander seeds, cracked

1 teaspoon lemon zest

12 tiny currant tomatoes

⅓ cup red onion, thinly sliced

Italian Seafood Salad

This salad gives you a great deal of latitude for using what is freshest in the market. This recipe is a starting place. You can substitute lobster for shrimp or use any kind of crabmeat. You can add other fresh herbs to change the flavor.

1. Set a large bowl next to the stove. In a large pot, mix together the water, wine, and lemon juice; bring to a boil. Poach the shrimp and sea scallops in the pot for 5 minutes. Remove to the large bowl. Place the bluefish into the water and allow to simmer for 4 minutes. Add to the bowl of seafood. Drop the crab leg pieces into the boiling water. Remove after 1 minute. Place in the bowl.

2. Poach the mussels for 2–4 minutes until they open. Place in the bowl.

3. To the bowl, add the Italian dressing and the rest of the ingredients. Toss gently to coat. Refrigerate covered for 2 hours. Serve chilled or at room temperature.

PER SERVING

Calories: 421	Sodium: . . . . 1,055 mg
Fat: . . . . 21 g	Fiber: . . . . 0 g
Protein: . . . . 46 g	Carbohydrate: . . . 8 g

INGREDIENTS | SERVES 4

½ pound squid rings

2 medium cucumbers

½ pound salad shrimp

1 (6-ounce) can chopped clams, drained

½ cup stalk celery, thinly sliced

½ cup white onion, finely chopped

1 inner stalk lemongrass, minced

1 small serrano chili, seeded and finely chopped

2 tablespoons fresh mint, chopped

1 garlic clove, minced

2 tablespoons green onion, thinly sliced

¼ cup fish sauce

Sugar, to taste

Bibb lettuce leaves

Thailand Seafood Salad

The different textures and flavors of the seafood in this recipe complement one another well. Still, don't hesitate to try other crustaceans in this recipe, such as bay scallops or lobster.

1. Poach the squid and let cool. Meanwhile, peel, seed, and thinly slice the cucumber. In a large mixing bowl, gently combine the cooled squid, shrimp, clams, cucumber, and celery; set aside.

2. In a small mixing bowl, stir together the onion, lemongrass, serrano chili, mint, garlic, green onion, and fish sauce. Add sugar to taste. Pour the dressing over the seafood mixture, tossing to coat. Cover and let sit for at least 30 minutes before serving.

3. To serve, place lettuce leaves in the center of 4 plates. Mound the seafood salad on top of the lettuce leaves.

PER SERVING

Calories: 144	Sodium: . . . . 1,502 mg
Fat: . . . . 2 g	Fiber: . . . . 2 g
Protein: . . . . 22 g	Carbohydrate: . . 10 g

Poaching Squid

To poach the squid, you need a large pot filled with water and a pinch of salt. Bring the water to a rolling boil over high heat and drop in the squid. Let the squid cook for 30 seconds. Quickly drain squid, moving the colander gently to help shake off excess water.

3 tablespoons sugar

4 tablespoons fish sauce

⅓ cup lime juice

2 tablespoons prepared chili sauce

¾ pound cooked shrimp

¼ cup fresh mint, chopped

½ cup red onion, thinly sliced

¼ cup green onions, thinly sliced

2 cups cucumber, peeled and thinly sliced

Bibb lettuce leaves

Spicy Shrimp Salad

The cooked shrimp add great color and texture to this salad, but it's equally tasty if you substitute cooked mussels or scallops.

1. In a small bowl, combine sugar, fish sauce, lime juice, and chili sauce. Stir until the sugar dissolves completely.

2. In a large bowl, combine all of the salad ingredients except the lettuce. Pour the dressing over and toss to coat.

3. To serve, place the lettuce leaves on individual plates. Mound a portion of the shrimp salad on top of the leaves. Serve immediately.

PER SERVING

Calories: 120
Fat: . . . . 1.5 g
Protein: . . . . 14 g

Sodium: . . . . 1,486 mg
Fiber: . . . . 0 g
Carbohydrate: . . 13 g

1 tablespoon fish sauce

⅓ cup water

1 inner stalk lemongrass, finely chopped

1 tablespoon lime zest

⅓ cup white onion, thinly sliced

5 teaspoons lime juice

2 red chili peppers, seeded and chopped

1 pound calamari, cleaned

15 mint leaves, chopped

6 sprigs cilantro, chopped

1 tablespoon green onion, thinly sliced

Baby greens (optional)

Grilled Calamari Salad

This recipe features calamari grilled with light vinaigrette to ensure the seafood complements the salad without taking over the other flavors.

1. Combine fish sauce, water, lemongrass, lime zest, onion, lime juice, and chili peppers in a small bowl; set aside.

2. Prepare a grill or broiler. Place the calamari on a broiler pan or in a grill basket and cook over high heat until tender, about 3 minutes per side. Let cool to room temperature.

3. Place the grilled calamari in a mixing bowl. Stir the dressing and pour it over the calamari.

4. If serving immediately, add the mint, cilantro, and green onions. Alternatively, allow the calamari to marinate for up to 1 hour before serving, and then add the additional ingredients.

5. To serve: Use individual cups or bowls to help capture some of the wonderful dressing. Alternatively, mound the calamari mixture over a bed of baby greens and spoon additional dressing over the top.

PER SERVING

Calories: 84	Sodium: . . . . . . 385 mg
Fat: . . . . 1 g	Fiber: . . . . 0 g
Protein: . . . . . . 14 g	Carbohydrate: . . . 3 g

What Is Calamari?

Calamari is squid. Sometimes you will see the smallest ones sold whole. Otherwise it comes in pearly white pieces that you slice into bite-sized morsels. Calamari has a sweet, mild flavor and only becomes chewy when overcooked.

2 tablespoons olive oil

1 pound medium shrimp, peeled and deveined

2 garlic cloves, minced

1 (15-ounce) can black beans, rinsed and drained

1 (16-ounce) can yellow corn, drained

1 (6-ounce) can green chilies, diced

⅓ cup green onions, chopped

¼ cup mayonnaise

¼ cup tomato salsa

2 tablespoons lime juice

1 teaspoon salt

¼ teaspoon black pepper, ground

¼ cup fresh cilantro, chopped

1 orange

Cuban Shrimp Salad

Use cooked salad shrimp instead of cooking your own if you want to whip up the recipe in a hurry. However, if you have a few minutes, cooking the shrimp yourself is easy and tastes much better.

1. Heat the oil in a large skillet over medium heat. Cook the shrimp and garlic 4 minutes until the shrimp are pink and thoroughly cooked. Drain and chill at least 2 hours.

2. When the shrimp is chilled, add the beans, corn, chilies, and onions; mix well. In a small bowl, combine the mayonnaise, salsa, lime juice, salt, and pepper. Add to the shrimp mixture and combine thoroughly. Chill at least 1 hour.

3. To serve, place the salad in a serving bowl and sprinkle cilantro on top. Cut the unpeeled orange in wedges and use as a garnish.

PER SERVING

Calories: 291	Sodium: . . . . . . 912 mg
Fat: . . . . 14 g	Fiber: . . . . 6 g
Protein: . . . . 17 g	Carbohydrate: . . 28 g

Preparing Shrimp

When it comes to buying raw, it's best to buy shrimp with shells. The shrimp shell protects the meat and preserves the fresh flavor until you're ready to cook. To prepare, grasp the underside of the shell with each hand and gently pull it apart to release the meat. Use a knife to scrape away the veins, rinse the shrimp clean, drain, and use as needed.

1 navel orange, large

1 cup curly endives, torn

3 cups Boston lettuce, torn

1 tablespoon white wine vinegar

1 tablespoon orange juice

12 dry sea scallops, large

¼ teaspoon kosher salt

¼ teaspoon black pepper, ground

1 tablespoon flat-leaf parsley, minced

2 teaspoons fresh rosemary, minced

1 teaspoon orange zest

2 tablespoons extra-virgin olive oil

2 teaspoons chives, sliced

Rosemary and Orange–Seared Scallop Salad

Use dry sea scallops, or scallops that have not been soaked in salt water, to ensure the juiciest texture and best taste. If you cannot find dry scallops, rinse the soaked ones in cold water and pat dry.

1. Remove peel, pith, and membranes from around each orange segment. Cut the segments into 1-inch chunks. Toss the prepared segments, curly endives, and Boston lettuce together in a large mixing bowl. Drizzle vinegar and orange juice over salad and toss well to coat.

2. Sprinkle scallops with salt and pepper. Toss parsley, rosemary, and orange zest together in a small bowl. Press one side of each scallop into the herb mixture to lightly coat.

3. Heat oil in a skillet over high heat. Add seasoned scallops to the hot skillet. Cook for 2 minutes on each side, turning once. Remove skillet from heat.

4. To serve, divide lettuce between 4 salad bowls. Divide the seared scallops between the bowls and drizzle each salad with the pan drippings. Garnish salads with chives and serve immediately.

PER SERVING

Calories: 137	Sodium: . . . . . . 263 mg
Fat: . . . . 7.5 g	Fiber: . . . . .2 g
Protein: . . . . 11 g	Carbohydrate: . . . 7 g

Successfully Searing Scallops

To sear scallops without overcooking, start with a very hot pan. This gives the scallop a crispy outside with a moist inside. Place the scallops on the pan and turn only once to get a nice sear without losing flavor.

Grilled Halibut Herb Salad

If you don't care for oranges, or don't have any fresh ones handy, use drained capers to garnish the entrée salad instead.

1. Place a large grill pan over medium-high heat. Sprinkle each fillet side with 1 teaspoon of orange juice and lightly rub it in. Brush both sides of each fillet with oil. Sprinkle each side with a little lemon pepper, garlic salt, and paprika.

2. Add fillets to hot grill pan and cook for 5 minutes on each side. Remove fillets from pan as soon as they are cooked and place on a plate. Let fillets rest for 3 minutes, then slice each one by width.

3. Combine romaine, parsley, basil, and chives in a large salad bowl. Toss to mix. Split salad between two plates. Top each salad with a sliced fillet. Squeeze an orange slice over each salad, garnish with slice and serve.

PER SERVING

Calories: 317
Fat: . . . . 23 g
Protein: . . . . 24 g

Sodium: . . . . . . 179 mg
Fiber: . . . . 2 g
Carbohydrate: . . . 5 g

8 (3-ounce) crab cakes

¼ cup mayonnaise

2 teaspoons water

2 teaspoons lemon juice

1 teaspoon spicy brown mustard

1 teaspoon fresh chives, finely minced

½ teaspoon honey

⅛ teaspoon kosher salt

3 cups butterhead lettuce, torn

½ cup fresh mustard greens, torn

½ cup red bell pepper, diced

4 teaspoons radish, diced

Crab Cake Salad

If you're short on time, substitute honey mustard salad dressing for the homemade dressing in the recipe.

1. Prepare crab cakes according to package instructions. Remove crab cakes from oven when done and let cool for 2 minutes.

2. While the crab cakes are cooking, combine mayonnaise, water, lemon juice, mustard, chives, honey, and salt in a small bowl. Stir until fully mixed. Cover bowl and chill in refrigerator until needed.

3. Toss the lettuce, greens, and bell pepper together in a large salad bowl. Split salad evenly between 4 plates. Cut the cool crab cakes in half and place 4 half-cakes on each plate. Remove dressing from refrigerator and drizzle over each salad. Garnish with radish and serve.

PER SERVING

Calories: 297	Sodium: . . . . . . 589 mg
Fat: . . . . 20 g	Fiber: . . . . 0.5 g
Protein: . . . . . . 26 g	Carbohydrate: . . . 3 g

The Key to Crab Cakes

Basic cakes consist of crabmeat, eggs, mayonnaise, herbs, and seasoned breadcrumbs. The patties are coated with flour or breadcrumbs and quickly fried on each side. It doesn't matter what recipe you follow, chilling the patties before frying is the key to making great crab cakes. Room temperature patties are much more likely to crumble during cooking, whereas chilled patties hold shape.

4 cups romaine lettuce, torn

2 cups lamb's lettuce

½ cup radicchio, shredded

⅓ cup creamy Italian vinaigrette dressing

⅔ cup plum tomato, sliced

24 anchovy fillets in oil, drained

½ cup seasoned croutons, small

2 tablespoons capers, drained

Anchovy and Tomato Salad

If you don't care for capers, this recipe also tastes amazing with Asiago, Romano, or Parmesan cheese grated over the top.

1. Combine romaine, lamb's lettuce, and radicchio in a large salad bowl. Add dressing to bowl and toss to coat. Add tomatoes to salad and toss gently to mix.

2. Split salad evenly between 6 plates. Slice fillets into 1-inch big pieces. Add 4 sliced anchovies over each salad. Garnish with croutons and capers. Serve immediately.

PER SERVING

Calories: 58	Sodium: . . . . . . 596 mg
Fat: . . . . 2.5 g	Fiber: . . . . 1 g
Protein: . . . . 5 g	Carbohydrate: . . . 5 g

CHAPTER 11

Quick Salads

Italian Garden Salad
194

Corny Ranch Ham Salad
194

Peachy Ham and Blue
Cheese Salad
195

Tomato, Feta, and Grape Salad
195

Pineapple Onion Salad
196

Easy Nacho Corn Salad
196

Tuna Caesar Salad
197

Crunchy Pepperoni Salad
197

Creamy Comfort Salad
198

Crisp Avocado Salad
198

Pecan and Goat Cheese Salad
199

Carrot and Cucumber
Ranch Salad
199

Raspberry-Cranberry
Spinach Salad
200

Sweet Bibb Salad
200

Cantaloupe, Pecan, and
Cheese Salad
201

Quick Cranberry Turkey Salad
201

Turkey Island Salad
202

Sweet and Savory Side Salad
202

Yellow Squash and Tomato Salad
203

Pickled Peppers and
Pickles Salad
203

Pastrami Mustard Salad
204

Beefy Mushroom Salad
204

2 cups iceberg lettuce, shredded

1 cup Roma tomatoes, diced

¼ cup white mushrooms, sliced

3 tablespoons black olives, diced

¼ cup shredded mozzarella cheese

¼ cup Italian salad dressing

Italian Garden Salad

Turn this simple side salad into a full meal with some sliced chicken breast or diced Italian lunchmeat, such as salami.

Toss lettuce, tomatoes, mushrooms, olives, and mozzarella together in a large salad bowl. Drizzle dressing over the salad. Toss gently to mix and serve immediately.

PER SERVING

Calories: 92	Sodium: . . . . . . 341 mg
Fat: . . . . 7 g	Fiber: . . . . 1 g
Protein: . . . . 3 g	Carbohydrate: . . . 5.5 g

2 cups iceberg lettuce, chopped

1 (15-ounce) can yellow corn, drained

1 cup ham lunchmeat, diced

½ cup Cheddar cheese, shredded

½ cup ranch salad dressing

Corny Ranch Ham Salad

Feel free to use canned white corn or fresh sweet corn for this recipe, it will still taste great.

Toss lettuce, corn, lunch meat, and cheese together in a mixing bowl. Add dressing and toss to mix. Serve immediately.

PER SERVING

Calories: 369	Sodium: . . . . . . 668 mg
Fat: . . . . 29 g	Fiber: . . . . 3 g
Protein: . . . . 11 g	Carbohydrate: . . 19 g

Peachy Ham and Blue Cheese Salad

This salad is as easy to make as a ham sandwich, especially if you use drained canned peaches, but is a far better tasting lunch than a plain sandwich.

Toss watercress, peaches, ham, and walnuts together in a large mixing bowl. Add dressing to salad and toss well to coat. Serve immediately.

PER SERVING

Calories: 341	Sodium: . . . . . . 705 mg
Fat: . . . . 30 g	Fiber: . . . . 2.5 g
Protein: . . . . 13 g	Carbohydrate: . . . 8.5 g

Tomato, Feta, and Grape Salad

This recipe goes well with steak or pasta entrées. If you want a richer tomato taste, replace the cherry tomatoes with plum or grape tomatoes.

1. Toss the grapes and tomatoes together in a medium salad bowl. Drizzle with lemon juice and toss to coat. Drizzle with oil and toss to coat.

2. Sprinkle with feta and toss to mix. Salt and pepper to taste. Serve immediately.

PER SERVING

Calories: 208	Sodium: . . . . . . 426 mg
Fat: . . . . 15 g	Fiber: . . . . 1.5 g
Protein: . . . . 7 g	Carbohydrate: . . 13 g

INGREDIENTS | SERVES 4

1 (8-ounce) can pineapple chunks

½ cup red onion, chopped

3 cups mixed baby greens

1 tablespoon lime juice

½ teaspoon kosher salt

Pineapple Onion Salad

This sweet and tangy recipe does not keep well, so make sure to throw it together right before eating. If you prefer a little more zing, add another tablespoon of lime juice and a sprinkle of cayenne pepper.

1. Drain juice from pineapple and place chunks in a large salad bowl. Mix onions and baby greens into the pineapple.

2. Sprinkle lightly with lime juice and salt. Toss to coat and serve immediately.

PER SERVING

Calories: 28	Sodium: . . . . . . 299 mg
Fat: . . . . 0 g	Fiber: . . . . 1 g
Protein: . . . . 0 g	Carbohydrate: . . . 5.5 g

INGREDIENTS | SERVES 6

1 (15-ounce) can sweet corn

3 cups iceberg lettuce, shredded

1 cup Cheddar cheese, shredded

⅓ cup salsa

¼ cup sour cream

Easy Nacho Corn Salad

This light recipe works well as a quick lunch. If you want to make it into a filling entrée, add some chopped avocado to the salad and serve with tortilla chips.

1. Drain water from corn and add drained corn to a large salad bowl. Toss the lettuce and cheese into the bowl.

2. In a small bowl, stir together the salsa and sour cream. Drizzle the dressing over the salad and toss to coat.

PER SERVING

Calories: 164	Sodium: . . . . . . 214 mg
Fat: . . . . 10 g	Fiber: . . . . 2 g
Protein: . . . . 8 g	Carbohydrate: . . 13 g

4 cups romaine lettuce, torn

¾ cup seasoned croutons

2 (6-ounce) cans tuna in water

⅓ cup Caesar salad dressing

2 tablespoons Parmesan cheese, grated

Tuna Caesar Salad

This versatile and easy recipe works with any kind of canned meat, be it tuna, turkey, chicken, or crab.

1. Toss lettuce and croutons together in a large salad bowl. Split salad evenly between 4 plates.

2. Drain tuna. Combine tuna and dressing in a small bowl. Mix well. Split tuna evenly over each plate. Garnish with cheese and serve.

PER SERVING

Calories: 257	Sodium: . . . . . . 638 mg
Fat: . . . . 15 g	Fiber: . . . . 1.5 g
Protein: . . . . . . 25 g	Carbohydrate: . . . 7 g

5 cups iceberg lettuce, chopped

¾ cup pepperoni, diced

½ cup mozzarella cheese, shredded

⅓ cup Italian vinaigrette salad dressing

⅓ cup seasoned croutons, crushed

Crunchy Pepperoni Salad

It's important to chop the lettuce for this recipe as opposed to shredding it. Chopping the iceberg leaves extra crunch, where shredding it reduces the crisp texture and causes the lettuce to blend in with the mozzarella too much.

Toss lettuce, pepperoni, and mozzarella together in a large salad bowl. Add dressing and toss to coat. Sprinkle with crushed croutons and serve.

PER SERVING

Calories: 125	Sodium: . . . . . . 233 mg
Fat: . . . . 9.5 g	Fiber: . . . . 1 g
Protein: . . . . 5.5 g	Carbohydrate: . . . 5 g

Creamy Comfort Salad

This recipe's simplicity betrays its amazing taste. It's easy to dress up with additional ingredients, but tastes best when left plain.

Combine lettuce and carrots in a large salad bowl. Grate eggs into salad using a grater or by pushing the eggs through a fine mesh sieve to break them into small chunks. Add the mayonnaise, salt, and pepper to the bowl. Gently stir the salad together and serve.

PER SERVING

Calories: 210	Sodium: . . . . . . 345 mg
Fat: . . . . 18 g	Fiber: . . . . 1.5 g
Protein: . . . . 7 g	Carbohydrate: . . . 5 g

Crisp Avocado Salad

This recipe tastes particularly good if served over, or with a side of, toasted focaccia bread. It also works well as a side dish to spicy Southwest or Mexican entrées.

Toss lettuce, avocado, onion, and olives together in a large salad bowl. Sprinkle salad with lime juice and salt. Toss well to coat. Sprinkle with pine nuts and serve.

PER SERVING

Calories: 189	Sodium: . . . . . . 322 mg
Fat: . . . . 17 g	Fiber: . . . . 6 g
Protein: . . . . 3 g	Carbohydrate: . . 10 g

Pecan and Goat Cheese Salad

This quick salad has a rich flavor that works in large portions as a side for a pasta dish or in small portions as an appetizer.

Mix greens and dressing together in a medium salad bowl. Toss well to coat. Add goat cheese and pecans to salad. Toss to mix and serve immediately.

PER SERVING

Calories: 257	Sodium: . . . . . . 158 mg
Fat: . . . . 24 g	Fiber: . . . . 2.5 g
Protein: . . . . 8 g	Carbohydrate: . . . 5 g

Carrot and Cucumber Ranch Salad

This sweet and creamy salad is a versatile dish that pairs well with anything from bacon cheeseburgers to eggplant lasagna.

Combine lettuce and dressing in a large salad bowl. Toss well to coat. Add carrots and cucumber to bowl. Toss to mix and coat. Serve immediately.

PER SERVING

Calories: 113	Sodium: . . . . . . 214 mg
Fat: . . . . 10 g	Fiber: . . . . 1 g
Protein: . . . . 1 g	Carbohydrate: . . . 4.5 g

INGREDIENTS | SERVES 4

4 cups baby spinach

⅔ cup red onion, sliced

½ cup dried cranberries, unsweetened

¼ cup raspberry vinaigrette salad dressing

Raspberry-Cranberry Spinach Salad

This simple spinach salad tastes particularly good with fall recipes, such as turkey and stuffing or pot roast and mashed potatoes.

Combine baby spinach, onion, and dried cranberries in a large salad bowl. Drizzle dressing over salad and toss well to coat. Serve immediately.

PER SERVING

Calories: 81	Sodium: . . . . 54 mg
Fat: . . . . 1 g	Fiber: . . . . 1.5 g
Protein: . . . . 1 g	Carbohydrate: . . 18 g

INGREDIENTS | SERVES 2

3 cups Bibb lettuce, torn

1 cup cherry tomatoes, halved

¼ cup carrot, shredded

2 tablespoons rice vinegar

½ teaspoon granulated sugar

1 tablespoon green onions, sliced

Sweet Bibb Salad

You can skip adding the sugar if you prefer, but the sweet hint the sugar adds is what really makes this recipe come together.

Toss lettuce, tomatoes, and carrots together in a large salad bowl. Sprinkle vinegar and sugar over salad. Toss to coat. Garnish with green onions and serve.

PER SERVING

Calories: 40	Sodium: . . . . 23 mg
Fat: . . . . 1 g	Fiber: . . . . 2.5 g
Protein: . . . . 2 g	Carbohydrate: . . . 8 g

Cantaloupe, Pecan, and Cheese Salad

This quick salad works as a light breakfast or served over mixed greens as a light lunch.

Toss cantaloupe, Gouda, and pecans together in a large mixing bowl. Sprinkle with vinaigrette and parsley. Toss well to mix and coat. Serve immediately.

PER SERVING

Calories: 247	Sodium: . . . . . . 263 mg
Fat: . . . . 18 g	Fiber: . . . . 3 g
Protein: . . . . 10 g	Carbohydrate: . . 14 g

Quick Cranberry Turkey Salad

Any kind of turkey lunchmeat works with this recipe, so try it with pepper-rubbed turkey, honey-roasted turkey, or even canned turkey breast meat.

Toss spinach, lunchmeat, and cranberries together in a large salad bowl. Add dressing and seeds to salad. Toss well to coat and mix. Serve immediately.

PER SERVING

Calories: 102	Sodium: . . . . . . 337 mg
Fat: . . . . 4 g	Fiber: . . . . 2 g
Protein: . . . . 6 g	Carbohydrate: . . 13 g

Turkey Island Salad

This easy lunch salad also tastes great with dried mango instead of dried pineapple.

Toss lettuce, turkey, celery, and dried pineapple together in a large salad bowl. Drizzle with dressing and toss to mix and coat. Serve immediately.

INGREDIENTS | SERVES 2

3 cups Bibb lettuce

½ cup peppered turkey lunchmeat, diced

⅓ cup celery, sliced

3 tablespoons dried pineapple, minced

¼ cup Thousand Island salad dressing

PER SERVING

Calories:	165	Sodium:	625 mg
Fat:	11 g	Fiber:	2 g
Protein:	6 g	Carbohydrate:	11 g

Sweet and Savory Side Salad

Drizzling the salad with concentrated pineapple juice turns the ordinary ingredients into a tantalizing side and pairs well with almost any kind of meal.

Toss lettuce, carrot, celery, and raisins together in a large salad bowl. Drizzle pineapple juice concentrate over salad and toss well to fully coat. Serve immediately.

INGREDIENTS | SERVES 2

1 cup Boston lettuce, finely torn

¾ cup carrot, shredded

⅓ cup celery, diced

2 tablespoons raisins

2 teaspoons pineapple juice concentrate

PER SERVING

Calories:	82	Sodium:	49 mg
Fat:	0 g	Fiber:	2.5 g
Protein:	1.5 g	Carbohydrate:	18 g

Yellow Squash and Tomato Salad

INGREDIENTS | **SERVES 2**

1 cup baby yellow squash, diced

1 cup grape tomatoes, quartered

2 cups oak leaf lettuce, torn

¼ cup Thousand Island salad dressing

⅓ cup garlic croutons

Use small yellow squash for the salad to ensure the vegetable is sweet and tender enough to eat raw.

Toss squash, tomatoes, and lettuce together in a large salad bowl. Drizzle dressing over salad and toss to coat. Sprinkle croutons over salad and toss to mix. Serve immediately.

PER SERVING

Calories: 181	Sodium: . . . . . . 376 mg
Fat: . . . . 13 g	Fiber: . . . . 2.5 g
Protein: . . . . 3 g	Carbohydrate: . . 16 g

Pickled Peppers and Pickles Salad

INGREDIENTS | **SERVES 4**

3 cups iceberg lettuce, chopped

1 cup oak leaf lettuce, torn

¼ cup ranch salad dressing

2 tablespoons pickled banana peppers, drained

1 tablespoon pickled jalapeño peppers, drained

½ cup dill pickles, diced

½ cup garlic croutons

This side dish recipe helps add a little zing to plain meat entrées, such as meatloaf and burgers.

Toss iceberg and oak leaf lettuce together in a large salad bowl. Add ranch dressing to bowl and toss well to coat. Dice banana peppers and jalapeño peppers. Add pickles, banana peppers, and jalapeño peppers to the salad. Toss gently to mix. Add croutons to salad, toss lightly, and serve.

PER SERVING

Calories: 111	Sodium: . . . . . . 443 mg
Fat: . . . . 9 g	Fiber: . . . . 1.5 g
Protein: . . . . 1.5 g	Carbohydrate: . . . 7 g

Pastrami Mustard Salad

INGREDIENTS | SERVES 2

2 cups green leaf lettuce, torn

½ cup pastrami lunchmeat, sliced

¼ cup white onion, diced

3 tablespoons honey mustard salad dressing

Serve this salad with small triangles of rye or pumpernickel bread. If you live near a gourmet grocer, look for rye or pumpernickel croutons to serve with the dish.

Toss ingredients together in a large mixing bowl. Toss well to coat. Split salad between 2 plates and serve.

PER SERVING

Calories:	54	Sodium:	197 mg
Fat:	0.5 g	Fiber:	0.5 g
Protein:	3.5 g	Carbohydrate:	4 g

Beefy Mushroom Salad

INGREDIENTS | SERVES 4

5 cups mixed baby greens

1 cup roast beef lunchmeat, sliced

½ cup white mushrooms, sliced

¼ cup red onion, diced

¼ cup honey mustard salad dressing

2 teaspoons prepared horseradish

This bistro-worthy salad recipe makes a great lunch and pairs well with a chunk of crusty bread.

Toss greens, roast beef, mushrooms, and onions together in a large salad bowl. Mix salad dressing and horseradish together in a small bowl. Drizzle over salad and toss to mix. Serve immediately.

PER SERVING

Calories:	130	Sodium:	62 mg
Fat:	4 g	Fiber:	1 g
Protein:	18 g	Carbohydrate:	3.5 g

CHAPTER 12

Gourmet Salads

Apple Watercress Salad with
Ginger Mustard Dressing
206

Peppery Grilled Portobello
and Leek Salad
207

Arugula, Pear, and
Avocado Salad
208

Asian Chopped Salad with
Crispy Noodles and Kimchi
209

Eggplant Arugula Salad
210

Escarole and Orange Salad
211

Radicchio Cabrales Salad
212

Turkey and Cranberry Salad on
Butternut Squash
213

Nutty Chanterelle Salad
214

Shaved Fennel Salad with
Toasted Hazelnuts
215

Grilled Shrimp Salad
215

Blood Orange Salad with Shrimp
and Baby Spinach
216

Fig and Parmesan Curl Salad
217

Lobster and Asparagus Salad
218

Fresh Crab with Arugula Salad
219

Wilted Amaretto Spinach Salad
220

Applewood Bacon and Brie
Frisee Salad
221

Almond and Pear Salad
with Gorgonzola
222

Sugared Flowers and
Greens Salad
223

Apricot and Fennel Sprout Salad
224

2 tablespoons apple cider vinegar

2 teaspoons Dijon mustard

1 teaspoon ginger root, finely minced

½ teaspoon roasted garlic paste

½ teaspoon soy sauce

¼ cup extra-virgin olive oil

1 cup diced Pink Lady apple

½ cup cucumber, peeled and thinly sliced

¼ cup leeks, diced

¼ cup palm hearts, diced

3 cups watercress, chopped

2 cups baby spinach leaves, torn

1 tablespoon toasted almond slices

½ teaspoon candied ginger, finely minced

Apple Watercress Salad with Ginger Mustard Dressing

Serve this flavorful salad before or after the entrée to prevent it from overwhelming the other selections.

1. Whisk vinegar, mustard, ginger, garlic, and soy sauce together in a small bowl. Mix well. Pour the mixture into a glass bottle.

2. Add oil to the bottle of dressing and twist the lid on tightly. Shake the dressing well and store in the fridge. Let the dressing mature for 1–24 hours before making the salad.

3. Toss the apples, cucumber, leeks, and palm hearts together in a salad bowl. Remove the matured dressing from the fridge and shake well. Drizzle the dressing over the salad and toss to coat.

4. Toss the watercress and spinach into the salad. Garnish with a sprinkle of almonds and candied ginger. Serve immediately.

PER SERVING

Calories: 107	Sodium: . . . . 63 mg
Fat: . . . . 9.5 g	Fiber: . . . . 1 g
Protein: . . . . 1 g	Carbohydrate: . . . 5 g

Keeping Apples the Right Color

Apples can turn brown if cut up and left to chill in a fruit salad. This browning is caused by the fruit's flesh reacting to the air and oxidizing. To prevent browning, lightly coat the fruit with lemon juice so that the acidic citrus juice can prevent oxidation. Fruit preservation products use ascorbic acid mixed with water to achieve the same results.

4 large Portobello mushroom caps

1 garlic clove

½ teaspoon black pepper, fresh ground

¼ teaspoon lemon zest

½ cup leeks, sliced

3 cups Boston lettuce, lightly packed

1 cup mixed micro greens, lightly packed

¼ cup honey mustard vinaigrette

¼ cup toasted pine nuts

Peppery Grilled Portobello and Leek Salad

Only use the sweeter, white bottom part of the leek in this salad, as the upper green leaves have a stronger flavor that can overpower the mushrooms.

1. Heat grill or grill pan to medium-high.

2. Place mushroom caps in a shallow baking dish, round side down. Add garlic clove to a garlic press and press garlic over the caps so that the juice sprays onto the mushrooms. Use clean hands to rub garlic juice and paste around each cap. Keep the coating light and discard excess garlic.

3. Drizzle oil over mushrooms and rub to ensure each cap is completely covered. Sprinkle ¼ teaspoon pepper over the caps. Flip the caps over so that the round side faces up. Sprinkle the lemon zest and remaining pepper over the caps.

4. Remove caps from dish and place on grill. Grill caps for 3 minutes on each side. Remove caps from grill, place back in dish, and set aside.

5. Combine Boston lettuce, micro greens, and leeks in a large salad bowl. Drizzle with vinaigrette and toss to coat. Slice cooled mushroom caps 1-inch thick and add to salad. Toss to mix and garnish with pine nuts. Serve immediately.

PER SERVING

Calories: 117	Sodium: . . . . 15 mg
Fat: . . . . 8 g	Fiber: . . . . 2 g
Protein: . . . . 5 g	Carbohydrate: . . . 7.5 g

3 cups arugula leaves

1 cup Asian pear, thinly sliced

½ cup avocado, diced

¼ cup grape tomatoes, diced

¼ cup sunflower seeds, lightly salted

1 tablespoon balsamic vinegar

¼ teaspoon black pepper, ground

½ teaspoon Dijon mustard

¼ teaspoon lemon zest

3 tablespoons extra-virgin olive oil

Arugula, Pear, and Avocado Salad

Use Bosc pears if Asian are not available. If Bosc pears are also unavailable, look for any kind of crisp pear. Avoid soft pears, as the texture will blend in with the avocado.

1. Toss the arugula, pear, avocado, tomato, and sunflower seeds together in a large salad bowl.

2. Whisk the vinegar, pepper, mustard, and lemon zest together in a small bowl. Whisk the oil into the dressing.

3. Drizzle the dressing over the salad and toss to coat. Serve salad immediately.

PER SERVING

Calories: 186
Fat: . . . . 17 g
Protein: . . . . 3 g
Sodium: . . . . 40 mg
Fiber: . . . . 4 g
Carbohydrate: . . . 8 g

INGREDIENTS | SERVES 4

2 bunches scallions, trimmed and thinly sliced

8 ounces Thai-flavored baked tofu, diced

2 cups baby spinach

1 cup water chestnuts, chopped

1 cup crispy chow mein noodles, crumbled

1 cup fresh shelled edamame

½ cup kimchi, drained and chopped

½ cup chopped baby corn

2 tablespoons toasted sesame seeds

Asian-style commercial salad dressing, to taste

Asian Chopped Salad with Crispy Noodles and Kimchi

Kimchi is a peppery condiment made from pickled and fermented cabbage and/or other vegetables and other assorted add-ins. Kimchi is available at well-stocked supermarkets in the refrigerated case of the produce section.

Combine all the ingredients in a large salad bowl. Add chosen dressing to taste and toss to coat. Serve immediately.

PER SERVING

Calories:	428	Sodium:	94 mg
Fat:	20 g	Fiber:	9.5 g
Protein:	30 g	Carbohydrate:	40 g

What Are Chow Mein Noodles and Baby Corn?

Chow mein noodles are deep-fried until crispy and add a zesty crunch to any salad mixture, but particularly to one that is Asian inspired. The baby corn that often turns up in Chinese stir-fries is corn that is harvested early, just after the silk is produced. The tiny cobs retain crispiness while adding a sweet undertone to other dishes. These are readily available canned.

3 medium eggplants

2 tablespoons olive oil

⅓ cup pine nuts

½ cup extra-virgin olive oil

¼ cup balsamic vinegar

¼ cup shallots, diced

2 tablespoons garlic cloves, minced

2 bunches arugula

2 cups peaches, pitted and sliced

5 ounces Parmesan cheese

½ teaspoon black pepper, ground

Eggplant Arugula Salad

Don't use a highly flavored dressing—it will overpower the delicate mix of flavors. A simple vinaigrette of extra-virgin olive oil and a good balsamic vinegar, like the one here, is perfect.

1. Preheat oven to 375°F. Slice the eggplants in half lengthwise.

2. Rub the eggplant with the 2 tablespoons olive oil. Place the eggplant halves face down in a baking pan and roast for approximately 45 minutes, until soft. Toast the pine nuts in the oven on a baking sheet for 6 minutes until lightly brown. Allow the eggplant and pine nuts to cool.

3. To prepare the vinaigrette, blend the extra-virgin olive oil and vinegar in a small bowl.

4. Scoop out the eggplant flesh and toss with the shallots and garlic. Mound on serving plates. Arrange the arugula on one side and the peaches on the other. Shave the Parmesan into thin curls using a vegetable peeler. Drizzle with the vinaigrette and sprinkle with the toasted pine nuts and black pepper. Serve immediately.

PER SERVING

Calories:..... 255	Sodium: ...... 233 mg
Fat:.......... 20 g	Fiber:.......... 5 g
Protein:........ 8 g	Carbohydrate: .. 15 g

Pitting Peaches

To remove the pits from peaches, slice the peach in half and poke the knife along the curve of the pit. Twist the peach halves in opposite directions to release the pit. Use a knife to pop the pit out if stubborn and slice the top stem area from the fruit.

1 head escarole

2 cups lamb's lettuce

2 seedless oranges, large

2 tablespoons fresh red or pink currants

2 tablespoons fresh lemon juice

2 teaspoons olive oil

2 tablespoons Perrier or other mineral water

⅛ teaspoon fleur de sel (French sea salt)

Escarole and Orange Salad

Also known as corn salad, lamb's lettuce leaves add a nutty flavor to this salad recipe. For an added touch, garnish the salad with radish "roses" before serving.

1. Wash the escarole, drain thoroughly, and shred. If using fresh lamb's lettuce, carefully rinse it under running water and drain. (If using prepackaged lamb's lettuce, there is no need to clean it.)

2. Peel the oranges, remove pith, remove membranes, and separate into segments. Rinse the currants and pat dry with paper towels.

3. Whisk together the lemon juice, olive oil, mineral water, and fleur de sel.

4. Combine escarole, lettuce, oranges, and currants in a large bowl. Drizzle the dressing over top. Serve immediately or cover and refrigerate until ready to serve.

PER SERVING

Calories: 35	Sodium: . . . . 91 mg
Fat: . . . . 2.5 g	Fiber: . . . . 1 g
Protein: . . . . 1.5 g	Carbohydrate: . . . 2.5 g

Radicchio Cabrales Salad

Adding blue cheese provides an interesting contrast to the slightly bitter taste of radicchio lettuce and endives in this recipe. Feel free to substitute Roquefort or Danish blue cheese if Cabrales is unavailable.

INGREDIENTS | SERVES 6–8

2 endives

6 cups radicchio, torn

2 tablespoons balsamic vinegar

2 tablespoons extra-virgin olive oil

1 teaspoon sugar

1 teaspoon Dijon mustard

8 ounces Cabrales cheese

¼ cup pine nuts, finely chopped

1. Remove the stem from each endive, cut in half, and cut into strips. Makes about 3 cups. Add endives and radicchio to a large salad bowl.

2. In a small bowl, whisk the balsamic vinegar, olive oil, sugar, and Dijon mustard together.

3. Crumble the Cabrales cheese over the salad. Drizzle with the vinaigrette. Sprinkle the pine nuts over salad and serve immediately.

PER SERVING

Calories: 204	Sodium: . . . . . . 212 mg
Fat: . . . . 15 g	Fiber: . . . . 4.5 g
Protein: . . . . 10 g	Carbohydrate: . . . 7.5 g

Why Cabrales Cheese?

Cabrales is considered one of the finest types of blue cheese. It is only made in the Asturias region of Spain and though specific recipes are tightly guarded, it generally contains cow's milk with a little goat's and/or sheep's milk mixed in. The artisan product is handmade, right down to the hand-salted rind, and is favored for its spicy flavor.

1 butternut squash

⅛ teaspoon kosher salt

⅛ teaspoon nutmeg, ground

12 ounces turkey (fresh roasted)

¾ cup cranberries

2 tablespoons extra-virgin olive oil

3 tablespoons orange juice

Salt and pepper, to taste

Turkey and Cranberry Salad on Butternut Squash

This recipe offers a new twist on an American classic with a Mediterranean flair. A sweet potato can be substituted for the butternut squash if desired.

1. Preheat oven to 350°F.

2. Peel the butternut squash and cut it in half lengthwise. Remove and rinse the seeds, and place the seeds on a baking sheet; toast for approximately 5–10 minutes, until golden. Sprinkle lightly with salt when done.

3. Thinly slice the butternut squash lengthwise into ¾ to 1-inch thick pieces. Brush another baking sheet with oil and lay out the squash slices; sprinkle with nutmeg. Roast the squash for approximately 20–30 minutes, until fork tender.

4. Let cool, then place the squash on plates. Arrange the turkey on top and sprinkle cranberries over the turkey. Drizzle with orange juice and oil. Season with pepper and salt to taste.

PER SERVING

Calories: 161	Sodium: . . . . . . 732 mg
Fat: . . . . 5 g	Fiber: . . . . 3.5 g
Protein: . . . . 10 g	Carbohydrate: . . 22 g

Canned or Fresh?

If using canned cranberries, drain first. If using fresh cranberries, steam and sprinkle lightly with sugar until they are slightly soft.

INGREDIENTS | SERVES 4

3 tablespoons butter

2 cups chanterelle mushrooms, sliced thick

½ teaspoon fresh rosemary, minced

⅛ teaspoon allspice, ground

⅓ cup hazelnuts, chopped

⅓ cup walnuts, chopped

4 cups mixed baby greens

1 (8-ounce) can sliced water chestnuts, drained

4 teaspoons apple cider juice

4 apple peel curls

½ teaspoon fresh chives, minced

Nutty Chanterelle Salad

Make sure to use apple cider juice for this recipe, not apple cider vinegar. The vinegar is a little too strong and sour for the herb and butter base.

1. Melt butter in a large frying pan over medium-high heat. Add mushrooms, rosemary, and allspice to pan. Sauté for 5 minutes.

2. Stir hazelnuts and walnuts into pan. Sauté for 30 seconds and remove pan from heat. Let mixture cool for 5 minutes.

3. Combine mixed greens, water chestnuts, and apple cider juice in a large salad bowl. Toss gently to coat well.

4. Gently toss the mushroom mixture, including drippings, into the salad. Split the salad between 4 plates. Garnish each plate with an apple peel curl and pinch of chives. Serve immediately.

PER SERVING

Calories:.....254	Sodium: ......106 mg
Fat:..........21 g	Fiber:..........4 g
Protein:........5 g	Carbohydrate:..15 g

Chanterelle Mushrooms

Chanterelles are wild mushrooms with a golden hue and sweet aroma. They tend to be expensive, so it's best to reserve their use for special occasion recipes. Look for chanterelles with firm flesh and good color. The caps tend to form bumps and folds, so it's important to both soak and gently scrub the mushrooms to make sure you get them clean.

INGREDIENTS | **SERVES 6**

3 bulbs fennel

6 oranges, large

1 teaspoon hazelnuts, finely chopped

⅓ cup fresh orange juice

2 tablespoons extra-virgin olive oil

1 tablespoon fresh orange zest

Shaved Fennel Salad with Toasted Hazelnuts

Tangelos, mandarin, or any easily sectioned citrus will work wonderfully with this recipe.

1. Finely slice the fennel bulbs. Remove the peel and pith from the oranges. With a paring knife, remove each section of the oranges.

2. Form a mound of shaved fennel on each serving plate and arrange the oranges on top. Sprinkle with nuts, then drizzle with the orange juice and oil. Finish with a sprinkle of zest.

PER SERVING

Calories: 172	Sodium: . . . . 61 mg
Fat: . . . . 5 g	Fiber: . . . . 7 g
Protein: . . . . 3 g	Carbohydrate: . . 32 g

INGREDIENTS | **SERVES 4**

16 jumbo shrimp, peeled and deveined

4 wooden skewers, presoaked in water for 1 hour

¼ cup olive oil

1 teaspoon curry powder

½ teaspoon granulated sugar

3 tablespoons fresh lemon juice

2 to 4 drops red pepper sauce

1 teaspoon kosher salt

4 cups mixed spring greens

Lemon wedges, for garnish

Grilled Shrimp Salad

This is an excellent first course, or with more shrimp, it makes a terrific summer supper.

1. Skewer shrimp. Stir together the olive oil, curry powder, granulated sugar, lemon juice, red pepper sauce, and salt in a bowl. Place the shrimp in a glass pan and cover with the dressing. Turn to coat.

2. Place the greens on serving plates. Grill the shrimp for about 60 seconds per side, or until they are pink. Place the shrimp over the greens and garnish with the lemon wedges.

PER SERVING

Calories: 160	Sodium: . . . . . . 641 mg
Fat: . . . . 14 g	Fiber: . . . . 0.5 g
Protein: . . . . 7 g	Carbohydrate: . . . 2 g

6 cups baby spinach

2 blood oranges

1¼ pounds shrimp, cleaned, cooked, and chilled

2 tablespoons fresh lemon juice

¼ cup extra-virgin olive oil

¼ teaspoon dry mustard

¼ cup stemmed, loosely packed parsley

Blood Orange Salad with Shrimp and Baby Spinach

For an elegant supper or luncheon salad, this is a crowd pleaser. The deep red flesh of the blood oranges contrasted with the saturated green of spinach and the bright pink shrimp makes for a dramatic presentation!

1. Place the spinach on individual serving plates.

2. Peel the oranges. Slice them crossways, about ¼-inch thick, picking out any seeds. Arrange on top of the spinach. Arrange the shrimp around the oranges.

3. Place the rest of the ingredients in the blender and puree until the dressing is a bright green. Pour over the salads. Serve chilled.

PER SERVING

Calories: 286	Sodium: . . . . . . 194 mg
Fat: . . . . 16 g	Fiber: . . . . 3 g
Protein: . . . . . . 24 g	Carbohydrate: . . 14 g

Fresh Spinach—Not Lettuce

When you can, substitute fresh baby spinach for less nutritious iceberg lettuce. White or pale green lettuce can be used as accents but have less nutritional substance than such greens as spinach, escarole, and watercress.

Fig and Parmesan Curl Salad

This mixture may sound a bit different, and it is. In addition to being unique, it is also very delicious!

1. Trim figs and cut in half. Remove stems from each spinach leaf and arrange leaves on serving dishes.

2. In a small bowl, whisk the olive oil, lemon juice, balsamic vinegar, honey, mustard, salt, and pepper together.

3. Make Parmesan curls over salad with a vegetable peeler and drizzle with dressing. Serve immediately.

PER SERVING

Calories:.....420	Sodium: ......253 mg
Fat:..........31 g	Fiber:..........4 g
Protein:........7 g	Carbohydrate: ..32 g

A Hidden Gem

Figs are a wonderfully nutritious food. Not only are they high in fiber and minerals, they also add tons of flavor to any recipe. Some cultures even claim that figs have medicinal value and healing potential.

INGREDIENTS | **SERVES 2**

1 garlic clove

2 anchovies, well drained

1 tablespoon fresh chives, diced

1 tablespoon fresh parsley, chopped

1 teaspoon fresh tarragon, chopped

½ cup mayonnaise

1 teaspoon tarragon vinegar

½ teaspoon salt

½ teaspoon black pepper, ground

2 tablespoons sour cream

1 pound asparagus spears

2 precooked lobster tails, shells discarded

2 cups mixed salad leaves

Lobster and Asparagus Salad

Use a basic lemon, garlic, and butter seasoning if you're cooking the lobster tails yourself. Sprinkle with a little lemon juice and garlic powder if you purchase the tails precooked.

1. Peel and crush the garlic clove. To make the dressing, combine the garlic, anchovies, and herbs in a food processor or blender; process until smooth. Add the mayonnaise; process to mix. Add the vinegar, salt, and pepper. Transfer to a bowl or other container, cover, and chill for at least 1 hour. Before serving, stir in the sour cream.

2. Trim off and discard the ends of the asparagus spears, making all the spears the same length. Use a vegetable peeler to peel off any tough outer layer on the stalks if necessary. Start about 1½ inches from the top when peeling. Cook the asparagus in a pan of salted, boiling water for 4–8 minutes, depending on the size, or until tender but still somewhat crisp and a vibrant green. Drain and rinse immediately under cold, running water, then drain again.

3. Slice the lobster tail meat into ½-inch rounds. Arrange the asparagus spears and lobster meat on a bed of the salad leaves on a chilled salad plate. Spoon a little of the dressing over the salad and serve immediately.

PER SERVING

Calories: 554	Sodium: . . . . . . 717 mg
Fat: . . . . 45 g	Fiber: . . . . 5 g
Protein: . . . . 28 g	Carbohydrate: . . 11 g

2½ pounds fresh cooked crabmeat

6 cups arugula

2 cups plums, pitted and halved

½ cup extra-virgin olive oil

¼ cup white wine vinegar

½ teaspoon salt

¼ teaspoon black pepper, ground

Fresh Crab with Arugula Salad

You can buy lump crabmeat in containers in the fresh fish section of the market. Just be sure you don't pick up artificial crabmeat—it is processed whitefish that is pressed and colored red.

1. If shelling the crab, make sure all bits of shell are removed from the meat. If not precut, cut the crabmeat into bite-sized cubes. Clean and dry the arugula.

2. To serve, mound the arugula on a serving platter and top with the crab and plums. Drizzle with the oil and vinegar, and sprinkle with salt and pepper.

PER SERVING

Calories:. 196	Sodium: . . . . .1,031 mg
Fat:. . . . . 12 g	Fiber:. . . . . .0.5 g
Protein:. . . . . . . 17 g	Carbohydrate: . . . 4 g

Cooking Crabmeat

Bring a large pot with salted water to a rolling boil. Drop the crabs into the pot, making sure the water covers the crabs completely. Bring the water back up to a boil and reduce heat to simmer. Cook large crabs for around 20 minutes and small crabs around 6 minutes. The crabs are done when the shell turns bright orange. Rinse crabs in cold water to stop the cooking process.

5 garlic cloves

2 tablespoons olive oil

1 tablespoon lemon juice

2 teaspoons Dijon mustard

1½ cups button mushrooms, sliced

1 tablespoon amaretto liqueur

1 pound fresh spinach

3 tablespoons Parmesan cheese, grated

Wilted Amaretto Spinach Salad

This salad tastes great alone, or you can serve it heaped over a juicy steak or pork chop.

1. Slice the garlic thinly. In a large, deep skillet with a lid, heat the oil over medium heat and sauté the garlic for about 1 minute.

2. Add the lemon juice and mustard, quickly mixing it directly in the skillet. Add the mushrooms and spread them thinly in the skillet. Add the amaretto, and mix. Let the mixture simmer for 3–4 minutes, stirring frequently, until the mushrooms are covered with sauce and soft.

3. Place the spinach on top of the mixture, but do not stir. Cover tightly. The steam will wilt the spinach in about 3 minutes. Remove from the heat.

4. In a serving dish, lightly toss the salad, and sprinkle with Parmesan cheese. Serve immediately.

PER SERVING

Calories: 80	Sodium: . . . . . . 111 mg
Fat: . . . . 6 g	Fiber: . . . . 2 g
Protein: . . . . 4 g	Carbohydrate: . . . 4.5g

Amaretto Liqueur

Amaretto, which means "bitter," is a strong Italian liqueur. It has an almond flavor, but usually does not contain almonds. Instead the liqueur is made with herbs and fruits soaked in apricot kernel oil. While the drink does have a bitter bite, it is relatively sweet with a rich taste.

8 ounces applewood bacon, sliced

6 ounces chilled brie cheese, diced

3 cups baby spinach

1 cup frisee, torn

½ cup palm hearts, sliced

¼ cup radicchio, shredded

1 tablespoon sherry vinegar

⅛ teaspoon kosher salt

Applewood Bacon and Brie Frisee Salad

Frisee, also known as curly endive, has lacy edges and a sharp flavor, so you only need to use a little to add zing and texture to the salad.

1. Cook bacon in large skillet until crisp. Pat each slice with a paper towel to remove excess grease. Crumble bacon into a large salad bowl.

2. Toss brie, spinach, frisee, palm hearts, and radicchio over the bacon. Toss gently to mix. Drizzle with vinegar and salt. Toss gently to coat thoroughly. Serve immediately.

PER SERVING

Calories: 443   Sodium: . . . . 1,233 mg
Fat: . . . . 37 g   Fiber: . . . . 1 g
Protein: . . . . 26 g   Carbohydrate: . . . 3 g

Brie Cheese

Brie is a soft and creamy French cheese made from cow's milk. Sold in wheels, brie is one of the few cheeses that ripens from the outside toward the middle. Although the rich cheese is usually served at room temperature, this recipe requires you to dice the brie while still chilled. The chilled cheese will be easier to cut and quickly warms to room temperature during mixing and serving.

3 red pears

⅓ cup orange juice

6 cups watercress

¼ cup almonds, slivered

3 ounces Gorgonzola cheese

1 tablespoon extra-virgin olive oil

Almond and Pear Salad with Gorgonzola

Any fine green can be used here. For a more peppery flavor, try arugula.

1. Slice the pears in half, then slice them thinly and place in a large mixing bowl. Mix the orange juice with enough ice water to cover the pears. Let pears marinate for at least 5 minutes.

2. Mound the watercress on individual plates or a serving platter.

3. Drain the pears and fan the slices on each plate around the watercress. Sprinkle with the almond slivers. Scatter the crumbled Gorgonzola on top. Drizzle a bit of extra-virgin olive oil over each serving, and serve.

PER SERVING

Calories: 159	Sodium: . . . . . . 201 mg
Fat: . . . . 8.5 g	Fiber: . . . . 3.5 g
Protein: . . . . 4 g	Carbohydrate: . . 18 g

12 small organic pansies, prepared

24 organic rose petals, prepared

3 tablespoons pasteurized egg whites

1½ teaspoons water

¼ teaspoon almond extract

3 tablespoons fine sugar

2½ cups mixed baby greens

1½ cups arugula leaves, torn

1 tablespoon orange juice

⅛ teaspoon kosher salt

Sugared Flowers and Greens Salad

This unusual salad is both beautiful to behold and exquisite to taste. Use a delicate touch with the flowers and petals to prevent bruising or ripping.

1. Whisk egg whites, water, and almond extract together in a small bowl. Use a small, sterile paintbrush to lightly coat each flower and petal, front and back. Use tweezers to help hold the delicate flowers and petals.

2. Sprinkle sugar over each flower and petal, front and back. Place on a cookie sheet lined with parchment paper. Let dry for 10 hours, gently turning the flower and petals over after 5 hours.

3. Toss greens and arugula together in a large salad bowl. Sprinkle with orange juice and salt. Toss well to coat. Add rose petals to bowl and toss gently to mix. Split salad between 4 plates and garnish each plate with 3 sugared pansies.

PER SERVING

Calories:	50	Sodium:	157 mg
Fat:	0 g	Fiber:	1.5 g
Protein:	5 g	Carbohydrate:	6.5 g

Preparing Flowers

Use homegrown organic flowers to ensure the ingredients are safe to eat. Remove any stems, leaves, or stamens from the flowers. Cut off the bottom of the rose petals to remove the area where the petal attaches due to its bitter taste. Place the flowers or petals in cold water to rinse, letting the flowers soak for 5 minutes. Gently shake the flowers/petals to remove excess water and place on a paper towel to dry.

3 tablespoons lemon juice

4 teaspoons orange juice

½ teaspoon kosher salt

⅛ teaspoon cayenne pepper, ground

⅛ teaspoon black pepper, finely ground

3 tablespoons sesame oil

2 cups fresh apricots, diced

⅓ cup fennel bulb, sliced

¼ cup dried apricots, diced

½ cup celery, sliced

2 cups iceberg lettuce, shredded

1 cup oak leaf lettuce, torn

1 cup alfalfa sprouts

¼ teaspoon orange zest

Apricot and Fennel Sprout Salad

This intricately flavored salad is best served before or after the entrée to avoid overwhelming your taste buds. Add strips of cooked chicken breast with light lemon-pepper seasoning to turn the salad into a full meal.

1. Whisk lemon juice, oil, orange juice, salt, cayenne pepper, and black pepper together in the bottom of a mixing bowl. Whisk until salt dissolves. Slowly pour oil into dressing and whisk until emulsified.

2. Add fresh apricots, fennel, dried apricots, and celery to the large bowl. Toss well to coat with dressing. Cover bowl and place in refrigerator. Let mixture marinate for 10 minutes.

3. Gently toss iceberg lettuce, oak leaf lettuce, and alfalfa sprouts together in a large salad bowl. Remove apricot mixture from fridge. Gently toss apricot mixture into salad, scraping the sides of the mixing bowl to make sure you get as much dressing as possible. Toss well to mix and coat. Garnish with a sprinkle of orange zest and serve.

PER SERVING

Calories: 111	Sodium: . . . . . . 209 mg
Fat: . . . . 7 g	Fiber: . . . . 2.5 g
Protein: . . . . 1.5 g	Carbohydrate: . . 12 g

Alfalfa Sprouts

Alfalfa sprouts used in salads are light, sweet, and crunchy baby sprouts with thin white stems topped with tiny green bulbs. The sprouts are harvested as early as 3 days after sprouting, so they are often grown on a pad right in the packaging. Remove the sprouts from the pad and rinse well before using.

CHAPTER 13

Creamy Salads/Slaws

Creamy Apple-Jicama Coleslaw
226

Broccoli Ranch Coleslaw
227

Tangy Cucumber Coleslaw
227

Sesame Orange Coleslaw
228

Mexican Coleslaw
229

Zesty Lime-Jicama Coleslaw
230

Light and Tangy Coleslaw
231

Jicama Fennel Slaw
232

Pineapple Coconut Coleslaw
233

Orange-Avocado Slaw
234

Overnight Coleslaw
235

Sesame and Soy Coleslaw
236

Dilly Pickle Coleslaw
236

Chinese Coleslaw
237

Black Bean Slaw
238

Veggie Slaw
239

Tangy Horseradish Coleslaw
240

Picnic Coleslaw
241

Carrot and Cabbage Slaw
242

Chicken Caesar Coleslaw
242

No-Mayo Apple Coleslaw
243

Spicy Coleslaw with Cashew
Mayonnaise
244

½ cup mayonnaise

3 tablespoons apple cider vinegar

2 tablespoons honey

1 tablespoon shallots, minced

2 teaspoons spicy brown mustard

¼ teaspoon kosher salt

¼ teaspoon black pepper, finely ground

3 cups green cabbage, shredded

1½ cups tart green apple, diced

1 cup peeled jicama, julienned

½ cup red cabbage, shredded

2 tablespoons parsley, diced

Creamy Apple-Jicama Coleslaw

The mellow flavor of jicama complements the tart apples and sweet cabbage to give this recipe a sophisticated flavor.

1. Stir mayonnaise, vinegar, honey, shallots, mustard, salt, and pepper together in a small mixing bowl. Mix well.

2. Toss green cabbage, apple, jicama, red cabbage, and parsley together in a large mixing bowl. Pour dressing into slaw and toss well.

3. Cover bowl with plastic wrap and chill in refrigerator for 30–60 minutes before serving. Mix well before serving.

PER SERVING

Calories: 140	Sodium: . . . . . . 161 mg
Fat: . . . . 11 g	Fiber: . . . . 2 g
Protein: . . . . 1 g	Carbohydrate: . . 10 g

Peeling Jicamas

Jicamas, root vegetables native to Central America, cannot be peeled like an apple or potato and will only cause frustration if you try. The best way to peel the "Mexican turnip" is to slice off the top and bottom, and then use a knife to cut away strips of peel from top to bottom.

1 (12-ounce) bag broccoli coleslaw

⅓ cup celery, diced

¼ cup sunflower seeds

¼ cup almond slivers

¼ cup Cheddar cheese, shredded

½ cup ranch salad dressing

2 cups green cabbage, shredded

1 cup red cabbage, shredded

1 cup cucumber, peeled and diced

⅓ cup green onion, diced

⅓ cup radicchio, shredded

¼ cup carrots, thinly sliced

½ cup Catalina salad dressing

Broccoli Ranch Coleslaw

This recipe also tastes great with traditional coleslaw dressing instead of ranch dressing. To lighten things up, try using reduced-fat cheese and low-fat ranch.

1. Mix the broccoli slaw, celery, sunflower seeds, almonds, and cheese together in a large bowl.

2. Drizzle salad dressing into the bowl and toss to coat. Serve immediately or chill in fridge for up to 12 hours before serving.

PER SERVING

Calories: 291	Sodium: . . . . . . 373 mg
Fat: . . . . 25 g	Fiber: . . . . 4.5 g
Protein: . . . . 8 g	Carbohydrate: . . 11 g

Tangy Cucumber Coleslaw

The radicchio adds a hint of bite to this recipe to help balance the mellow cucumbers. However, you can leave the radicchio out if you prefer a lighter flavor.

Toss everything except the dressing together in a large mixing bowl. Drizzle with dressing and toss well to coat. Serve immediately or store in fridge for up to 24 hours.

PER SERVING

Calories: 136	Sodium: . . . . . . 162 mg
Fat: . . . . 9.5 g	Fiber: . . . . 3 g
Protein: . . . . 2 g	Carbohydrate: . . 13 g

3 medium oranges

1 (8-ounce) can water chestnuts, diced

2 cups red cabbage, shredded

½ cup green onions, sliced

¼ cup radicchio, shredded

3 tablespoons orange juice

1 tablespoon lemon juice

2 teaspoons soy sauce

1 teaspoon toasted sesame seeds

2 tablespoons sesame oil

Sesame Orange Coleslaw

Select ripe navel oranges for this salad, as their sweet juice is what really makes this recipe spectacular.

1. Use a sharp knife to remove peel and pith (white stuff) from each orange. Remove seeds and slice membrane from around each segment. Slice each segment in half. You should end up with around 2 cups of prepared orange segments. Discard peels, pith, seeds, and membranes.

2. Drain the water from the canned water chestnuts. Combine the prepared oranges, drained chestnuts, cabbage, onion, and radicchio in a large mixing bowl.

3. Whisk orange juice, lemon juice, soy sauce, and sesame seeds together in a small bowl. Whisk oil into bowl. Mix until emulsified. Drizzle dressing over coleslaw and toss well to coat. Serve immediately or chill up to 4 hours before serving.

PER SERVING

Calories:.....121	Sodium: ......114 mg
Fat:..........5 g	Fiber:..........4 g
Protein:........2 g	Carbohydrate:..19 g

Toasting Seeds

The quickest way to toast sesame seeds is in a skillet on the stove. Add the seeds to a small skillet over medium heat to toast. Stir seeds often and remove from heat when they turn golden. Let the seeds cool before using them in a recipe or storing them for later.

INGREDIENTS | SERVES 6

3 tablespoons salad oil

½ cup cider vinegar

2 tablespoons granulated sugar

1½ teaspoons salt

1 teaspoon sweet Hungarian paprika

½ teaspoon dry mustard

1 teaspoon celery seeds

4 cups green cabbage, shredded

½ cup green bell pepper, diced

⅓ cup yellow onion, diced

¼ cup canned diced pimientos

½ cup pitted black olives, sliced

Mexican Coleslaw

Serve as a salad with barbecued pork ribs or with juicy steaks. If you want to sweeten the recipe up a bit, replace the yellow onions with white and the green bell peppers with red or orange.

1. In a small container with a cover, combine the salad oil, cider vinegar, white sugar, salt, paprika, dried mustard, and celery seed. Cover and shake until well mixed.

2. In a large serving bowl, combine the cabbage, bell pepper, onion, pimientos, and black olives; toss gently until well mixed.

3. Pour the dressing on top and toss gently until well covered. Cover and refrigerate for at least 1 hour before serving.

PER SERVING

Calories: 119	Sodium: . . . . . . 677 mg
Fat: . . . . 9 g	Fiber: . . . . 2 g
Protein: . . . . 1 g	Carbohydrate: . . 10 g

2 cups red cabbage, shredded

1½ cups peeled jicama, julienned

½ cup green onions, sliced

¼ cup lime juice

1 teaspoon granulated sugar

¼ teaspoon kosher salt

¼ teaspoon sweet Hungarian paprika

¼ teaspoon red pepper sauce

Zesty Lime-Jicama Coleslaw

Lime and jicama are a classic combination. In fact, one of the most popular ways to eat jicamas is raw with a little lime juice and red pepper sprinkled over top.

1. Toss cabbage, jicama, and onions together in a large mixing bowl.

2. Stir lime juice, sugar, salt, paprika, and red pepper sauce together in a small bowl. Mix until sugar and salt dissolve fully.

3. Drizzle dressing over coleslaw and toss well to coat. Cover bowl and chill coleslaw for 30–60 minutes before serving. Mix well before serving.

PER SERVING

Calories:. 28	Sodium: . . . . . . 107 mg
Fat:. . . . . 0 g	Fiber: . . . . 2.5 g
Protein:. . . . . . . 1 g	Carbohydrate: . . . 7 g

¼ cup rice vinegar

2 teaspoons Dijon mustard

1 teaspoon artificial sweetener

½ teaspoon celery seed

⅛ teaspoon dried rosemary, crushed

1 tablespoon extra-virgin olive oil

2 cups green cabbage, shredded

2 cups red cabbage, shredded

1 cup carrot, peeled and chopped

1 cup celery, chopped

¼ cup flat-leaf parsley, chopped

¼ cup green onions, diced

Light and Tangy Coleslaw

This dieter-friendly coleslaw has a refreshing crunch and full flavor ideal for any summer barbecue.

1. Whisk the vinegar, mustard, sweetener, celery seed, and rosemary together in a large mixing bowl. Whisk oil into bowl and mix until emulsified.

2. Add green cabbage, red cabbage, carrots, celery, parsley, and onions to the bowl. Toss to mix and coat.

3. Cover bowl with lid and chill in fridge for at least 20 minutes before serving. Mix well before serving.

PER SERVING

Calories: 39	Sodium: . . . . . . 182 mg
Fat: 1.5g	Fiber: . . . . 1.5 g
Protein: . . . . 1 g	Carbohydrate: . . . 5 g

Koolsla or Coleslaw

The dish now known as coleslaw finds its roots with Dutch settlers in the Americas. Hearty cabbage was a popular garden item for Dutch farmers and koolsla, or cold cabbage salad, was a popular easy dish. The salad caught on in America, and with the invention of mayonnaise in the eighteenth century, soon evolved into the basic dish that's still used in modern times.

½ cup cashews

3 tablespoons lime juice

1 teaspoon lime zest

¼ teaspoon salt

Water, for the sauce

1 cup jicama, peeled and grated

1 cup fennel bulb, peeled and grated

1 cup green cabbage, shredded

2 tablespoons poppy seeds

Jicama Fennel Slaw

This is a creamy and crunchy slaw that is great for picnics and road trips. Good substitutes for the lime juice include apple cider vinegar, lemon juice, or orange juice. Good substitutes for the poppy seeds include sesame seeds or hemp seeds.

1. In a blender place the cashews, lime juice, lime zest, and salt and blend. Slowly add the water until it blends to the consistency of whipped cream.

2. Toss the jicama, fennel, and cabbage with the prepared cashew cream and poppy seeds. This recipe will stay fresh for up to 3 days in the refrigerator.

PER SERVING

Calories: 302	Sodium: . . . . . . 332 mg
Fat: . . . . 21 g	Fiber: . . . . 7.5 g
Protein: . . . . 8.5 g	Carbohydrate: . . 27 g

½ teaspoon salt

3 cups green cabbage, grated

1 cup carrot, grated

1 cup cashews, soaked

¾ cup dried coconut

1 cup pineapple, cut into small chunks

2 tablespoons agave nectar

Water, as needed

Pineapple Coconut Coleslaw

This coleslaw has a sweet, tropical twist. Jicama is a good substitute for the carrot. Fresh pineapple juice could be substituted for the water. This is a good side dish to serve with a veggie burger.

1. In a medium bowl, sprinkle salt onto the grated cabbage and carrots and stir.

2. Using a food processor or blender, blend together the cashews, ¼ cup dried coconut, ¼ cup pineapple, and agave nectar. Add just enough water so you can blend it.

3. Toss together the remaining pineapple and dried coconut with the grated cabbage and carrot. Add the blended dressing to the bowl and stir until well mixed. Serve immediately.

PER SERVING

Calories: 373	Sodium: . . . . . . 192 mg
Fat: . . . . 25 g	Fiber: . . . . 6 g
Protein: . . . . 7 g	Carbohydrate: . . 36 g

Soaking Cashews

Soaking cashews in water for several hours makes a difference in texture if you're trying to turn the nuts into butter without loading up on oil. As the cashews absorb the water, their flesh becomes softer and mixes fluidly when blended to create a creamy butter. Using dry cashews can result in a gritty texture and can keep the nutty flavor from blending with other ingredients.

INGREDIENTS | **SERVES 10**

1 avocado

¼ cup orange juice

½ teaspoon curry powder

⅛ teaspoon cumin, ground

¼ teaspoon granulated sugar

1 teaspoon white wine vinegar

1 tablespoon olive oil

5 cups broccoli slaw mix

½ teaspoon sea salt

¼ teaspoon freshly ground black pepper

Orange-Avocado Slaw

Use as a unique complement to backyard barbecues or as the perfect potluck surprise.

1. Peel the avocado, remove the pit, and chop the meat into ¼-inch pieces.

2. In a medium-sized bowl, whisk together the orange juice, curry powder, cumin, sugar, and vinegar. Add the oil in a stream, whisking until emulsified.

3. In a large bowl, toss the avocado with the slaw mix. Drizzle with the vinaigrette. Chill until ready to serve, and season with the salt and pepper.

PER SERVING

Calories: 55	Sodium: . . . . . . 132 mg
Fat: . . . . 3.5 g	Fiber: . . . . 2.5 g
Protein: . . . . 2 g	Carbohydrate: . . . 5.5 g

Making Broccoli Slaw

Broccoli coleslaw consists of broccoli stems shredded and mixed with carrots and/or cabbage. To make your own slaw, use large and tender broccoli stems. Cut away the woody bottoms and leaves. Shred the stems until you have the amount needed. You can also break and crumble the broccoli heads into the slaw.

4 cups green cabbage, shredded

2 cups carrots, shredded

¾ cup green onions, thinly sliced

¾ cup unsweetened apple juice

⅔ cup cider vinegar

1 tablespoon prepared mustard

1½ teaspoons paprika

1 teaspoon mustard seeds

½ teaspoon garlic salt

½ teaspoon celery seeds

½ teaspoon black pepper, ground

Overnight Coleslaw

This is a perfect dish to take to a barbecue or party. Prepare it the night before and just grab it out of the fridge when you're ready to go!

1. In a large bowl, combine cabbage, carrots, and green onions.

2. In a jar with a secure lid, combine apple juice, vinegar, mustard, paprika, mustard seeds, garlic salt, celery seeds, and pepper. Tightly screw jar lid and shake vigorously.

3. Pour over coleslaw mixture. Toss lightly to coat.

4. Cover and refrigerate overnight. Toss well before serving.

PER SERVING

Calories: 41	Sodium: . . . . 88 mg
Fat: . . . . 0.5 g	Fiber: . . . . 2.5 g
Protein: . . . . 1 g	Carbohydrate: . . . 9.5 g

Icing Cabbage

If you want really crispy coleslaw, immerse the head(s) of cabbage in ice water before shredding. After you've shredded the icy cabbage, refrigerate it. That way it's chilly and crisp when you serve it!

4 cups Napa cabbage, shredded

¼ cup carrot, grated

¼ cup green onions, chopped

⅔ cup red bell pepper, sliced thin

2 tablespoons olive oil

2 tablespoons apple cider vinegar

2 teaspoons soy sauce

½ teaspoon sesame oil

2 tablespoons maple syrup

2 tablespoons sesame seeds (optional)

⅓ cup mayonnaise

2 tablespoons pickle juice

1 tablespoon fine sugar

1 tablespoon water

2 teaspoons fresh chives, minced

¼ teaspoon garlic salt

⅛ teaspoon black pepper, ground

4 cups white cabbage, shredded

1 cup radicchio, shredded

½ cup dill pickle, finely chopped

⅓ cup carrot, shredded

¼ cup red bell pepper, diced

Sesame and Soy Coleslaw

You don't need mayonnaise to make a coleslaw dish. This recipe mixes oil, vinegar, and maple syrup to add flavor without adding milk or egg products.

1. Toss together the cabbage, carrot, green onions, and bell pepper in a large bowl.

2. In a separate small bowl, whisk together the olive oil, vinegar, soy sauce, sesame oil, and maple syrup until well combined.

3. Drizzle dressing over cabbage and veggies, add sesame seeds, and toss well to combine.

PER SERVING

Calories: 117	Sodium: . . . . . . 173 mg
Fat: . . . . 7.5 g	Fiber: . . . . .1 g
Protein:. . . . . . . .2 g	Carbohydrate: . . 12 g

Dilly Pickle Coleslaw

This refreshing salad is ideal for any menu in need of a family-friendly dish that fuses creamy, crunchy, tangy, and sweet.

1. Stir mayonnaise, pickle juice, sugar, water, chives, garlic salt, and pepper together in medium mixing bowl. Mix well.

2. Toss cabbage, radicchio, pickle, carrot, and bell pepper together in a large mixing bowl. Add dressing to slaw and mix well. Cover bowl, place in refrigerator, and chill for at least 1 hour before serving. Mix well before serving.

PER SERVING

Calories: 55	Sodium: . . . . . . 143 mg
Fat: . . . . .4.5 g	Fiber: . . . . .1 g
Protein:. . . . . . . .0.5 g	Carbohydrate: . . .4 g

5 cups Chinese cabbage, coarsely chopped

1 cup carrots, shredded

½ cup green onions, chopped

1 (8-ounce) can sliced water chestnuts

2 tablespoons toasted sesame seeds

¼ cup olive oil

1 teaspoon dark sesame oil

2 tablespoons granulated sugar

1 tablespoon fresh cilantro, minced

½ teaspoon black pepper, ground

½ cup white wine vinegar

1 tablespoon soy sauce

Chinese Coleslaw

With water chestnuts and sesame seeds, this coleslaw has a crunch to it that will wake up your palate!

1. Toss veggies and sesame seeds together.

2. In a small bowl, whisk together oils, sugar, cilantro, pepper, vinegar, and soy sauce. Pour dressing over slaw. Toss until well mixed.

3. Refrigerate at least two 2 hours before serving. Toss at serving time.

PER SERVING

Calories:......78	Sodium: ......105 mg
Fat:..........5.5 g	Fiber:..........1.5 g
Protein:........1 g	Carbohydrate: ...7 g

Chinese Cabbage

Chinese cabbage, also known as bok choy, is very healthy. In fact, Chinese cabbage is higher in calcium than other cabbage. It looks different because it grows in white celery-like stalks with dark green leaves instead of forming a head. It's yet another veggie to add to your ongoing list of ways to get your calcium requirements without lactose concerns.

Black Bean Slaw

2½ cups green cabbage, finely shredded

1 (15-ounce) can black beans, rinsed and drained

½ cup carrot, shredded

½ cup red onion, chopped

¼ cup fresh cilantro, chopped

½ cup plain yogurt

½ cup salsa

2 tablespoons mayonnaise

2 teaspoons white wine vinegar

2 teaspoons lime juice

Fresh cilantro sprigs (optional)

And you thought coleslaw was just shredded cabbage! There are hundreds of different kinds of cabbage, and adding different ingredients and dressings gives you a variety of tasty options.

1. In a large bowl, combine cabbage, beans, carrot, onion, and chopped cilantro. Toss well.

2. In a small bowl, combine yogurt, salsa, mayonnaise, vinegar, and lime juice. Stir well. Pour over cabbage mixture and gently toss.

3. Tightly cover. Refrigerate at least 2 hours. Garnish with fresh cilantro sprigs, if desired, and serve.

PER SERVING

Calories:	92	Sodium:	232 mg
Fat:	3 g	Fiber:	3.5 g
Protein:	4 g	Carbohydrate:	12 g

1½ cups red cabbage, shredded

1 cup carrot, shredded

¾ cup yellow squash, shredded

¾ cup zucchini, shredded

½ cup green bell pepper, chopped

⅓ cup white onion, finely chopped

¼ cup unsweetened pineapple juice

1½ tablespoons sugar

3 tablespoons cider vinegar

2 tablespoons water

½ teaspoon chicken-flavored bouillon granules

¼ teaspoon paprika

¼ teaspoon celery seeds

⅛ teaspoon garlic powder

⅛ teaspoon red pepper, ground

Veggie Slaw

A dish with fresh red cabbage always makes a pretty addition to a table setting, and it's a double win when it tastes great too.

1. In a large bowl, combine cabbage, carrot, yellow squash, zucchini, green pepper, and chopped onion.

2. In a small bowl, combine pineapple juice, sugar, vinegar, water, bouillon, paprika, celery seeds, garlic powder, and red pepper. Stir well. Pour over vegetable mixture. Toss gently.

3. Cover tightly and refrigerate at least 4 hours before serving. Toss gently at serving time.

PER SERVING

Calories:	66	Sodium:	41 mg
Fat:	0 g	Fiber:	2.5 g
Protein:	1.5 g	Carbohydrate:	15 g

Red Cabbage Trivia

Some people call red cabbage by a slightly different name—purple cabbage. Its color does change according to the environment it's in; it will even turn blue if served with non-acidic food. All colors aside, red cabbage happens to be much higher in vitamin C than other types of cabbage.

4 cups green cabbage, coarsely shredded

2 cups heirloom tomato, chopped

1½ cups frozen whole kernel corn, thawed

1 cup red cabbage, coarsely shredded

1 cup green bell pepper, chopped

1 cup plain yogurt

2 tablespoons Dijon mustard

4 teaspoons prepared horseradish

¼ teaspoon salt

¼ teaspoon hot sauce

¼ cup Cheddar cheese, shredded

Tangy Horseradish Coleslaw

No horsing around with this recipe! If you love horseradish, feel free to add more than what's called for in this recipe. The combination of colors in this coleslaw is truly beautiful.

1. In a large bowl, combine green cabbage, chopped tomato, corn, red cabbage, and green pepper. Gently toss.

2. In a small bowl, combine yogurt, mustard, horseradish, salt, and hot sauce, stirring well.

3. Add to cabbage mixture, tossing gently until cabbage mixture is well coated. Cover tightly and refrigerate for at least 1 hour before serving.

4. Just before serving, sprinkle Cheddar cheese over slaw.

PER SERVING

Calories: 92	Sodium: . . . . . . 149 mg
Fat: . . . . 2 g	Fiber: . . . . 3 g
Protein: . . . . 5 g	Carbohydrate: . . 15 g

8 cups green cabbage, shredded

1 cup carrot, finely grated

1 cup sweet onion, chopped

1 cup green bell pepper, chopped

12 green olives, chopped

⅓ cup firmly packed brown sugar

½ teaspoon salt

1 teaspoon celery seed

1 teaspoon Dijon mustard

⅛ teaspoon black pepper, coarsely ground

4 teaspoons olive oil

⅔ cup balsamic vinegar

Picnic Coleslaw

This coleslaw isn't made with mayonnaise so it keeps very well for about a week in the refrigerator and it also travels nicely for a picnic.

1. Combine cabbage, carrot, onion, bell pepper, and chopped olives in a large bowl.

2. Combine brown sugar, salt, celery seed, mustard, ground pepper, oil, and vinegar in a small saucepan. Bring to a boil over high heat. Reduce heat and simmer for 3 minutes.

3. Pour warm dressing over cabbage mixture. Toss gently, coating evenly.

4. Cover and refrigerate for at least 6 hours before serving. Toss the coleslaw a couple of times while it's chilling. Serve chilled.

PER SERVING

Calories: 146	Sodium: . . . . . . 510 mg
Fat: . . . . 5.5 g	Fiber: . . . . 3.5 g
Protein: . . . . 2 g	Carbohydrate: . . 25 g

Mayonnaise Maze

When a recipe calls for mayo, think about substituting yogurt. It's a healthy and comfy option for people with lactose intolerance. However, only yogurt with probiotics work to ease lactose problems and regular yogurt can be just as bad as mayo. In addition, you'll find that yogurt usually makes the dish you're preparing even creamier!

2 cups green cabbage, shredded

1 cup carrots, shredded

½ cup raisins

¼ cup toasted slivered almonds

½ cup vanilla yogurt

2 teaspoons lemon juice

⅛ teaspoon nutmeg

Carrot and Cabbage Slaw

If you have young children, you might want to serve the toasted almonds on the side for the adults as they could be a choking hazard for little ones.

1. Combine cabbage, carrots, raisins, and almonds in a large bowl.

2. Combine yogurt, lemon juice, and nutmeg in a small bowl, stirring until mixed well.

3. Add dressing to slaw, gently toss, cover, and chill in refrigerator for at least 30 minutes. Toss before serving.

PER SERVING

Calories: 96	Sodium: . . . . 35 mg
Fat: . . . . 2.5 g	Fiber: . . . . 2.5 g
Protein: . . . . 3 g	Carbohydrate: . . 18 g

2 cups green cabbage, shredded

1 cup celery, chopped

½ cup red cabbage, shredded

½ cup red onion, chopped

8 ounces cooked chicken breast, shredded

½ cup Caesar salad dressing

Chicken Caesar Coleslaw

As long as it's cooked and shredded, this recipe works with rotisserie, leftover, or canned chicken breast.

1. Combine the green cabbage, celery, red cabbage, and red onion together in a large mixing bowl. Toss to mix.

2. Stir together the chicken and salad dressing in a small mixing bowl. Pour the chicken mixture into the cabbage. Mix well. Serve immediately or chill for up to 24 hours in the fridge.

PER SERVING

Calories: 221	Sodium: . . . . . . 345 mg
Fat: . . . . 17 g	Fiber: . . . . 2 g
Protein: . . . . 11 g	Carbohydrate: . . . 5 g

No-Mayo Apple Coleslaw

3 cups green cabbage, shredded

⅓ cup apple, diced small

1 (15-ounce) can pineapple, drained (reserve 2 tablespoons of juice)

1 tablespoon apple cider vinegar

2 tablespoons olive oil

1 tablespoon tahini

2 tablespoons agave nectar

2 tablespoons sunflower seeds

There's nothing wrong with grabbing a store-bought pre-shredded coleslaw mix from the produce section to make this vegan salad, just double the dressing if you find it's not enough.

1. In a large bowl, combine the cabbage, apple, and pineapple.

2. In a separate small bowl, whisk together 2 tablespoons of the pineapple juice with the cider vinegar, olive oil, and tahini. Pour over cabbage and apples, tossing gently to coat.

3. Drizzle with agave nectar, again tossing to coat.

4. Cover and chill for at least 30 minutes before serving, and toss with sunflower seeds.

PER SERVING

Calories: 194	Sodium: . . . . 18 mg
Fat: . . . . 11 g	Fiber: . . . . 3.5 g
Protein: . . . . 2 g	Carbohydrate: . . 25 g

Make It Vegan!

If you have a favorite family coleslaw recipe, there's no need to give it up when eating vegan. Just use a store-bought or homemade vegan mayonnaise or dressing. Whatever recipe you use, coleslaw works best if it sits for several hours to soften up the cabbage, so make this recipe in advance if possible. The night before would be best.

Spicy Coleslaw with Cashew Mayonnaise

For a little more kick add ¼ teaspoon mustard powder. Add more oil as needed when making the cashew butter to ensure creamy results.

1. Add cashews and oil to a food processor and process until smoothed into butter. Scrape cashew butter from processor into a small bowl. Add mayonnaise into bowl. Mix well.

2. Combine cabbages, carrot, onion, and radish in a large mixing bowl. Sprinkle the salt onto the shredded vegetables and mix together.

3. Pour on the apple cider vinegar, black pepper, and the cashew mayonnaise and mix everything together.

PER SERVING

Calories: 254	Sodium: . . . . . . 373 mg
Fat: . . . . 20 g	Fiber: . . . . 1.5 g
Protein: . . . . 2.5 g	Carbohydrate: . . 16 g

Raw Apple Cider Vinegar

There are numerous health and beauty benefits associated with apple cider vinegar (ACV). Whole books have been written about it, the most famous being *Apple Cider Vinegar: Miracle Health System* by natural health pioneer Patricia Bragg. The unpasteurized brands by Bragg or Spectrum are recommended.

CHAPTER 14

Spicy Salads

Fire-Kissed Cantaloupe Salad
246

Chipotle Avocado and
Cheese Salad
247

Peppered Cilantro and
Tomato Salad
248

Spiced Italian Corn Salad
249

Spicy Papaya Salad
250

Zesty Banana Pepper Salad
250

Spiced Taro Salad
251

Spicy Shrimp with Lemon Yogurt
on Wilted Greens
252

Pepper Jack Caesar Salad
253

Curried Cauliflower and
Peanut Salad
254

Wasabi Pea Salad
255

Flaming Pineapple Salad
256

Zesty Cheese Salad
257

Fiery Beef Salad
258

Spicy Rice Salad
259

Spicy-Sweet Cucumber Salad
260

Spicy Herb Salad
261

Zesty Pecan Chicken and
Grape Salad
262

East African Kachumbari Salad
263

Flaming Taco Salad Supreme
264

2 tablespoons mango juice

1 tablespoon walnut oil

¼ teaspoon chipotle pepper sauce

⅛ teaspoon sweet Hungarian paprika

⅛ teaspoon red pepper, ground

⅛ teaspoon kosher salt

3 cups cantaloupe, cubed

½ cup red onion, diced

Fire-Kissed Cantaloupe Salad

Garnish this light and spicy salad with fresh cilantro or a slice of mango. Serve it as a side to any filling bean, meat, or rice dish with a Southwest flavor.

1. Whisk mango juice, oil, pepper sauce, paprika, red pepper, and salt together in a small bowl. Whisk until salt dissolves and oil is emulsified.

2. Add cantaloupe and red onion to a large mixing bowl. Pour dressing over salad. Toss well to mix and coat. Cover salad and let chill in refrigerator for 15 minutes. Remove bowl from refrigerator, toss salad gently to mix, and serve.

PER SERVING

Calories: 291	Sodium: . . . . 97 mg
Fat: . . . . 27 g	Fiber: . . . . 1.5 g
Protein: . . . . 1.5 g	Carbohydrate: . . 11 g

Pepper Sauces

Making your own chipotle pepper sauce is an easy way to save money and find the perfect recipe for your taste buds. Mix 1 cup of your favorite vinegar, 4 teaspoons of chipotle puree, a pinch of garlic powder, pinch of sugar, and a pinch of salt in a bottle. Shake the bottle to mix and adjust to taste. Chill in refrigerator to let flavors develop.

2 cups avocado, diced

1 cup green cabbage, shredded

⅔ cup Monterey jack cheese, diced

½ cup red onion, chopped

2 tablespoons chipotles in adobo sauce

1 tablespoon lime juice

¼ cup Catalina salad dressing

2 tablespoons sour cream

2 tablespoons sharp Cheddar, shredded

Chipotle Avocado and Cheese Salad

Serve this dish as a salad, or dice up the ingredients into tiny bits and serve it as a dip with tortilla chips.

1. Add avocado, cabbage, jack cheese, and onions to a large salad bowl. Toss gently to mix.

2. Place the chipotles and adobo sauce in a small bowl. Carefully mince the chipotle into tiny bits. Use a small spoon or whisk to mix the lime juice, salad dressing, and sour cream into the bowl. Mix until fully blended.

3. Pour chipotle dressing over salad. Toss gently to mix and coat. Cover and chill for up to 12 hours before serving or serve immediately. Sprinkle with Cheddar garnish before serving.

PER SERVING

Calories:	406	Sodium:	392 mg
Fat:	34 g	Fiber:	7 g
Protein:	10 g	Carbohydrate:	20 g

Chipotles and Adobo

Chipotle peppers are smoked red jalapeño peppers with a mild bite and rich flavor. The peppers are often packaged with adobo sauce, a mix of vinegar, tomato sauce, and spices. The sauce adds extra flavor to the chilies, as well as absorbing the chilies' flavor, which means it's useful for spreading a hint of the spice throughout the dish.

1 tablespoon lemon juice

¼ teaspoon black pepper, ground

¼ teaspoon chipotle pepper, ground

⅛ teaspoon white pepper, ground

¼ teaspoon salt

3 tablespoons salad oil

2 cups grape tomatoes, chopped

2 cups plum tomatoes, chopped

¼ cup green bell pepper, diced

¼ cup pickled banana peppers, drained and diced

3 tablespoons fresh cilantro, chopped

Peppered Cilantro and Tomato Salad

Pickled banana peppers add a hint of sweet and tangy flavor to this spicy salad.

1. Whisk together the lemon juice, black pepper, chipotle pepper, white pepper, and salt in a small bowl. Whisk the oil into the bowl. Set bowl aside.

2. Gently toss the grape tomatoes, plum tomatoes, bell peppers, banana peppers, and cilantro together in a large salad bowl.

3. Drizzle oil dressing over the mixture. Toss gently, but mix well. Serve alone or on a bed of shredded lettuce. Serve immediately or chill up to 24 hours before serving.

PER SERVING

Calories: 136	Sodium: . . . . . . 162 mg
Fat: . . . . 12 g	Fiber: . . . . 2.5 g
Protein: . . . . 2 g	Carbohydrate: . . . 9 g

½ cup Italian vinaigrette salad dressing

1 tablespoon fresh cilantro, minced

¼ teaspoon Hungarian paprika

¼ teaspoon chili powder

⅛ teaspoon black pepper, ground

⅛ teaspoon chipotle pepper, ground

⅛ teaspoon cumin, ground

2 (15-ounce) cans whole kernel yellow sweet corn

1 (15-ounce) can whole kernel white sweet corn

⅓ cup Parmesan cheese, grated

Spiced Italian Corn Salad

To make the dish ahead of time, mix the corn and dressing only. Chill the salad until needed, up to 36 hours, and mix in the Parmesan up to 30 minutes before serving.

1. Whisk the salad dressing, paprika, chili powder, black pepper, chipotle pepper, and cumin together in a large mixing bowl. Mix well.

2. Drain the liquid from each can of corn. Empty the kernels into the mixing bowl. Mix well to coat each kernel with dressing.

3. Sprinkle Parmesan over salad and toss to mix. Serve immediately and store leftovers in fridge.

PER SERVING

Calories: 121	Sodium: . . . . . . 201 mg
Fat: . . . . 4.5 g	Fiber: . . . . 2 g
Protein: . . . . 3.5 g	Carbohydrate: . . 20 g

What Is Sweet Corn?

Corn is native to South America and has been used by man for thousands of years. The difference between basic corn and sweet corn is the sugar and water content, which is much higher in sweet corn than it is other types of corn, including dent, flour, and flint varieties.

Spicy Papaya Salad

INGREDIENTS | SERVES 4

2 tablespoons fresh lemon juice

½ teaspoon black salt

1 tablespoon finely chopped cilantro

½ teaspoon sugar

½ cup papaya, diced

½ cup mango, diced

½ cup kiwi, diced

¼ cup strawberries, chopped

This salad looks magnificent as a centerpiece on the table during summertime. Use seasonal fruit of your choice to make variations.

1. In a large bowl, combine the lemon juice, black salt, cilantro, and sugar. Mix well.

2. Add the papaya, mango, kiwi, and strawberries, and gently toss. Chill for about 30 minutes, then serve.

PER SERVING

Calories:	40	Sodium:	292 mg
Fat:	0 g	Fiber:	2 g
Protein:	1 g	Carbohydrate:	10 g

Zesty Banana Pepper Salad

INGREDIENTS | SERVES 4

½ cup pickled banana peppers, drained

3 cups iceberg lettuce, shredded

⅓ cup red bell pepper, diced

¼ cup celery, diced

⅓ cup ranch salad dressing

¼ cup pitted black olives, sliced

Pickled banana peppers give this recipe a mix of tangy, sweet, and spicy flavors that stand out against the mellow iceberg lettuce.

1. Chop banana peppers into bite-size pieces and place in large salad bowl. Add lettuce, bell peppers, and celery to bowl.

2. Drizzle dressing over salad and toss well to coat. Add olives to salad and toss well to mix. Serve salad immediately, as leftovers do not keep well.

PER SERVING

Calories:	126	Sodium:	265 mg
Fat:	12 g	Fiber:	1.5 g
Protein:	1.5 g	Carbohydrate:	5 g

2 taro roots, peeled

2 potatoes, peeled

2 tablespoons fresh lemon juice

½ teaspoon black salt

2 tablespoons minced cilantro, plus extra for garnish

Spiced Taro Salad

You can spike up this mild salad with a pinch of red chili powder. If you cannot find taro, try yams or sweet potatoes.

1. Place the taro roots and potatoes in a pot with enough water to cover; boil for 15 minutes until just fork-tender. Drain and let cool.

2. Cut the taro and potatoes into cubes and place them in a large bowl. Add the lemon juice, black salt, and cilantro to the bowl and mix well. Serve immediately.

PER SERVING

Calories:......88	Sodium:......296 mg
Fat:...........0 g	Fiber:..........2.5 g
Protein:........1.5 g	Carbohydrate:..20 g

Tale of the Taro

Also known as dasheen, taro is a member of the tuber family. The starchy root is toxic if eaten raw, so it's important to always cook the root thoroughly before adding it to any dish. Use gloves to peel away the hairy, thick outer skin to reveal the nutty-flavored flesh. Make sure to boil the root until it's soft all the way through to ensure it's fully cooked.

1 cup nonfat plain yogurt

¼ cup fresh lemon zest

6 cups bitter greens (collard, kale, etc.)

12 large peeled shrimp, tails on

2 cloves garlic, finely minced

1 teaspoon olive oil

⅛ teaspoon black pepper, ground

¼ cup black olives, thinly sliced

1 lemon, cut into wafer-thin slices

Spicy Shrimp with Lemon Yogurt on Wilted Greens

The yogurt must be prepared a day in advance, but after trying this recipe, you will never want just lemon on your shrimp again!

1. Prepare the yogurt the night before by mixing together the yogurt and zest in a small bowl, then cover and refrigerate overnight.

2. Wilt the greens in a steamer, place in a bowl, and chill immediately (this can be done the night before).

3. Butterfly the shrimp by cutting them down the center, almost but not completely through, and then pushing down the halves to form a butterfly shape. Place the shrimp in a bowl and coat with the garlic, oil, and pepper. Grill or broil until just done, about 1 minute per side (they should turn white and pink and be firm to the touch).

4. Place the greens in mounds on serving plates and add the shrimp. Dollop lemon yogurt on top of the shrimp. Sprinkle with the olives and garnish with the lemon slices.

PER SERVING

Calories: 69

Fat: . . . . 2.5 g

Protein: . . . . 7 g

Sodium: . . . . . . 106 mg

Fiber: . . . . 2 g

Carbohydrate: . . . 6.5 g

1 (6-ounce) grilled chicken breast

1 tablespoon fat-free Caesar dressing

1 teaspoon green pepper sauce

2 cups romaine lettuce

2 tablespoons fat-free garlic croutons

1 tablespoon reduced fat pepper jack cheese, shredded

Pepper Jack Caesar Salad

Traditional Caesar salads are based on romaine lettuce drenched in fattening Caesar dressing and topped with Parmesan cheese. Make these modest modifications and you'll enjoy all of the flavor with less fat.

1. Cut chicken into cubes.

2. In a small bowl, blend Caesar dressing and green pepper sauce.

3. In a large bowl, combine lettuce, chicken, croutons, and dressing.

4. Sprinkle with cheese and serve.

PER SERVING

Calories: 483	Sodium: . . . . . . 281 mg
Fat: . . . . 8.5 g	Fiber: . . . . 2.5 g
Protein: . . . . 94 g	Carbohydrate: . . . 9 g

Preparing Cheese

To shred a soft or semisoft cheese, pop it in the freezer for about 30 minutes before grating to make it easier to handle. It also won't stick to the grater or the counter as much.

2 cups cauliflower florets

1 cup dry-roasted peanuts, chopped

1 cup bok choy, diced

½ cup raisins

3 tablespoons white wine vinegar

1 teaspoon yellow curry powder, mild

¼ teaspoon turmeric, ground

¼ teaspoon garlic powder

⅛ teaspoon kosher salt

3 tablespoons sesame oil

Curried Cauliflower and Peanut Salad

The light curry taste gives this crunchy salad a spicy flair without overpowering the other flavors. The salad pairs particularly well with a chicken or beef entrée.

1. Break washed cauliflower florets into bite-size pieces and place in a large salad bowl. Add peanuts and bok choy to bowl.

2. Whisk vinegar, curry powder, turmeric, garlic powder, and salt together in a small bowl. Whisk oil into bowl. Drizzle mixture over salad and mix very well. Cover bowl and place in refrigerator. Let salad chill for 30 minutes. Mix well before serving.

PER SERVING

Calories: 255	Sodium: . . . . 68 mg
Fat: . . . . 19 g	Fiber: . . . . 4 g
Protein: . . . . 7 g	Carbohydrate: . . 19 g

Creating Yellow Curry Powder

Basic yellow curry powder consists of turmeric, fenugreek, coriander, cumin, clove, mustard seed, cardamom, and white/black peppers ground to powder. The exact ratios for the spices vary according to preference, but about two parts mustard seed, cumin, and coriander to one part everything else provides a base powder you can then adjust according to taste.

1 cup baby sweet peas, frozen

1 (8-ounce) can water chestnuts, diced

3 cups iceberg lettuce, shredded

1 tablespoon honey

2 tablespoons white wine vinegar

¼ teaspoon kosher salt

3 tablespoons salad oil

¾ cup wasabi peas

Wasabi Pea Salad

You can increase the heat of this spicy and crunchy salad even more by using "extra hot" wasabi peas instead of regular wasabi peas.

1. Fill a pot with 3 inches of water and place a steam basket in the middle. Bring the water to a boil over medium-high heat. Add the frozen peas to the basket and cover pot with lid. Steam peas for 4 minutes, or until just heated through. Remove peas from basket and rinse under cold water.

2. Place drained peas in a large mixing bowl. Drain water chestnuts. Add water chestnuts and lettuce to bowl.

3. Whisk honey, vinegar, and salt together in a small bowl. Whisk oil into bowl and mix until emulsified. Drizzle dressing over salad and toss very well to coat.

4. Add wasabi peas to salad and toss to mix. Serve immediately.

PER SERVING

Calories: 200	Sodium: . . . . . . 200 mg
Fat: . . . . 11 g	Fiber: . . . . 5.5 g
Protein:. . . . . 4 g	Carbohydrate: . . 24 g

Wasabi Peas Please

Wasabi is spicy Japanese green horseradish. It's much hotter than common white horseradish and is often served with sushi. Wasabi peas are fried green peas coated with a wasabi sauce and dried. The crunchy, salty, sweet, and spicy peas are popular snacks used in the same way as chips or peanuts.

Flaming Pineapple Salad

This recipe mixes sweet and hot flavors that wake up your taste buds. The juice in the canned pineapples is an important part of the dressing, so make sure to use canned pineapples as opposed to fresh cut pineapple.

INGREDIENTS | SERVES 4

1 (15-ounce) can pineapple chunks

2 cups iceberg lettuce, shredded

1 cup red leaf lettuce, torn

½ cup red bell pepper, julienned

1 small jalapeño

2 tablespoons white balsamic vinegar

¼ teaspoon sweet Hungarian paprika

⅛ teaspoon kosher salt

⅛ teaspoon black pepper, finely ground

1 teaspoon fresh chives, sliced

1. Drain juice from pineapple into a small mixing bowl. Place drained pineapple in a large mixing bowl. Add iceberg, red leaf, and bell pepper to drained pineapple.

2. Remove seeds from jalapeño and finely mince the flesh. Add jalapeño to pineapple juice. Stir vinegar, paprika, salt, and pepper into the juice. Mix well.

3. Drizzle dressing over salad. Toss well to mix and coat. Chill salad for 10 minutes before serving. Gently toss salad, garnish with a sprinkle of chives, and serve.

PER SERVING

Calories: 48	Sodium: . . . . 85 mg
Fat: . . . . 0 g	Fiber: . . . . 2 g
Protein: . . . . 1 g	Carbohydrate: . . 11 g

2 small poblano chilies

1 medium jicama

1 pound mozzarella cheese

¾ cup red onion, diced

¾ cup avocado, julienned

⅓ cup fresh cilantro leaves, chopped

4 garlic cloves, minced

1 teaspoon ground cumin

½ teaspoon fresh oregano

⅔ cup olive oil

½ teaspoon salt

½ teaspoon ground black pepper

½ cup lime juice

Zesty Cheese Salad

This recipe is great with grilled swordfish, trout, or tilapia. Let the salad chill in the refrigerator for a few hours before serving if you want to increase the intensity of the flavor.

1. Remove the stem and seeds from the chilies and cut into ¼-inch pieces. Peel the jicama and cut into pieces about the size of matchsticks. Cut the mozzarella into ½-inch cubes.

2. In a large mixing bowl, combine the onion, avocado, cilantro, chilies, jicama, and cheese. Toss until well mixed.

3. In a medium-sized container with a lid, combine the garlic, cumin, oregano, olive oil, salt, black pepper, and lime juice. Cover and shake until well mixed.

4. Pour the dressing over the vegetables and cheese; toss lightly and serve.

PER SERVING

Calories: 136	Sodium: . . . . . . 111 mg
Fat: . . . . 14 g	Fiber: . . . . 1.5 g
Protein: . . . . 1 g	Carbohydrate: . . . 2 g

How to Substitute Dry Spices

Because dry spices have the water taken out of them, you usually substitute half the amount of dry for the fresh variety. However, many spices lose their flavor when dried, so it's best to use what the recipe calls for if at all possible.

¼ cup basil leaves

2 tablespoons serrano chilies, chopped

2 garlic cloves

2 tablespoons brown sugar

2 tablespoons fish sauce

¼ teaspoon black pepper, ground

¼ cup lemon juice

1 pound beef steak

1 inner stalk lemongrass, finely sliced

⅔ cup red onion, finely sliced

1 cup cucumber, finely sliced

½ cup tomato, finely sliced

½ cup mint leaves

Bibb lettuce leaves

Fiery Beef Salad

This entrée salad is somehow hearty and light at the same time. If the weather doesn't permit grilling, the steak can be broiled instead.

1. Combine basil, serrano chilies, garlic, brown sugar, fish sauce, black pepper, and lemon juice in a blender and process until well incorporated; set aside.

2. Season the steak to taste with salt and pepper. Over a hot fire, grill to medium-rare (about 4 minutes per side), or to your liking. Transfer the steak to a platter, cover with foil, and let rest for 5–10 minutes before carving.

3. Slice the beef across the grain into thin slices.

4. Place the beef slices, any juices from the platter, and the remaining salad ingredients, except the lettuce, in a large mixing bowl. Add the dressing and toss to coat.

5. To serve, place lettuce leaves on individual plates and mound the beef mixture on top of the lettuce.

PER SERVING

Calories:	343	Sodium:	753 mg
Fat:	24 g	Fiber:	1 g
Protein:	20 g	Carbohydrate:	11 g

Preparing Serrano Chilies

Serrano chilies can be red or green in color, but they're always extremely hot and sharp in flavor. To prepare a serrano chili, you need to slice away the stem and cap, as well as remove the seeds. Check the flesh and cut away any damaged areas. Slice the chili flesh as needed and be careful to wash your hands before you touch your face.

½ cup rice wine vinegar

½ cup fish sauce

¼ cup sesame oil

¼ cup hot chili oil

¼ cup lime juice

2 cups long-grained rice

½ cup green onions, thinly sliced

⅓ cup carrots, peeled and diced

½ cup red bell pepper, seeded and diced

1 serrano chili pepper, seeded and minced

¼ cup fresh mint, chopped

¼ cup cilantro, chopped

1 pound cooked shrimp

⅓ cup unsalted peanuts, chopped, for garnish

Lime wedges, for garnish

Spicy Rice Salad

This salad is equally delicious with shredded chicken or turkey instead of the shrimp. Or if you would prefer a vegetarian salad, simply omit the shrimp and fish sauce.

1. Whisk vinegar, fish sauce, sesame oil, hot chili oil, and lime juice together in a medium mixing bowl; set aside.

2. Cook the rice according to the package directions. Fluff the rice, then transfer it to a large mixing bowl. Allow the rice to cool slightly.

3. Pour approximately ⅓ of the dressing over the rice and fluff to coat. Continue to fluff the rice every so often until it is completely cooled.

4. Add the green onions, carrots, red pepper, serrano chili pepper, mint, cilantro, and shrimp to the rice. Toss with the remaining dressing to taste.

5. To serve, place on individual plates and garnish with peanuts and lime wedges.

PER SERVING

Calories:.....346	Sodium: .....1,743 mg
Fat:..........22 g	Fiber: ....1 g
Protein:.......16 g	Carbohydrate: .. 19 g

Vinegar Distinctions

Rice wine vinegar has a much more subtle flavor than distilled white vinegar and matches particularly well with sesame oil.

1 cup cucumbers, thinly sliced

¾ teaspoon salt

¼ cup rice wine vinegar

1 teaspoon sugar

1 teaspoon sesame oil

¼ teaspoon red pepper flakes

½ cup white onion, thinly sliced

Spicy-Sweet Cucumber Salad

Japanese cucumber salad is cool and refreshing, but with a bit of spice. Enjoy it as a healthy afternoon snack, or as a fresh accompaniment to take-out.

1. In a large, shallow container or baking sheet, spread the cucumbers in a single layer and sprinkle with salt. Allow to sit at least 10 minutes.

2. Drain any excess water from the cucumbers and place cucumbers in a bowl.

3. In a small bowl, whisk together the rice wine vinegar, sugar, oil, and red pepper flakes.

4. Pour dressing over the cucumbers, add onions, and toss gently.

5. Allow to sit at least 10 minutes before serving to allow flavors to mingle.

PER SERVING

Calories: 47	Sodium: . . . . . . 873 mg
Fat: . . . . 2 g	Fiber: . . . . 0.5 g
Protein: . . . . 0.5 g	Carbohydrate: . . . 4.5 g

INGREDIENTS | SERVES 4

5 cups romaine leaves, finely torn

⅓ cup fresh mint leaves

¼ cup fresh basil leaves

1 tablespoon fresh oregano, chopped

¼ cup green onions, finely chopped

¼ cup olive oil

2 teaspoons red wine vinegar

2 tablespoons water

½ teaspoon salt

1 teaspoon horseradish mustard

¼ cup garlic croutons

Spicy Herb Salad

Select fresh and healthy herbs for this salad, as the quality of the flavor depends entirely on the quality of the herbs.

1. Combine the romaine with the mint, basil, oregano, and green onions in a large bowl. Toss to mix well.

2. In a jar with a lid, mix the olive oil, red wine vinegar, water, salt, and mustard. Shake well until completely blended. Drizzle half the vinaigrette over the salad and gently toss to mix well. Add more vinaigrette if needed. Garnish with croutons and serve.

PER SERVING

Calories:	144	Sodium:	331 mg
Fat:	14 g	Fiber:	2 g
Protein:	1 g	Carbohydrate:	4 g

Using Oregano

Oregano is a potent herb that stands out regardless of the other flavors in a dish. The two main types of oregano are Italian and Greek. Cuban and Mexican oreganos are not the same plant as European oreganos, but the spices are utilized in the same manner. When a recipe asks for oregano, it usually means Italian or Greek, unless otherwise specified.

¼ cup pecans, chopped

1 teaspoon chili powder

¼ cup olive oil

1½ pounds boneless, skinless chicken breasts

1½ cups white grapes

6 cups salad greens

Zesty Pecan Chicken and Grape Salad

Coating your chicken with nuts adds a crispy skin to keep the breast inside moist and tender.

1. Preheat oven to 400°F.

2. In a blender, mix the chopped nuts and chili powder. Pour in the oil while the blender is running. When the mixture is thoroughly combined, pour it into a shallow bowl.

3. Coat the chicken with the pecan mixture and place on racked baking dish; roast for 40–50 minutes, until the chicken is thoroughly cooked. Remove from oven, let cool for 5 minutes, and thinly slice.

4. Slice the grapes and tear the greens into bite-size pieces. To serve, fan the chicken over the greens and sprinkle with sliced grapes.

PER SERVING

Calories: 220	Sodium: . . . . 11 mg
Fat: . . . . 13 g	Fiber: . . . . 1 g
Protein: . . . . 21 g	Carbohydrate: . . . 5.5 g

Toasting Nuts for Fresher Flavor and Crispness

To wake the natural flavor of the nuts, heat them on the stovetop or in the oven for a few minutes. For the stovetop, spread nuts in a dry skillet, and heat over a medium flame until their natural oils come to the surface. For the oven, spread the nuts in a single layer on a baking sheet, and toast for 5–10 minutes at 350°F, until the oils are visible. Cool nuts before serving.

1 medium jalapeño pepper

2 cups green cabbage, shredded

1½ cups tomatoes, thinly sliced

¾ cup red onion, thinly sliced

½ teaspoon salt

3 tablespoons lemon juice

3 tablespoons fresh cilantro, chopped

East African Kachumbari Salad

Jalapeño peppers work well for this traditional coleslaw/salsa dish, but you can also use banana, cherry, or serrano peppers, depending on how hot you want the salad.

1. Slice the jalapeño open, remove stem, and remove seeds. Finely mince the jalapeño flesh. Add the jalapeño, cabbage, tomatoes, and onion to a large mixing bowl.

2. Sprinkle the salad with salt, lemon juice, and cilantro. Toss gently to mix and coat. Serve immediately or cover and chill in refrigerator up to 4 hours before serving.

PER SERVING

Calories:	23	Sodium:	203 mg
Fat:	0 g	Fiber:	1.5 g
Protein:	1 g	Carbohydrate:	4 g

Traditional Kachumbari

Kachumbari is a popular dish in East Africa and is like a mix between a salsa and coleslaw. The exact recipe changes from family to family, but the basic dish consists of shredded and chopped raw vegetables. Most kachumbari recipes call for cabbage, tomatoes, onions, and some sort of hot chili pepper mixed with vinegar or citrus juice. The dish may also include cucumbers, cilantro, and oil.

1 pound ground beef

1 (1-ounce) packet taco seasoning

¾ teaspoon chipotle pepper sauce

4 fried tortilla salad shells, large

2 cups iceberg lettuce, chopped

1 cup canned pinto beans, drained

1 cup Cheddar cheese, shredded

¾ cup spicy salsa

½ cup beefsteak tomato, diced

¼ cup sliced green chili peppers, drained

4 teaspoons pitted black olives, minced

¼ cup guacamole or sour cream

Flaming Taco Salad Supreme

Change the salsa in the recipe to give the salad your own twist. The dish works with lime-chipotle salsa, mango salsa, or pineapple salsa.

1. Brown the meat in a large skillet over medium-high heat. Use taco seasoning according to package instructions. Stir chipotle pepper sauce into skillet and set seasoned beef aside.

2. To create each salad, fill a salad shell with ½ cup lettuce, ¼ cup beans, and 4 ounces of beef. Add ¼ cup cheese, 3 tablespoons salsa, 2 tablespoons tomato, and 1 tablespoon chili peppers. Top with 1 tablespoon guacamole or sour cream, sprinkle with 1 teaspoon olives, and serve.

PER SERVING

Calories: 564	Sodium: . . . . . . 742 mg
Fat: . . . . 32 g	Fiber: . . . . 5 g
Protein: . . . . . . 45 g	Carbohydrate: . . 23 g

CHAPTER 15

Dessert Salads

Caramel Apple Salad with
Cinnamon Raisin Croutons
266

Chocolate-Kissed Berry Salad
267

Banana Split Salad
267

Valencia Orange Salad with
Orange-Flower Water
268

Raspberry and Nectarine
Macaroon Salad
269

Creamy Apricot Gelatin Salad
270

Cherry Ambrosia Fruit Salad
271

Butterscotch Banana
Praline Salad
272

Cherry Rocky Road Salad
272

Very Berry Cheesecake Salad
273

Sparkling Fruit Salad
274

Light Lemon Blueberry Salad
274

Orange-Pineapple Sherbet Salad
275

Gingered Citrus Salad
276

Cranberry Peach Salad
277

Spumoni Salad
278

Southern Grilled Peach and
Pecan Salad
279

Holiday Gelatin Salad
280

Strawberry Gelatin Salad
281

Tropical Watermelon Salad in
Strawberry-Ginger Sauce
282

Blackberry Pear Salad with
Tangerine Wine Dressing
283

Orange-Mango
Pomegranate Salad
284

6 slices cinnamon raisin bread

Butter-flavor cooking spray

2 cups Washington apples, cored and chopped

2 cups Granny Smith apples, cored and chopped

⅓ cup pecans, chopped

⅓ cup caramel sauce

2 teaspoons lemon juice

2 tablespoons hot water

Caramel Apple Salad with Cinnamon Raisin Croutons

The hot water in this recipe helps thin and liquefy the caramel sauce so that it coats the apples evenly.

1. Preheat the oven to 350°F. Chop bread slices into 1-inch cubes and place in large mixing bowl. Lightly coat cubes with butter-flavored cooking spray. Spread cubes on nonstick cookie sheet and place in oven. Bake for 10–5 minutes, or until dry and golden. Place croutons in a bowl and set aside until needed.

2. Toss together the Washington apples, Granny Smith apples, and pecans in a large salad bowl.

3. In a mixing bowl, stir together the caramel sauce, lemon juice, and hot water. Mix well. Drizzle the caramel sauce over the salad and mix well.

4. Add the croutons to the salad and toss lightly. Serve salad immediately. Salad does not store well, but the dried croutons will keep for at least a week if stored alone.

PER SERVING

Calories: 218	Sodium: . . . . . . 155 mg
Fat: . . . . 7 g	Fiber: . . . . 3.5 g
Protein: . . . . 3.5 g	Carbohydrate: . . 38 g

Flavored Cooking Sprays

It's important to use a high-quality cooking spray to coat the bread before drying it into croutons. A high-quality spray with a light and natural butter flavor enhances the croutons, but a cheap cooking spray will make the croutons, and thus the entire salad, taste like chemicals.

INGREDIENTS | SERVES 10

2 cups fresh strawberries, chopped

1 cup fresh raspberries or blackberries

1 cup fresh cherries, pitted and halved

⅓ cup dark chocolate, shaved

⅓ cup semi-sweet chocolate, shaved

⅓ cup walnuts, finely chopped

¼ cup whipped cream, for garnish

Chocolate-Kissed Berry Salad

This recipe tastes best when served immediately. You can store the salad in the fridge for a few hours, but the berries get soggy if left for several hours.

Toss ingredients together in a large mixing bowl. Garnish with a dollop of whipped cream and serve.

PER SERVING

Calories: 162	Sodium: . . . . 9.5 g
Fat: . . . . 9 g	Fiber: . . . . 3.5 g
Protein: . . . . 2.5 g	Carbohydrate: . . 20 g

INGREDIENTS | SERVES 6

1 cup banana, sliced

2 cups strawberries, chopped

¼ cup dark chocolate chips, finely chopped

¼ cup caramel chips, finely chopped

¼ cup Spanish peanuts, chopped

1 (8-ounce) can pineapple chunks

Banana Split Salad

This mixed fruit salad provides all the flavor of a banana split sundae without all the extra calories.

1. Toss the banana, strawberries, chocolate chips, caramel chips, and peanuts together in a large mixing bowl. Add pineapple (including the juice) to the bowl and toss to mix.

2. Chill up to 2 hours before serving. Do not store overnight, as leftovers tend to get soggy.

PER SERVING

Calories: 236	Sodium: . . . . 38 mg
Fat: . . . . 9 g	Fiber: . . . . 4.5 g
Protein: . . . . 4 g	Carbohydrate: . . 38 g

2 Valencia oranges, large

1 teaspoon orange-flower water

2 tablespoons pistachios, chopped

Valencia Orange Salad with Orange-Flower Water

Oranges are given an exotic treatment with fragrant orange-blossom essence and pistachios.

1. Slice the tops and bottoms off the Valencia oranges and set them on one of the cut surfaces.

2. With a sharp knife, cut the peel and pith off the oranges in downward strips around each orange to reveal the flesh. Cut the oranges into thin slices across the width, making round wheel slices. Remove any seeds.

3. Arrange the orange slices on a plate and sprinkle the orange-flower water over them. Scatter the pistachios over the slices.

PER SERVING

Calories: 129	Sodium: . . . . 0 mg
Fat: . . . . 3.5 g	Fiber: . . . . 4.5 g
Protein: . . . . 3.5 g	Carbohydrate: . . 24 g

About Oranges

Valencia oranges are sweet oranges that are often employed in juice making. Seville oranges are bitter oranges and are used to make marmalade and liqueurs. Navel oranges are sweet oranges that have no seeds.

Raspberry and Nectarine Macaroon Salad

INGREDIENTS | SERVES 8

1½ cups fresh raspberries, chilled

1 cup fresh nectarine, diced

1 tablespoon lemon juice

2 cups coconut macaroons, quartered

2 cups vanilla pudding

Chilling berries before mixing them into a salad helps keep each one firm so that it doesn't break during mixing and turn to mush.

1. Add raspberries and nectarines to a medium mixing bowl. Drizzle with lemon juice and toss gently to fully coat. Add macaroons to salad and toss to mix.

2. Add ¼ cup pudding to a dessert bowl and top with ½ cup salad. Repeat process to prepare remaining servings.

PER SERVING

Calories: 171	Sodium: . . . . . . 108 mg
Fat: . . . . 5 g	Fiber: . . . . 2.5 g
Protein: . . . . 2 g	Carbohydrate: . . 31 g

Marvelous Macaroons

The term *macaroon* covers several different types of cookies, the original being a fluffy almond and meringue delicacy. The coconut version of the cookies became popular in Jewish communities because they use egg white for leavening, making them kosher for holidays, particularly Passover. Coconut macaroons are easier to package and transport than meringue, so the coconut version quickly grew in popularity.

2 cups apricot nectar, divided

1 egg, beaten

⅔ cup sugar, divided

3 tablespoons flour

2 (0.25-ounce) packages unflavored gelatin

2 (15-ounce) cans apricot halves

2 cups orange juice, divided

1 cup frozen low-fat whipped topping, thawed

Creamy Apricot Gelatin Salad

This creamy salad makes a perfect side to a cold soup, or serve it alongside waffles for a great brunch.

1. In small saucepan, combine 1 cup apricot nectar with egg, ⅓ cup sugar, and flour; beat well with wire whisk. Cook over low heat 6–8 minutes, stirring constantly, until mixture boils and thickens. Remove from heat and chill until cold.

2. In large bowl, combine gelatin and ⅓ cup sugar and set aside.

3. Drain apricot halves, discarding juice. Chop apricots into small pieces and set aside.

4. Pour 1 cup orange juice over gelatin mixture. Stir to combine.

5. Combine 1 cup orange juice and 1 cup apricot nectar in microwave-safe glass measuring cup. Microwave on full power until boiling, about 5 minutes. Immediately pour into gelatin mixture. Stir until sugar and gelatin are completely dissolved. Add chopped apricots, then chill in refrigerator for 1½ hours, or until syrupy.

6. When apricot mixture is syrupy, beat the chilled flour mixture until smooth. Fold into the apricot mixture along with whipped topping. Pour into 1½-quart casserole dish, cover, and chill until set, about 4–5 hours. Cut into squares to serve.

PER SERVING

Calories: 184	Sodium: . . . . 25 mg
Fat: . . . . 1.5 g	Fiber: . . . . 1.5 g
Protein: . . . . 4 g	Carbohydrate: . . 40 g

INGREDIENTS | SERVES 8

1 (6-ounce) can maraschino cherries, without stems

¾ cup vanilla pudding

1 cup strawberries, sliced

1 cup bananas, sliced

½ cup Pink Lady apple, peeled and diced

½ cup peach, diced

¾ cup fresh cherries, pitted and halved

¼ cup whipped cream

Cherry Ambrosia Fruit Salad

You can use packaged or homemade vanilla pudding for this sweet recipe, as long as it's prepared pudding and not just dry pudding mix.

1. Drain the syrup from the cherries into a large mixing bowl. Set cherries aside. Stir vanilla pudding into the bowl. Mix well.

2. Add strawberries, bananas, apple, peach, and fresh cherries to the bowl. Stir gently to mix.

3. Add drained cherries to the bowl. Gently fold the cherries into the salad. Garnish salad with whipped cream and serve.

PER SERVING

Calories: 145	Sodium: . . . . 62 mg
Fat: . . . . 2 g	Fiber: . . . . 3 g
Protein: . . . . 2 g	Carbohydrate: . . 31 g

What Makes a Cherry Maraschino?

Maraschino cherries were traditionally Italian black cherries preserved in maraschino liqueur. These days, the treat is made with pitted cherries, usually Queen Anne cherries, soaked in sugary syrup. Red maraschino cherries usually have almond flavor added to the syrup and green maraschino cherries usually have mint flavor added.

2 cups banana, sliced

1 cup pecans, chopped

3 tablespoons lemon juice

½ cup butterscotch pudding

Butterscotch Banana Praline Salad

This super-sweet salad is best served in small portions. Keep leftovers chilled to serve as a small snack the next day.

1. Mix bananas and pecans together in a medium mixing bowl. Drizzle lemon juice into bowl and mix.

2. Gently stir pudding into the bowl. Mix well and serve.

PER SERVING

Calories: 212	Sodium: . . . . 19 mg
Fat: . . . . 14 g	Fiber: . . . . 4 g
Protein: . . . . 2.5 g	Carbohydrate: . . 24 g

2 cups fresh cherries, pitted and halved

1 cup mini marshmallows

¾ cup dry-roasted peanuts, chopped

1 cup milk chocolate pudding

1 tablespoon dark chocolate shavings

Cherry Rocky Road Salad

Use thawed frozen cherries if fresh are not available, but do not use canned cherry filling. The filling is too soft and turns the "salad with pudding dressing" into just pudding.

Gently fold the ingredients except the chocolate shavings together in a large mixing bowl. Serve immediately or cover and chill up to 12 hours before serving. Sprinkle with dark chocolate shavings before serving.

PER SERVING

Calories: 224	Sodium: . . . . 58 mg
Fat: . . . . 12 g	Fiber: . . . . 3 g
Protein: . . . . 6 g	Carbohydrate: . . 27 g

¼ cup fresh lemon juice

3 tablespoons superfine sugar

1 teaspoon fresh lemon zest

1 teaspoon vanilla extract

⅓ cup cream cheese, softened

2 cups fresh strawberries, diced

1 cup fresh blueberries

1 cup fresh raspberries

¼ cup graham crackers, crushed

Very Berry Cheesecake Salad

It's important to use real cream cheese, lemon juice, and lemon zest in this recipe to give the dressing the right taste and texture.

1. Stir lemon juice, superfine sugar, zest, and vanilla together in a medium mixing bowl. Mix well, making sure the sugar dissolves fully. Stir cream cheese into the bowl and mix well.

2. Toss strawberries, blueberries, and raspberries together in a large salad bowl. Add cream cheese dressing to bowl and toss well to coat evenly. Split salad evenly between 4 bowls, garnish with graham cracker crumbs, and serve.

PER SERVING

Calories: 199	Sodium: . . . . 90 mg
Fat: . . . . 8 g	Fiber: . . . . 5.5 g
Protein: . . . . 4 g	Carbohydrate: . . 32 g

Types of Granulated Sugar

Granulated white sugar crystals come in many different sizes. The common "granulated sugar" mentioned in recipes actually means medium "table" size sugar crystals. Fine granulated sugar consists of small sugar crystals, making it easier to mix. Superfine sugar consists of tiny crystals, making it quick to dissolve in liquid.

Sparkling Fruit Salad

In this easy salad, the gelatin retains the bubbles from the soda, so it really sparkles!

1. Drain pineapple, reserving juice in a large saucepan. Add enough water to juice to equal 1½ cups. Bring to a boil over high heat. In large bowl, combine gelatin and boiling liquid; stir until gelatin is completely dissolved.

2. Stir in sparkling soda and chill until the mixture is syrupy, about 45 minutes. Add fruits and stir gently. Pour into 9" × 13" pan and chill until set. Cut into squares to serve.

PER SERVING

Calories: 78	Sodium: . . . . 66 mg
Fat: . . . . 0 g	Fiber: . . . . 0.5 g
Protein: . . . . 1 g	Carbohydrate: . . 18 g

Light Lemon Blueberry Salad

Indulge your sweet tooth while still eating healthy. Switch around the ingredients if you like; the salad works with any mix of fresh berries.

1. Place blackberries in a large mixing bowl and sprinkle with sugar. Gently toss to coat. Add blueberries to the bowl and toss to mix.

2. Stir yogurt, vanilla, and zest together in a mixing bowl. Pour mixture over berries and gently fold until the berries are evenly coated.

PER SERVING

Calories: 144	Sodium: . . . . 37 mg
Fat: . . . . 1 g	Fiber: . . . . 4 g
Protein: . . . . 4 g	Carbohydrate: . . 31 g

Orange-Pineapple Sherbet Salad

Place raspberries in the freezer for 15 minutes before making the recipe to ensure the berries are very cold, but not frozen.

1. Drain syrup from pineapple and oranges into a large mixing bowl. Stir sherbet into bowl and mix well.

2. Stir pineapple and oranges into sherbet. Mix well. Gently fold raspberries into the bowl and serve. Chill salad in freezer for 20–30 minutes if soupy, but be careful not to let it freeze completely.

PER SERVING

Calories: 86	Sodium: . . . . 10 mg
Fat: . . . . 1 g	Fiber: . . . . 3.5 g
Protein: . . . . 1 g	Carbohydrate: . . 20 g

Ice Cream, Sherbet, and Sorbet

Though often mistaken as assorted names for the same dessert, ice cream, sherbet, and sorbet are three different kinds of frozen dessert. Ice cream contains large amounts of milk and/or cream and sorbet is more like a fruit ice without any dairy product. Sherbet falls into the middle area and contains fruit with a small amount of dairy, usually no more than 3 percent.

3 large naval oranges

1 medium Ruby Red grapefruit

1 large lime

1 large lemon

¼ teaspoon kosher salt

¼ cup granulated sugar

1 teaspoon candied ginger, finely minced

Gingered Citrus Salad

Serve this fruit salad alone for a light dessert or serve it over a scoop of raspberry sorbet for an indulgent dessert.

1. Remove the peel from each orange and break into segments. Cut the pith and membrane from around each segment. Remove the seeds from each segment. Cut each segment into bite-size pieces and place in large mixing bowl. You should end up with about 3 cups orange pieces.

2. Repeat preparation process with grapefruit, lime, and lemon. You should end up with about 1 cup grapefruit, ½ cup lime, and ½ cup lemon pieces. Add grapefruit, lime, and lemon to the bowl.

3. Sprinkle salad with salt. Toss well to mix. Sprinkle sugar and candied ginger over salad. Toss well to mix. Serve immediately or chill in refrigerator up to 1 hour before serving.

PER SERVING

Calories: 150	Sodium: . . . . . . 146 mg
Fat: . . . . 0.5 g	Fiber: . . . . 6 g
Protein: . . . . 2.5 g	Carbohydrate: . . 41 g

2 (3-ounce) packages peach-flavored gelatin

2 cups boiling water

¼ cup orange juice

1 (8-ounce) can crushed pineapple, drained

1 (16-ounce) can whole berry cranberry sauce

1 (15-ounce) can peach slices, drained and chopped

½ cup chopped walnuts

Cranberry Peach Salad

Old-fashioned molded salads are great for entertaining because they must be made ahead of time. And leftovers are delicious for breakfast!

1. In large bowl, combine gelatin and boiling water; stir until gelatin is completely dissolved.

2. Add remaining ingredients to bowl and mix well. Pour into 2-quart mold or glass baking dish and chill in refrigerator until firm, about 2 hours. Cut into squares to serve.

PER SERVING

Calories: 190	Sodium: . . . . 94 mg
Fat: . . . . 4 g	Fiber: . . . . 1.5 g
Protein: . . . . 2 g	Carbohydrate: . . 38 g

Gelatin Salads

There are a few tricks to making gelatin salads. First, be sure to completely dissolve the gelatin in the boiling liquid in the first step. Spoon up a small amount and make sure you can't see any grains of sugar or gelatin. And never use fresh or frozen pineapple, kiwi, or guava in gelatin salads; they will keep it from setting.

INGREDIENTS | SERVES 6

1 (8-ounce) container whipped topping

1 (3-ounce) packet instant pistachio pudding

2 cups fresh cherries

½ cup dark chocolate chips, roughly chopped

¼ cup shelled pistachios, chopped

Spumoni Salad

Buy mini dark chocolate chips instead of regular dark chocolate chips and you won't have to bother with chopping the chips into smaller chunks.

1. Stir whipped topping and pudding mix together in a large mixing bowl. Mix well, making sure the mix dissolves completely into the topping.

2. Remove the stems and pits from the cherries. Chop cherries into quarters. You should end up with about 1 cup chopped cherries. Add cherries to bowl.

3. Stir chips and pistachios into the salad. Mix well. Serve immediately or cover and chill in refrigerator until serving time.

PER SERVING

Calories:. 274	Sodium: . . . . . . 277 mg
Fat:. . . . . 12 g	Fiber: . . . . 2.5 g
Protein:. . . . . 3.5 g	Carbohydrate: . . 40 g

Spectacular Spumoni

Classic spumoni is molded Italian ice cream containing a layer of chocolate and a layer of vanilla with candied fruits and nuts in a whipped cream layer. However, modern spumoni is an American-Italian ice cream that evolved from the classic dessert. Most modern spumoni ice creams contain a chocolate layer, a cherry layer with candied cherries, and a pistachio layer with chopped pistachios.

INGREDIENTS | SERVES 4

6 firm freestone peaches

1 tablespoon red wine vinegar

1 teaspoon honey

⅛ teaspoon kosher salt

1 tablespoon canola oil

3 tablespoons brown sugar

½ teaspoon cinnamon, ground

½ cup pecans, chopped

¼ cup caramel syrup

Southern Grilled Peach and Pecan Salad

Make sure to select peaches that are ripe, but still firm, for this recipe. If a peach is soft and overripe, it will simply fall through the grates when grilled.

1. Preheat your grill to medium-high or high. Whisk vinegar, honey, and salt together in a small bowl. Mix well.

2. Cut open 4 peaches and remove the pits. Set the other 2 peaches aside for later. Place peach halves on a baking sheet. Drizzle each of the 8 peach halves with a little of the vinegar mixture. Place baking sheet in refrigerator and let peaches marinate for 5 minutes.

3. Meanwhile, brush the grill lightly with a little canola oil. Remove the peach halves from the refrigerator. Place each half on the grill, skin up. Turn peaches after 3 minutes. Let peaches cook, skin-side down, for 2 minutes. Remove peaches from grill and place on baking sheet. Sprinkle grilled peaches with brown sugar and cinnamon.

4. Slice open the two reserved peaches and remove pits. Dice the raw peaches and place in a mixing bowl. Gently stir pecans into bowl.

5. To serve, cut each grilled peach half into quarters. Split grilled peach quarters between 4 dessert bowls. Split pecan mixture evenly and sprinkle over each bowl. Drizzle a little caramel syrup over each salad and serve.

PER SERVING

Calories:	329	Sodium:	123 mg
Fat:	15 g	Fiber:	6 g
Protein:	4.5 g	Carbohydrate:	50 g

1 (3-ounce) package orange-flavored gelatin

1 (3-ounce) package cranberry-flavored gelatin

1½ cups boiling water

1 (8-ounce) can crushed pineapple

1 cup cranberry-orange sauce

1 cup lemon-lime soda

Holiday Gelatin Salad

This sparkling dessert tastes great after any meal. The cranberry flavors make it suitable for fall or winter meals and the orange flavors make it suitable for spring or summer, so you can serve this dish all year long.

1. In a bowl, dissolve both packages of gelatin in the boiling water. Add the pineapple (do not drain) and stir in the cranberry-orange sauce. Chill until thick but not set.

2. Slowly stir in the soda and pour into a mold or an 8" × 11" glass dish. Chill until set.

3. Cut set salad into cubes and serve on lettuce leaves.

PER SERVING

Calories: 133	Sodium: . . . . 92 mg
Fat: . . . . 0 g	Fiber: . . . . 0.5 g
Protein: . . . . 1 g	Carbohydrate: . . 33 g

Make Your Own Soda

If you don't want to deal with a high price or preservatives in soda, try making your own. Mix ⅔ cup carbonated water, 3 tablespoons lemon juice, 2 tablespoons lime juice, and fine sugar to taste. Mix well and adjust as needed.

1 (10-ounce) package frozen strawberries

2 (3-ounce) packages strawberry-flavored gelatin

2 cups water

2 firm bananas

4 ounces sour cream

1 (8-ounce) can crushed pineapple

Strawberry Gelatin Salad

Use frozen strawberries, as this recipe includes the water content of the frozen berries.

1. Allow the strawberries to thaw partially.

2. In a bowl, dissolve 1 package of the gelatin in 1 cup boiling water. Add the strawberries (do not drain) plus ⅓ cup cold water. Stir until the strawberries are completely thawed and well distributed, then turn into an 8" × 11" dish. Slice the bananas on top, pressing lightly to cover in the liquid. Chill until firm.

3. When the mixture is firm, bring the sour cream to room temperature. Spread it evenly over the gelatin, then return to the refrigerator until the sour cream is thoroughly chilled.

4. In a bowl, dissolve the second package of gelatin in 1 cup boiling water. Add the pineapple (do not drain) plus 6 ice cubes. Stir until the ice cubes are dissolved.

5. Refrigerate for no longer than ½ hour, or until the mixture has gelled slightly but can still be stirred. Carefully pour over the sour cream and chill until firm. Cut into squares and serve in a dessert bowl.

PER SERVING

Calories: 147	Sodium: . . . . 86 mg
Fat: . . . . 2.5 g	Fiber: . . . . 2 g
Protein: . . . . 2 g	Carbohydrate: . . 30 g

J-E-L-L-O!

Jell-o, the first fruit-flavored gelatin dessert, was invented in 1897 by a cough-syrup manufacturer from New York. By the 1930s, more than a third of all recipes in most cookbooks were gelatin based!

⅔ cup strawberries, diced

¼ cup water

3 tablespoons lime juice

3 tablespoons granulated sugar

1½ teaspoons candied ginger, finely minced

⅛ teaspoon kosher salt

3 cups seedless watermelon balls, small

1 cup honeydew melon balls, small

1 cup mango, diced

Tropical Watermelon Salad in Strawberry-Ginger Sauce

This recipe works best if you chill the sauce in the refrigerator for at least 15 minutes before pouring it over the salad.

1. Combine strawberries, water, lime juice, sugar, ginger, and salt in a small saucepan over medium heat. Bring to a simmer, stirring occasionally, and reduce heat to low. Cover and let mixture simmer for 5 minutes. Remove pan from heat, remove lid, mix, and let sauce cool for 5–10 minutes.

2. Pour cooled sauce into a blender. Blend on low until almost smooth.

3. Gently combine watermelon balls, honeydew balls, and mango in a large mixing bowl. Pour strawberry sauce over salad and toss gently to coat.

4. Garnish salad with slices of strawberry and a sprig of mint. Serve immediately.

PER SERVING

Calories:. 84	Sodium: . . . . 57 mg
Fat:. . . . . 0 g	Fiber: . . . . 1.5 g
Protein:. . . . . . . 1.5 g	Carbohydrate: . . 22 g

3 tangerines

2 cups fresh blackberries, chilled

1 cup diced Asian pear

¼ cup sweet white wine

1 tablespoon lemon juice

½ teaspoon lemon zest

⅛ teaspoon kosher salt

2 tablespoons toasted almond slices

Blackberry Pear Salad with Tangerine Wine Dressing

Fresh blackberries have a wonderful tangy quality that helps balance the sweet pears, tangerines, and white wine in this dessert recipe.

1. Peel and remove membrane from each tangerine segment. Chop each segment in half. You should end up with about 1¼ cups tangerine pieces. Add 1 cup of the tangerine to a large mixing bowl with blackberries and Asian pears. Toss gently, cover with plastic wrap, and chill salad in refrigerator until needed.

2. Stir wine, lemon juice, lemon zest, and salt into a small saucepan over medium-low heat. Lightly chop or smash the remaining tangerine and add to saucepan. Bring mixture to a simmer, stirring occasionally. Reduce heat to low. Simmer for 5 minutes, or until tangerine flesh breaks down and dressing thickens, stirring occasionally.

3. Remove pot from heat and let dressing cool for 10 minutes. Pour dressing into a lidded container and chill in fridge for at least 15 minutes before using.

4. Remove dressing from refrigerator and mix well. Remove salad from refrigerator, add dressing, and toss well to mix and coat. Garnish with sliced almonds and a curl of lemon peel. Serve immediately.

PER SERVING

Calories: 77		Sodium: . . . . 52 mg	
Fat: . . . . 1.5 g		Fiber: . . . . 5 g	
Protein: . . . . 2 g		Carbohydrate: . . 16 g	

INGREDIENTS | SERVES 6

1 large navel orange

2 tablespoons grapefruit juice

3 tablespoons honey

⅛ teaspoon cinnamon, ground

⅛ teaspoon nutmeg, ground

⅛ teaspoon kosher salt

2 cups pomegranate seeds

1 cup mango, diced

1 cup green apple, diced

Orange-Mango Pomegranate Salad

Buy a bottle of orange juice if you'd rather not do the juicing yourself, but make sure it's heavy on pulp or the sauce will be too thin.

1. Slice orange in half and juice with a hand juicer. Remove any seeds from the juice, but keep the pulp. You should end up with about ½ cup pulpy juice. Grate rind from orange, which should yield about 1 tablespoon zest.

2. Add orange juice, orange zest, grapefruit juice, honey, cinnamon, nutmeg, and salt together in a small bowl. Mix until honey is fully dissolved.

3. Combine pomegranate, mango, and apples in a large bowl. Add dressing to bowl and toss well to coat fully.

4. Cover bowl and chill in refrigerator for at least 1 hour. Mix well before serving. Garnish with a slice of orange and a cinnamon stick.

PER SERVING

Calories: 113	Sodium: . . . . 53 mg
Fat: . . . . 0 g	Fiber: . . . . 2 g
Protein: . . . . 1 g	Carbohydrate: . . 29 g

Juicing By Hand

Even if you don't own a hand juicer, you can still juice an orange. Roll the orange along a hard surface, cut it open, and squeeze each half over a bowl. Use a strong metal spoon to scrape the inside of each orange half to scoop out the pulp, being careful not to scoop out membrane. Remove seeds from juice, leaving as much pulp as possible, and use juice as needed.

Classic Salad Combinations

Ambrosia Fruit Salad: apples, grapes, banana, and vanilla pudding

Caesar Salad: romaine lettuce, Parmesan cheese, croutons, and garlic vinaigrette

Chef's Salad: lettuce, deli ham, sliced turkey, hard-boiled eggs, Cheddar cheese, carrots, onions, celery, and tomatoes

Cobb Salad: chicken, bacon, hard-boiled eggs, tomatoes, avocados, lettuce, and blue cheese vinaigrette

Coleslaw: cabbage, carrots, mayonnaise, vinegar, sugar, celery seed, and salt

Cucumber Onion Salad: cucumber, red onion, vinegar, salt, pepper, and sugar

German Potato Salad: potatoes, onions, hard-boiled eggs, mayonnaise, and mustard

Greek Salad: tomato, cucumber, red onion, feta, kalamata olives, and olive oil dressing

Niçoise Salad: green beans, potatoes, olives, and vinaigrette

Oriental Chicken Salad: iceberg lettuce, breaded chicken, toasted almonds, crispy noodles, and sweet oriental dressing

Panzanella Salad: bread, tomatoes, onion, basil, pepper, and oil

Russian Salad: chicken, potatoes, green beans, pickles, carrots, and mayonnaise

Spinach Bacon Salad: baby spinach, bacon, red onions, hard-boiled egg, and vinaigrette

Spinach Salad: baby spinach, button mushrooms, onions, celery, tomatoes, hard-boiled egg, vinegar, olive oil, and salt

Tabbouleh Salad: bulgur wheat, tomatoes, onion, parsley, mint, and lemon oil dressing

Taco Salad: tortilla shell, iceberg lettuce, tomatoes, onions, olives, ground beef, refried beans, Cheddar cheese, and sour cream

Tomato and Mozzarella Salad: tomatoes, mozzarella, basil, and Italian vinaigrette

Tossed Salad: iceberg lettuce, tomatoes, cucumber, and carrots

Waldorf Salad: apples, celery, walnuts, lemon juice, and mayonnaise

Produce Buying Guide

Your ability to select quality produce can make or break a good salad before you even begin. Finding out that recently purchased produce is bad not only ruins your recipe plans, it wastes your grocery budget.

Selecting Produce

As a rule of thumb, you want to purchase your salad ingredients at a grocer that keeps the produce at the proper cool temperature and lightly moistened throughout the day. Produce stored in warm and dry places are more likely to carry germs, develop bruises, dry out, and lose flavor. Farmer's markets are safe if they offer local produce delivered the same morning or afternoon. Farmer's markets that keep produce on display for days or weeks at a time are best avoided.

The first thing you want to do is check assorted produce for bruising. It doesn't matter if you're buying iceberg lettuce or red apples; almost all forms of produce are susceptible to bruises. Feel each piece of produce to check for soft or mealy spots that may not yet show bruising. Judge the overall color, scent, and texture of each item to decide if it's worth purchasing. If the item does have small bruises or blemishes, you may be able to cut away the damaged area and use the rest of the ingredient.

Avoid produce with any visible cuts or cracks, as any opening makes the inner flesh vulnerable to bacteria. Judge the weight of the produce in your hand to determine hydration. Produce that feels heavier than it should for its type and size is filled with juice. Produce that feels lighter than it should for its type and size is likely old and dried out.

JUDGING PRODUCE
- Apples, bell peppers, lemons, limes, grapefruit, pears, bananas, onions, oranges, and tomatoes should feel firm but not hard. The skin should be smooth and free of pockmarks or wrinkles.
- Apricots, berries, mangoes, plums, peaches, nectarines, figs, kiwis, and avocados should be slightly soft, giving a little when pressed, but still relatively firm.
- Avoid slimy carrots, lettuce, greens, cucumbers, celery, radishes, cabbages, green onions, and mushrooms. These vegetables are best when firm and crisp. Green onions and mushrooms should be moist, but not slimy, and slightly springy.
- Melons, potatoes, jicamas, pineapples, coconuts, turnips, and squashes should be hard with consistent skin texture. Scratch the stem-end of the melon to check the scent. The melon will taste as sweet, bitter, or sour as it smells.

Produce Seasons

The easiest way to guarantee you'll receive the best produce for the lowest price is to buy in-season items. Produce always tastes better, costs less, and causes less environmental damage if it doesn't have to be forced into maturity or grown under artificial conditions. Even if the produce is organic, it has to be shipped from far away to arrive at your table out-of-season.

PRODUCE BY SEASON

- **Spring** produce includes apricots, artichokes, asparagus, beets, bell peppers, lettuce, mangoes, papayas, strawberries, sugar snap peas, sweet peas, and watercress.
- **Summer** produce includes arugula, berries, corn, cucumbers, figs, green beans, melons, peaches, plums, summer squash, and tomatoes.
- **Fall** produce includes apples, broccoli, cauliflower, cranberries, dates, grapes, mushrooms, onions, pears, pomegranates, potatoes, spinach, Swiss chard, and winter squash.
- **Winter** produce includes avocados, cabbage, chicory, fennel, grapefruit, kale, leeks, parsnips, radicchio, and turnips.

Produce Storage

It's important to store certain ingredients in separate areas if you want to keep your raw produce in the best possible condition for use in a salad. Refrigerators have separate fruit and produce compartments partially due to ethylene gas. Many fruits, especially apples, pears, and bananas, produce high levels of the gas to help regulate the ripening process. Many vegetables, especially lettuce and cucumber, produce low levels of this gas. Exposure to high levels of ethylene causes the low-level producers to over-ripen and turn brown, bitter, or mushy. Tomatoes can also produce high levels of the gas, and store best in a separate container in the fruit drawer or on an open shelf above the produce drawers.

Standard U.S./Metric Measurement Conversions

VOLUME CONVERSIONS

U.S. Volume Measure	Metric Equivalent
⅛ teaspoon	0.5 milliliters
¼ teaspoon	1 milliliters
½ teaspoon	2 milliliters
1 teaspoon	5 milliliters
½ tablespoon	7 milliliters
1 tablespoon (3 teaspoons)	15 milliliters
2 tablespoons (1 fluid ounce)	30 milliliters
¼ cup (4 tablespoons)	60 milliliters
⅓ cup	90 milliliters
½ cup (4 fluid ounces)	125 milliliters
⅔ cup	160 milliliters
¾ cup (6 fluid ounces)	180 milliliters
1 cup (16 tablespoons)	250 milliliters
1 pint (2 cups)	500 milliliters
1 quart (4 cups)	1 liter (about)

WEIGHT CONVERSIONS

U.S. Weight Measure	Metric Equivalent
½ ounce	15 grams
1 ounce	30 grams
2 ounces	60 grams
3 ounces	85 grams
¼ pound (4 ounces)	115 grams
½ pound (8 ounces)	225 grams
¾ pound (12 ounces)	340 grams
1 pound (16 ounces)	454 grams

OVEN TEMPERATURE CONVERSIONS

Degrees Fahrenheit	Degrees Celsius
200 degrees F	100 degrees C
250 degrees F	120 degrees C
275 degrees F	140 degrees C
300 degrees F	150 degrees C
325 degrees F	160 degrees C
350 degrees F	180 degrees C
375 degrees F	190 degrees C
400 degrees F	200 degrees C
425 degrees F	220 degrees C
450 degrees F	230 degrees C

BAKING PAN SIZES

American	Metric
8 × 1½ inch round baking pan	20 × 4 centimeter cake tin
9 × 1½ inch round baking pan	23 × 4 centimeter cake tin
1 × 7 × 1½ inch baking pan	28 × 18 × 4 centimeter baking tin
13 × 9 × 2 inch baking pan	30 × 20 × 5 centimeter baking tin
2 quart rectangular baking dish	30 × 20 × 3 centimeter baking tin
15 × 10 × 2 inch baking pan	30 × 25 × 2 centimeter baking tin (Swiss roll tin)
9 inch pie plate	22 × 4 or 23 × 4 centimeter pie plate
7 or 8 inch springform pan	18 or 20 centimeter springform or loose bottom cake tin
9 × 5 × 3 inch loaf pan	23 × 13 × 7 centimeter or 2 lb narrow loaf or pate tin
1½ quart casserole	1.5 liter casserole
2 quart casserole	2 liter casserole

Index

Note: Page numbers in **bold** indicate recipe category lists.

Agave nectar, 17
Alfalfa sprouts, 224
Amaretto liqueur, 220
Apples
    about: keeping right color, 206; produce buying guide, 286–87
    Apple Watercress Salad with Ginger Mustard Dressing, 206
    Apple with Mascarpone, 81
    Caramel Apple Salad with Cinnamon Raisin Croutons, 266
    Gorgonzola, Apple, and Apricot Fruit Salad, 75
    Holiday Dried Fruit and Apple Salad, 74
    No-Mayo Apple Coleslaw, 243
    Prosciutto Charoses Salad, 84
    Sweet and Fruity Salad, 77
    Swiss Apple Potato Salad, 95
Apricots
    about: produce buying guide, 286–87
    Apricot and Fennel Sprout Salad, 224
    Creamy Apricot Gelatin Salad, 270
    Gorgonzola, Apple, and Apricot Fruit Salad, 75
Artichokes
    Pearl Onion and Artichoke Bean Salad, 148
    Tomato and Artichoke-Feta Pasta Salad, 112
Asian Dressing, Creamy, 39
Asparagus
    Lobster and Asparagus Salad, 218
    Smoked Salmon and Asparagus Salad, 173
Avocados
    about: produce buying guide, 286–87
    Chipotle Avocado and Cheese Salad, 247
    Creamy Avocado-Herb Dressing, 35
    Crisp Avocado Salad, 198
    Marinated Avocado and Mushroom Salad, 66
    Marinated Kale and Avocado Salad, 60
    Orange-Avocado Slaw, 234
Balsamic Vinaigrette, Basic, 35
Bananas, 78, 79, 267, 271, 272, 281, 286, 287
Beans and legumes, **127–48**
    about: dry vs. canned chickpeas, 92; fava beans, 148; lentils, 147; snow pea pods, 117; soaking beans, 128; wax beans, 146
    Asian Green and Yellow Bean Salad, 139
    Aunt Gloria's Italian Green Bean Salad, 141
    Black Bean Slaw, 238
    Cannellini Bean Salad, 138
    Chickpea Herb Salad Dressing, 30
    Citrus Green-Bean Salad, 142
    Crunchy Stir-Fry Salad, 56
    Cuban Three-Bean Salad, 132
    Cucumber-Parsley Edamame Bean Salad, 144
    Deli-Style Macaroni Salad, 123
    Easy Four-Bean Salad, 142
    Flaming Taco Salad Supreme, 264

Four-Bean Salad, 129
    Green Bean Almondine Salad, 140
    Italian Double-Tomato Bean Salad, 136
    Kidney Bean and Chickpea Salad, 145
    Lemon-Parmesan Four-Bean Salad, 134
    Marinated Pea and Bean Salad, 133
    Palm Heart and Herb Bean Salad, 147
    Pasta Salad with Shrimp and Snow Pea Pods, 117
    Pearl Onion and Artichoke Bean Salad, 148
    Potato and Chickpea Curry Salad, 92
    Southwest Black Bean Salad, 128
    Spicy Southwestern Two-Bean Salad, 143
    Sweet Bacon Bean Salad, 131
    Sweet Lime Three-Bean Salad, 130
    Tex-Mex Bean Salad, 137
    Traditional Three-Bean Salad, 146
    Wasabi Pea Salad, 255
    White and Black Bean Salad, 135
Beef, **149**
    about: resting cooked meat, 154
    Beef and Horseradish Salad, 166
    Beefy Mushroom Salad, 204
    Fiery Beef Salad, 258
    Filet Mignon Caesar, 160
    Flaming Taco Salad Supreme, 264
    Grilled Teriyaki Steak and Watercress Salad, 154
    Pot Roast and Oyster Mushroom Salad, 167
    Sirloin Steak Salad, 161
Beets, in Russian Beet and Micro Greens Salad, 58
Berries
    about: canned cranberries, 213; produce buying guide, 286–87; strawberry garnish, 168
    American Fruit Salad, 76
    Blackberry Pear Salad with Tangerine Wine Dressing, 283
    Cherry Ambrosia Fruit Salad, 271
    Cranberry Peach Salad, 277
    Crisp Strawberry Spinach Salad, 64
    Good Gouda Fruit Salad, 86
    Light Lemon Blueberry Salad, 274
    Macadamia Strawberry–Star Fruit Salad, 86
    Minty Blueberry Melon Salad, 70
    Rainbow Fruit Salad, 79
    Raspberry and Nectarine Macaroon Salad, 269
    Raspberry and Red Onion Vinaigrette, 36
    Raspberry-Cranberry Spinach Salad, 200
    Sparkling Fruit Salad, 274
    Strawberry Chicken Salad, 168
    Strawberry Gelatin Salad, 281
    Tangy Ruby Raspberry Salad, 72
    Tropical Strawberry Kiwi Salad, 73
    Tropical Watermelon Salad in Strawberry-Ginger Sauce, 282
    Turkey and Cranberry Salad on Butternut Squash, 213
    Very Berry Cheesecake Salad, 273
Blanching vegetables, 116

Broccoli
    Broccoli and Pasta Salad, 116
    Broccoli Ranch Coleslaw, 227
    Broccoli Slaw, 234
    Creamy Broccoli Bacon Salad, 155
    Garden Glory Pasta Salad, 114
    Green Goddess Salad, 51
Buttermilk Dressing, 45
Cabbage and slaws. See Creamy salads/slaws
Cactus Salad, 57
Caesar salads, 285
    about: origins of, 93
    Easy Caesar Potato Salad, 93
    Pepper Jack Caesar Salad, 253
    Tuna Caesar Salad, 197
Carrots
    about: produce buying guide, 286–87
    Carrot and Cabbage Slaw, 242
    Carrot and Cucumber Ranch Salad, 199
    Veggie Slaw, 239
Cauliflower
    Curried Cauliflower and Peanut Salad, 254
    Garden Glory Pasta Salad, 114
    Green Goddess Salad, 51
Celery leaves, 30
Charoses, 84
Cheese
    about: blue, 89; brie, 221; Cabrales, 212; mascarpone, 81; Parmesan and Parmigiano-Reggiano, 134; queso fresco, 121; shredding soft/semisoft, 253
    Almond and Pear Salad with Gorgonzola, 222
    Applewood Bacon and Brie Frisee Salad, 221
    Asiago Cucumber and Olive Pasta Salad, 126
    Bacon and Tomato Pasta Salad, 124
    Blue Cheese Dressing, 23
    Chipotle Avocado and Cheese Salad, 247
    Chunky Blue Cheese Salad Dressing, 47
    Cottage Cheese and Fruit Salad, 77
    Creamy Blue Cheese Potato Salad, 89
    Creamy Feta Salad Dressing, 39
    Garlic Parmesan Salad Dressing, 32
    Good Gouda Fruit Salad, 86
    Gorgonzola, Apple, and Apricot Fruit Salad, 75
    Pecan and Goat Cheese Salad, 199
    Radicchio Cabrales Salad, 212
    Smoky Cheddar Potato Salad, 98
    Zesty Cheese Salad, 257
Cherries, 271, 272, 278
Chicken. See Poultry
Chives, in Light and Creamy Chive Dressing, 16
Chocolate, 267, 272, 278
Chow mein noodles, 209
Cilantro
    about, 18
    Cilantro and Red Onion Dressing, 18
    Cilantro-Lime Tofu Dressing, 20
    Peppered Cilantro and Tomato Salad, 248

Citrus
  about: juicing, 284; mandarin oranges, 152;
    oranges, 268; produce buying guide, 286–87;
    selecting grapefruit, 164; squeezing lime
    juice, 130
  Blood Orange Salad with Shrimp and Baby
    Spinach, 216
  Citrus Green-Bean Salad, 142
  Escarole and Orange Salad, 211
  Gingered Citrus Salad, 276
  Grapefruit-and-Chicken Salad, 164
  Grapefruit-Pomegranate Salad, 80
  Lemon-Almond Dressing, 46
  Lemon-Ginger Poppy Seed Dressing, 22
  Light Lemon Blueberry Salad, 274
  Orange Cashew Salad Dressing, 42
  Orange-Mango Pomegranate Salad, 284
  Orange-Pineapple Sherbet Salad, 275
  Orange Sesame Vinaigrette, 33
  Sesame Orange Coleslaw, 228
  Sugar-Snapped Mandarin Chicken Salad, 152
  Sweet Lime Three-Bean Salad, 130
  Tangerine Wine Dressing, 283
  Tangy Lemon-Garlic Tomato Dressing, 27
  Tangy Ruby Raspberry Salad, 72
  Thai Orange Peanut Dressing, 48
  Tropical Orange Salad, 70
  Valencia Orange Salad with Orange-Flower
    Water, 268
Cobb Salad Vinaigrette Dressing, 21
Corn
  about: baby corn, 209; grilled, 170; sweet, 249
  Blackened Corn and Sweet Shallot Pasta
    Salad, 110
  Corn and Pepper Salad with Ham, 170
  Corny Ranch Ham Salad, 194
  Deli-Style Macaroni Salad, 123
  Easy Nacho Corn Salad, 196
  Spiced Italian Corn Salad, 249
Couscous Salad with Fresh-Grilled Tuna, 181
Creamy salads/slaws, 225–44
  about: Chinese cabbage, 237; icing cabbage,
    235; koosla and coleslaw, 231; mayonnaise
    options, 24, 241; red cabbage, 239; vegan
    coleslaw, 243
  Black Bean Slaw, 238
  Broccoli Ranch Coleslaw, 227
  Broccoli Slaw, 234
  Carrot and Cabbage Slaw, 242
  Chicken Caesar Coleslaw, 242
  Chinese Coleslaw, 237
  Creamy Apple-Jicama Coleslaw, 226
  Dilly Pickle Coleslaw, 236
  Jicama Fennel Slaw, 232
  Light and Tangy Coleslaw, 231
  Mexican Coleslaw, 229
  No-Mayo Apple Coleslaw, 243
  Orange-Avocado Slaw, 234
  Overnight Coleslaw, 235
  Picnic Coleslaw, 241
  Pineapple Coconut Coleslaw, 233

  Sesame and Soy Coleslaw, 236
  Sesame Orange Coleslaw, 228
  Spicy Coleslaw with Cashew Mayonnaise, 244
  Tangy Cucumber Coleslaw, 227
  Tangy Horseradish Coleslaw, 240
  Veggie Slaw, 239
  Zesty Lime-Jicama Coleslaw, 230
Croutons, 150
Cuban dishes, 132
Cucumbers
  about: English, 51; produce buying guide,
    286–87; removing seeds from, 15
  Asiago Cucumber and Olive Pasta Salad, 126
  Carrot and Cucumber Ranch Salad, 199
  Cucumber-Parsley Edamame Bean Salad, 144
  Cucumber Vinaigrette Salad Dressing, 15
  Spicy-Sweet Cucumber Salad, 260
  Tangy Cucumber Coleslaw, 227
Curry powder, creating, 254
Dessert salads, 265–84
Dressings. See Salad dressings recipes
Eggplant Arugula Salad, 210
Eggs
  Creamy Comfort Salad, 198
  Fresh Summer Potato Salad, 106
  Pickle Lover's Egg Pasta Salad, 118
Fats, 27
Fennel
  Apricot and Fennel Sprout Salad, 224
  Jicama Fennel Slaw, 232
  Shaved Fennel Salad with Toasted Hazelnuts,
    215
Fig and Parmesan Curl Salad, 217
Fish and seafood, 171–92. See also Quick salads
  about: boiling shrimp, 183; calamari, 187;
    cooking crabmeat, 219; cooking lobster, 179;
    crab cakes, 191; frozen, 178; Norway fare,
    176; poaching squid, 185; preparing shrimp,
    188; seafood cocktail history, 172; searing
    scallops, 189
  Anchovy and Tomato Salad, 192
  Cajun Shrimp and Mango Salad, 174
  Couscous Salad with Fresh-Grilled Tuna, 181
  Crab Cake Salad, 191
  Cuban Shrimp Salad, 188
  Dilled Shrimp and Watercress Salad, 183
  Fresh Crab with Arugula Salad, 219
  Grilled Calamari Salad, 187
  Grilled Halibut Herb Salad, 190
  Grilled Shrimp Salad, 215
  Hollywood Lobster Salad, 179
  Italian Seafood Salad, 184
  Lemon Roll-Up Fillet Salad, 175
  Lime-Poached Flounder, 178
  Lobster and Asparagus Salad, 218
  Norwegian Salmon Salad, 176
  Pasta and King Crab Salad, 182
  Pasta Salad with Shrimp and Snow Pea Pods,
    117
  Rosemary and Orange–Seared Scallop Salad,
    189

  Salmon-Spinach Salad, 177
  Salmon Tortellini Salad, 180
  Shrimp and Melon Salad, 177
  Smoked Salmon and Asparagus Salad, 173
  Spicy Shrimp Cocktail Salad, 172
  Spicy Shrimp Salad, 186
  Spicy Shrimp with Lemon Yogurt on Wilted
    Greens, 252
  Thailand Seafood Salad, 185
  Tuna Macaroni Salad, 122
Flowers, Sugared, and Greens Salad, 223
French Dressing, Classic, 33
Fruits. See also specific fruits
  dried, 71
  produce buying guide, 286–87
  salad recipes, 69–86, 274
Garlic Parmesan Salad Dressing, 32
Gelatin salads, 270, 274, 277, 280, 281
Gourmet Salads, 205–24
  Almond and Pear Salad with Gorgonzola, 222
  Apple Watercress Salad with Ginger Mustard
    Dressing, 206
  Applewood Bacon and Brie Frisee Salad, 221
  Apricot and Fennel Sprout Salad, 224
  Arugula, Pear, and Avocado Salad, 208
  Asian Chopped Salad with Crispy Noodles
    and Kim Chee, 209
  Blood Orange Salad with Shrimp and Baby
    Spinach, 216
  Eggplant Arugula Salad, 210
  Escarole and Orange Salad, 211
  Fig and Parmesan Curl Salad, 217
  Fresh Crab with Arugula Salad, 219
  Grilled Shrimp Salad, 215
  Lobster and Asparagus Salad, 218
  Nutty Chanterelle Salad, 214
  Peppery Grilled Portobello and Leek Salad,
    207
  Radicchio Cabrales Salad, 212
  Shaved Fennel Salad with Toasted Hazelnuts,
    215
  Sugared Flowers and Greens Salad, 223
  Turkey and Cranberry Salad on Butternut
    Squash, 213
  Wilted Amaretto Spinach Salad, 220
Grapefruit. See Citrus
Grapes
  about: types of, 76
  American Fruit Salad, 76
  Middle Eastern Fruit Salad, 71
  Rainbow Fruit Salad, 79
  Sparkling Fruit Salad, 274
  Tomato, Feta, and Grape Salad, 195
  Zesty Pecan Chicken and Grape Salad, 262
Greek Pasta Salad, 122
Green Goddess Dressing, 38
Green salads, 49–68. See also Quick salads
  about: collard greens, 61; kale, 60; lettuce, 53;
    preparing greens, 63; sea vegetables, 59;
    wilting greens, 65
  Apple Walnut Spinach Salad, 50

Cactus Salad, 57
Country Garden Salad, 64
Crisp Strawberry Spinach Salad, 64
Crunchy Stir-Fry Salad, 56
Green Goddess Salad, 51
Greens with Jalepeño Dressing, 63
Kale and Sea Vegetables with Orange Sesame
    Dressing, 59
Leafy Zucchini Salad, 52
Lettuce Lover's Salad Delight, 53
Marinated Avocado and Mushroom Salad, 66
Marinated Kale and Avocado Salad, 60
Mediterranean Tomato Salad, 50
Mushroom Lover's Green Salad, 68
Pomegranate Green Salad, 62
Russian Beet and Micro Greens Salad, 58
Spiced Collards Salad, 61
Spring Greens with Berries, 54
Sweet Spring Baby Salad, 54
Tarragon Arugula-Peanut Salad, 55
Tofu Tossed Salad, 67
Wilted Kale Salad with Roasted Shallots, 65
Herb Salad, Spicy, 261
Horseradish
    about: types of, 94
    Beef and Horseradish Salad, 166
    Creamy Horsey Potato Salad, 94
    Light and Creamy Horseradish Dressing, 16
    Tangy Horseradish Coleslaw, 240
Italian Herb Dressing, Creamy, 40
Italiano Salad Dressing, 41
Jicamas
    about: peeling, 226; produce buying guide,
        286–87
    Creamy Apple-Jicama Coleslaw, 226
    Jicama Fennel Slaw, 232
    Tofu Tossed Salad, 67
    Zesty Cheese Salad, 257
    Zesty Lime-Jicama Coleslaw, 230
Kachumbari Salad, 263
Kiwi
    Papaya and Kiwi Fruit Salad, 82
    Spicy Papaya Salad, 250
    Tropical Strawberry Kiwi Salad, 73
Lemon. See Citrus
Lemongrass, using, 96
Liquid smoke, 98
Litchis, 78, 83
Macaroons, 269
Mangoes
    about: produce buying guide, 286–87
    Cajun Shrimp and Mango Salad, 174
    Curried Chicken and Mango Salad, 165
    Orange-Mango Pomegranate Salad, 284
    Rainbow Fruit Salad, 79
Mayonnaise options, 24, 241
Melons
    about: produce buying guide, 286–87
    American Fruit Salad, 76
    Cantaloupe, Pecan, and Cheese Salad, 201
    Creamy Fruit Salad, 82

Fire-Kissed Cantaloupe Salad, 246
    Melon Pineapple Salad, 75
    Minty Blueberry Melon Salad, 70
    Shrimp and Melon Salad, 177
    Tropical Watermelon Salad in Strawberry-
        Ginger Sauce, 282
Mushrooms
    about: chanterelle, 214; oyster, 167; produce
        buying guide, 286–87; varieties of, 68
    Beefy Mushroom Salad, 204
    Marinated Avocado and Mushroom Salad, 66
    Mushroom Lover's Green Salad, 68
    Nutty Chanterelle Salad, 214
    Peppery Grilled Portobello and Leek Salad,
        207
    Portobello Penne Pasta Salad, 120
    Pot Roast and Oyster Mushroom Salad, 167
Mustard
    Dijon Vinaigrette, 41
    Walnut Honey-Mustard Vinaigrette, 34
Nuts and seeds
    about: adding seeds to salads, 158; making
        peanut butter, 48; soaking cashews, 233;
        tahini, 28; toasting nuts, 156, 262; toasting
        seeds, 228; working with walnuts, 34
    Butterscotch Banana Praline Salad, 272
    Cashew-Garlic Ranch Dressing, 45
    Curried Cauliflower and Peanut Salad, 254
    Green Bean Almondine Salad, 140
    Lemon-Almond Dressing, 46
    Macadamia Strawberry–Star Fruit Salad, 86
    Nutty Chanterelle Salad, 214
    Orange Cashew Salad Dressing, 42
    Pecan and Goat Cheese Salad, 199
    Southern Grilled Peach and Pecan Salad, 279
    Spicy Coleslaw with Cashew Mayonnaise, 244
    Spumoni Salad, 278
    Thai Orange Peanut Dressing, 48
    Tropical Fruit Salad with Pecans, 78
    Walnut Honey-Mustard Vinaigrette, 34
    You Are a Goddess Dressing, 28
    Zesty Pecan Chicken and Grape Salad, 262
Oils, 40, 42
Olives, 126
Onions
    about: cutting without crying, 36; produce
        buying guide, 286–87; red, 141
    Asian Chopped Salad with Crispy Noodles
        and Kim Chee, 209
    Garden Glory Pasta Salad, 114
    Pearl Onion and Artichoke Bean Salad, 148
    Pineapple Onion Salad, 196
    Raspberry and Red Onion Vinaigrette, 36
Oranges. See Citrus
Papaya
    Papaya and Kiwi Fruit Salad, 82
    Spicy Papaya Salad, 250
    Tropical Fruit Salad with Pecans, 78
Parsley, flat-leaf, 32
Pasta salads
    about: flavor secrets, 123; fresh pasta and, 124;

penne pasta and, 120
    recipes, 109–26, 143, 180, 182
Peaches and nectarines
    about: 85; pitting, 210; produce buying guide,
        286–87
    Cranberry Peach Salad, 277
    Eggplant Arugula Salad, 210
    Peachy Ham and Blue Cheese Salad, 195
    Raspberry and Nectarine Macaroon Salad,
        269
    Southern Grilled Peach and Pecan Salad, 279
    Sweet and Creamy Peach Fruit Salad, 85
Pears
    about: produce buying guide, 286–87
    Almond and Pear Salad with Gorgonzola, 222
    Arugula, Pear, and Avocado Salad, 208
    Blackberry Pear Salad with Tangerine Wine
        Dressing, 283
    Spinach, Pear, and Smoked Ham Salad, 162
Peas. See Beans and legumes
Pepper, fresh-cracked black, 107
Peppers. See also Spicy salads
    about: chipotles, 247; pepper sauces, 246;
        preparing Serrano chilies, 258; produce
        buying guide, 286–87; selecting and storing,
        115
    Corn and Pepper Salad with Ham, 170
    Pasta Salad with Hot Peppers and Sweet Red
        Pepper Dressing, 115
    Pickled Peppers and Pickles Salad, 203
    Tex-Mex Pasta Salad, 121
    Zesty Banana Pepper Salad, 250
Pesto and Potato Salad, 88
Pesto Pasta Salad, 125
Pineapple
    about: produce buying guide, 286–87
    Asian Pineapple and Sweet Potato Salad, 108
    Flaming Pineapple Salad, 256
    Melon Pineapple Salad, 75
    Orange-Pineapple Sherbet Salad, 275
    Pineapple Coconut Coleslaw, 233
    Pineapple Onion Salad, 196
    Sparkling Fruit Salad, 274
    Tropical Fruit Salad with Pecans, 78
    Tropical Strawberry Kiwi Salad, 73
Pomegranates
    about: seeding, 62, 80
    Grapefruit-Pomegranate Salad, 80
    Orange-Mango Pomegranate Salad, 284
    Pomegranate Green Salad, 62
Poppy seeds
    about, 22
    Lemon-Ginger Poppy Seed Dressing, 22
Pork, 149
    about: chopping bacon, 101; resting cooked
        meat, 154
    Applewood Bacon and Brie Frisee Salad, 221
    Bacon and Tomato Pasta Salad, 124
    Chinese Barbecued Pork Salad, 163
    Corn and Pepper Salad with Ham, 170
    Creamy Broccoli Bacon Salad, 155

Creamy Salsa and Chorizo Pasta Salad, 113
Prosciutto Charoses Salad, 84
Roasted Ham and Sweet Potato Salad, 107
Sausage and Sauerkraut Potato Salad, 102
Spinach, Pear, and Smoked Ham Salad, 162
Swiss-Herb Pork Loin Salad, 169
Wild Rice Ham Salad, 157
Potatoes
about: keeping skins on, 103; preparing for
salads, 104; produce buying guide, 286–87;
substituting, 100; varieties of, 92
salad recipes, **87**–108, 251
Poultry, **149**. *See also* Quick salads
Chicken BLT Salad, 150
Chicken Caesar Coleslaw, 242
Chinese Chicken Salad, 158
Curried Chicken and Mango Salad, 165
Dijon Apricot Chicken Salad, 151
Fall Turkey Sandwich Salad, 153
Golden Raisin Smoked Turkey Salad, 159
Grapefruit-and-Chicken Salad, 164
Pepper Jack Caesar Salad, 253
Strawberry Chicken Salad, 168
Sugar-Snapped Mandarin Chicken Salad, 152
Tex-Mex Pasta Salad, 121
Turkey and Cranberry Salad on Butternut
Squash, 213
Turkey and Nectarine Bib Salad, 153
Turkey Waldorf Salad, 156
Zesty Pecan Chicken and Grape Salad, 262
Quick salads, **193**–204
Beefy Mushroom Salad, 204
Cantaloupe, Pecan, and Cheese Salad, 201
Carrot and Cucumber Ranch Salad, 199
Corny Ranch Ham Salad, 194
Creamy Comfort Salad, 198
Crisp Avocado Salad, 198
Crunchy Pepperoni Salad, 197
Easy Nacho Corn Salad, 196
Italian Garden Salad, 194
Pastrami Mustard Salad, 204
Peachy Ham and Blue Cheese Salad, 195
Pecan and Goat Cheese Salad, 199
Pickled Peppers and Pickles Salad, 203
Pineapple Onion Salad, 196
Quick Cranberry Turkey Salad, 201
Raspberry-Cranberry Spinach Salad, 200
Sweet and Savory Side Salad, 202
Sweet Bib Salad, 200
Tomato, Feta, and Grape Salad, 195
Tuna Caesar Salad, 197
Turkey Island Salad, 202
Yellow Squash and Tomato Salad, 203
Radicchio Cabrales Salad, 212
Ranch dressings, 21, 24, 45
Raspberries. *See* Berries
Rice
Spicy Rice Salad, 259
Wild Rice Ham Salad, 157
Salad dressings
about, 6–8; bottled vs. homemade, 160; creamy,

7–8; flavored vinegars and, 161; food
processors vs. blenders for, 8; pepper sauces,
246; types of, 7–8; vinaigrettes, 7
Ginger Mustard Dressing, 206
Lemon Yogurt, 252
light. *See* Salad dressings (light)
rich. *See* Salad dressings (rich)
Strawberry-Ginger Sauce, 282
Tangerine Wine Dressing, 283
Salad dressings (light), **13**–30
Agave-Lemon Ginger Salad Dressing, 17
Asian Ranch Dressing, 21
Blue Cheese Dressing, 23
Chickpea Herb Salad Dressing, 30
Cilantro and Red Onion Dressing, 18
Cilantro-Lime Tofu Dressing, 20
Cobb Salad Vinaigrette Dressing, 21
Creamy Miso Sesame Dressing, 26
Creamy Wasabi-Tofu Dressing, 19
Cucumber Vinaigrette Salad Dressing, 15
Dairy-Free Ranch Dressing, 24
Italian Dill Vinaigrette Dressing, 14
Lemon-Ginger Poppy Seed Dressing, 22
Light and Creamy Chive Dressing, 16
Light and Creamy Horseradish Dressing, 16
Low-Cal Spinach Pesto Vinaigrette, 25
Sherry Vinaigrette, 14
Tangy Honey Mustard Salad Dressing, 29
Tangy Lemon-Garlic Tomato Dressing, 27
You Are a Goddess Dressing, 28
Salad dressings (rich), **31**–48
Basic Balsamic Vinaigrette, 35
Buttermilk Dressing, 45
Cashew-Garlic Ranch Dressing, 45
Chunky Blue Cheese Salad Dressing, 47
Classic French Dressing, 33
Creamy Asian Dressing, 39
Creamy Avocado-Herb Dressing, 35
Creamy Feta Salad Dressing, 39
Creamy Italian Herb Dressing, 40
Dijon Vinaigrette, 41
Garlic Parmesan Salad Dressing, 32
Green Goddess Dressing, 38
Honey-Wasabi Vinaigrette, 43
Italiano Salad Dressing, 41
Lemon-Almond Dressing, 46
Orange Cashew Salad Dressing, 42
Orange Sesame Vinaigrette, 33
Raspberry and Red Onion Vinaigrette, 36
Roasted Tomato Catalina Dressing, 37
Tarragon Salad Dressing, 44
Thai Orange Peanut Dressing, 48
Walnut Honey-Mustard Vinaigrette, 34
Salsa, 113
Seasonal produce, 287
Sherbet, 275
Sherry Vinaigrette, 14
Slaws. *See* Creamy salads/slaws
Soda, making, 280
Sour cream, mock, 23
Soy products. *See also* Tofu

about: eating edamame, 144
Creamy Miso Sesame Dressing, 26
Cucumber-Parsley Edamame Bean Salad, 144
Spicy salads, 143, 172, 186, 244, **245**–64
Spinach. *See also* Green salads
about: substituting for iceberg lettuce, 216
Blood Orange Salad with Shrimp and Baby
Spinach, 216
Low-Cal Spinach Pesto Vinaigrette, 25
Raspberry-Cranberry Spinach Salad, 200
Salmon-Spinach Salad, 177
Spinach, Pear, and Smoked Ham Salad, 162
Spinach and Orzo Pasta Salad, 118
Wilted Amaretto Spinach Salad, 220
Spumoni Salad, 278
Squash
about: produce buying guide, 286–87;
zucchinis, 52
Leafy Zucchini Salad, 52
Turkey and Cranberry Salad on Butternut
Squash, 213
Veggie Slaw, 239
Yellow Squash and Tomato Salad, 203
Sweet potato salads, 107–8, 251
Tabbouleh Pasta Salad, 119
Taro Salad, Spiced, 251
Tarragon
about: taste of, 55
Tarragon Arugula-Peanut Salad, 55
Tarragon Salad Dressing, 44
Tofu
about: creation of, 67; taste of, 20
Asian Chopped Salad with Crispy Noodles
and Kim Chee, 209
Cilantro-Lime Tofu Dressing, 20
Creamy Wasabi-Tofu Dressing, 19
Tangy Honey Mustard Salad Dressing, 29
Tofu Tossed Salad, 67
Tomatoes
about: plum tomatoes, 112; produce buying
guide, 286–87; storing roasted, 37
Anchovy and Tomato Salad, 192
Bacon and Tomato Pasta Salad, 124
Mediterranean Tomato Salad, 50
Peppered Cilantro and Tomato Salad, 248
Roasted Tomato Catalina Dressing, 37
Tangy Lemon-Garlic Tomato Dressing, 27
Tomato, Feta, and Grape Salad, 195
Tomato and Artichoke-Feta Pasta Salad, 112
Yellow Squash and Tomato Salad, 203
Turkey. *See* Poultry
Vegan foods, 24, 104, 105, 123, 243
Vegetables. *See also specific vegetables*
about: blanching, 116
produce buying guide, 286–87
Vinegars, 161, 244, 259
Wasabi
about: paste, 43
Honey-Wasabi Vinaigrette, 43
Wasabi Pea Salad, 255

We Have
EVERYTHING®
on Anything!

With more than 19 million copies sold, the Everything® series has become one of America's favorite resources for solving problems, learning new skills, and organizing lives. Our brand is not only recognizable—it's also welcomed.

The series is a hand-in-hand partner for people who are ready to tackle new subjects—like you!

For more information on the Everything® series, please visit *www.adamsmedia.com*

The Everything® list spans a wide range of subjects, with more than 500 titles covering 25 different categories:

Business	History	Reference
Careers	Home Improvement	Religion
Children's Storybooks	Everything Kids	Self-Help
Computers	Languages	Sports & Fitness
Cooking	Music	Travel
Crafts and Hobbies	New Age	Wedding
Education/Schools	Parenting	Writing
Games and Puzzles	Personal Finance	
Health	Pets	